FROM THE SLAVE SHIP

TO THE SPACESHIP

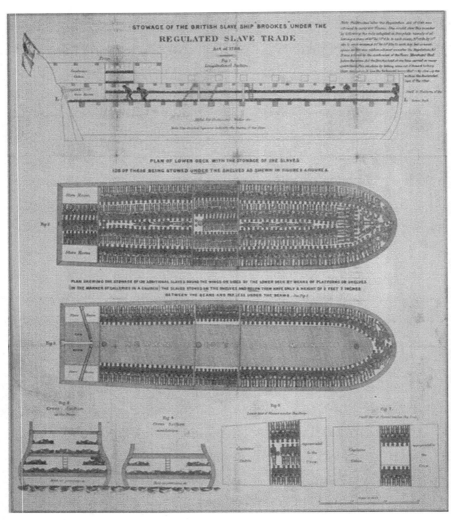

Slaves stowed on the British slave ship Brookes under the
regulated slave trade act of 1788

FROM THE SLAVE SHIP

TO THE SPACESHIP

African American History in Vignettes

Betty Swan

To order additional copies of this book, contact:
Xlibris Corporation
1-888-795-4274
www.Xlibris.com
Orders@Xlibris.com
52803

CONTENTS

DEDICATION

In special memory of my mother, Martha Newport Swan, who patiently read everything I gave her and provided me very valuable input.

I also dedicate *From the Slave Ship to the Space Ship* to my family and my daughters, Tiffany and Laini, who have always encouraged me. A special thanks to Johnny, who always believed in me.

PREFACE

As an African American and a teacher, I love exploring and sharing African American history. However, I have become deeply concerned that most Americans are only aware of what I term "the maximum ten." This is usually the maximum number of famous African Americans in history that people know. The list typically includes Martin Luther King Jr., Rosa Parks, Harriet Tubman, Frederick Douglass, Jackie Robinson, Malcolm X, Thurgood Marshall, George Washington Carver, Jesse Owens, and Garrett Morgan. Ask about A. Philip Randolph, Pap Singleton, Fannie Lou Hamer, or blacks in the West, and knowledge begins to wane.

When the average American is asked, "What kind of work did enslaved people do?" The first and sometimes only response is, "Pick cotton in the South." Slave labor consisted of much more than Southern agricultural work. Many in the North were shipbuilders and domestic servants. In western Virginia, some slaves were coal miners. Farther west some were cooks, cowboys, and explorers. Some even played key roles in the expansion of our country, such as York, who was the slave of William Clark of the famous Lewis and Clark expedition. It seems apparent that where there was a need, it was filled with slave labor. This is why African Americans played such a diverse and significant role in United States history.

Our country must develop an interest in African American history. This history does not only pertain to African Americans, but to the United States and its people as a whole. Carter Woodson initiated our study. He was the first person to document the contributions of African Americans.

He is called the Father of Black History. It is my hope that this book will inspire people of all races and ages to desire to learn more about African American history and remember it well.

How to Use This Book

This book is designed to teach through reading and reenactments. The vignettes can be used for personal interest, classroom teaching, or school assembly programs. The material in each chapter is organized chronologically according to when an event took place, or when a historical figure began to make his or her mark in history. Each piece varies in length and complexity thus enabling everyone from pre-K to adult to participate and have fun. The monologues, skits, and poems are diverse and informal with minimal stage directions and clothing descriptions. The purpose is to keep them simple and written in a manner that can easily be modified to suit the director and performers. Many of the characters use racial terms that are now archaic. The purpose was to remain as true as possible to the language used during the era in which the character lived.

Most of the characters in this book are real people who made significant contributions to history. The characters Henry Simmons Newport, in the chapter Military, and Mrs. Rosa, in the chapter Medicine, were relatives of the author. This book also contains fictional characters that reflect the importance of a true event rather than a real person. Any resemblance to an actual person, living or dead, is entirely coincidental.

The information used for these vignettes has been extensively researched to compile the most accurate sources possible. The entries offer a stimulus for further extensive study. The bibliography includes suggested resources for additional knowledge. All photographs are courtesy of the Library of Congress.

ACKNOWLEDGMENTS

I would like to acknowledge my history professors at Kentucky State University, especially Dr. Henry E. Cheaney and Dr. Harold S. Smith. They stimulated my love for history. They were walking textbooks and great teachers and role models. A special thanks to Joi Gilliam, who helped with the initial edits. Many thanks to Michele Louhisdon, who graciously shared her knowledge of dramatic writing. Too many thanks to my daughter Laini, who stuck with me and worked around the clock to copyedit and finalize my book. Without her it would have been impossible.

SLAVE SHIPS

The *White Lion* and the *Treasurer*

(SPEAKER recounts the roles of the White Lion and the Treasurer in bringing Africans to America.)

SPEAKER

The *White Lion* was the first ship to bring Africans to a British colony. In 1619 two British pirate ships—the *White Lion*, which was flying a Dutch flag, and the *Treasurer*—overtook the Portuguese slave ship *San Juan Bautista* in the South Atlantic off the coast of Mexico. The *Bautista* was carrying about 350 kidnapped Africans from Luanda, Angola. It was destined for Veracruz, Mexico, to sell its captives. The pirates each took between twenty to thirty Africans. The *White Lion* then sailed north.

In late August 1619, the *White Lion* arrived in Jamestown, Virginia, and traded the Africans for provisions. Four days later, the *Treasurer* docked in Jamestown and traded the Africans they had taken. No one knows the exact number of people who were traded from the *White Lion*, but they were referred to as the "twenty and odd." These "twenty and odd" Africans, who became indentured servants, were the initial victims of what evolved into over two hundred years of African American enslavement.

The *Desire*

(SPEAKER *recounts the Desire's role in furthering the slave trade.*)

SPEAKER

The *Desire* was the first slave ship built in North America. It was constructed in 1636 in Marblehead, Massachusetts. It weighed twelve tons and was seventy-nine feet long. In 1638 it sailed from Salem, Massachusetts, to the West Indies. It returned later that year with a cargo of Africans, cotton, salt, and tobacco. The success of the *Desire* marked the beginning of a long and prosperous enterprise of slave-ship building in the North.

The *Clotilde*

(SPEAKER *recounts the Clotilde's illegal importation of slaves.*)

SPEAKER

When the *Clotilde*—also known as the *Clotilda*—arrived in Mobile Bay, Alabama in 1859, it brought the last known cargo of enslaved Africans to the United States. The *Clotilde* recorded a vessel license in 1855. It was eighty-six feet long, twenty-three feet wide, and had two masts. However, it became an illegal ship in 1859, because it was used to import slaves. The U.S. Congress passed a law that made it illegal to bring slaves into the United States or build ships for the purpose of selling or disposing of slaves. The law took effect after January, 1, 1808.

Timothy Meaher, owner of the *Clotilde*, made a wager with some men that he could "bring a ship full of n—— right into Mobile Bay under the officers' noses." Meaher hired Captain William Foster to commandeer the ship. He sailed to the Kingdom of Dahomey and purchased between 110 and 160 Africans. They ranged in age, size, and gender, from small children to young women and men. On his return, Foster learned that federal authorities received word of his mission. He waited until late night and maneuvered the *Clotilde* into Mobile Bay. Captain Foster continued to outwit officials by unloading his human cargo into a riverboat. He then burned the ship before sinking it to destroy any evidence.

When the Civil War ended slavery, the captives from Dahomey banned together and chose to establish a segregated community in the Mobile area. They named the place Africa Town. The inhabitants wanted to preserve their African heritage. They spoke in their native language, practiced their African customs, and maintained their social traditions until the twenty-first century. Cudjo Kazoola Lewis was the last survivor from the *Clotilde*. Kazoola died in 1935.

EARLY SETTLERS AND PROTESTERS

The First Africans in the British Colonies

Characters:
ANTHONY, *male, indentured servant*
ISABELLA, *female, indentured servant*
Costumes:
Typical attire for indentured servants
Props:
Baby doll wrapped in a blanket

(ANTHONY and ISABELLA describe their arrival to the colonies.)

ANTHONY
My name is Anthony, and this is my wife Isabella. We were among the first twenty Africans to arrive to an English colony. We came to Jamestown, Virginia, in late August 1619. We were here over a year before the Pilgrims landed in Massachusetts.

ISABELLA
We were not slaves. We were indentured servants, which meant we could work for our freedom. This is our son William.
(Turns the baby toward the audience.)
He was the first black child to be born in the British colonies.

(End scene.)

John Punch
(dates undetermined)
Slave

(JOHN explains how he became the first slave in the colonies.)

JOHN

My name is John Punch. I was brought to Virginia as an indentured servant. In 1640 two white indentured servants and I ran away. We were caught, returned to our masters, and whipped for trying to escape. At the trial, the two white servants had five extra years added to their service. As for me, I was made a servant for life. This made me the first slave in the colonies.
(Hangs his head.)

James Forten
(1766–1846)
Abolitionist, Businessman

(JAMES describes what prompted him to become an abolitionist and a businessman.)

JAMES

My name is James Forten. I was blessed enough to be born free in Philadelphia, Pennsylvania. I always believed every man should be free, and I fought for those rights for colonists and Negroes.

During the Revolutionary War, when I was about twelve years old, I volunteered to be a powder boy aboard an American warship. Unfortunately, the British captured the ship. Ordinarily, they sold black prisoners of war to slave holders in the West Indies; however, the captain's son and I had become friends, and I was transferred to a prison ship instead. Seven months passed before I was rescued. I returned to Philadelphia and became an apprentice to a sailmaker named Robert Bridges. When he retired, I took over the business. Within twenty years of owning the company, I employed forty men—black and white—and accrued a fortune of $100,000. During the War of 1812, I seized another opportunity to help America gain its freedom. I personally recruited 2,500 Negroes to help protect Philadelphia from the British.

I not only fought for colonists, I fought for black people's rights too. In 1813 I wrote "A Series of Letters by a Man of Color." In these letters, I opposed legislation that required all Negroes in Philadelphia to be registered. I knew that if this law were passed, it would be easy for slave catchers to locate runaways living in the city. Information like this needed to be shared with the black community. I had become a friend of the reverends Richard Allen and Absalom Jones, who were the two most influential ministers in Philadelphia. Reverend Allen allowed me to use his church on several occasions to inform black people about important issues that affected them. I also supported William Lloyd Garrison's newspaper, the *Liberator*, and personally recruited subscribers.

I was also one of the people responsible for organizing the first Negro Convention held in Philadelphia in 1830. The convention members expressed the political and social opinions of Northern free blacks. I was also president of the American Moral Reform Society. This organization actively promoted education, temperance, and abolition. I did, however, oppose the American Colonization Society, which encouraged free blacks to return to Africa. I felt the colonization movement would undermine the antislavery movement by relocating successful blacks to Africa. I believed that most of us would rather remain in America and live as free men.

If anyone were to ask me what I would want my legacy to be, I would tell them that I don't want to be remembered as a rich black man; I want to be remembered as a black man who enriched others' lives by fighting for their social rights and freedom.

Paul Cuffe
(1759–1817)
Businessman

Paul Cuffe

(PAUL explains how he used his wealth to help African Americans.)

PAUL

My name is Paul Cuffe. I was born free and lived in New Bedford, Massachusetts. My father was a slave, which made me more sensitive to the slaves' plight. I decided to make it my duty to help them.

When I was sixteen, I went to sea for a number of years. When I returned, I bought a farm in Massachusetts with $3,500 that I had saved. After a few years, I built a boat and later bought other vessels. I soon owned a fleet with ships of all sizes. I made money by shipping and hauling goods to various parts of the world. I was blessed and amassed a fortune. I was probably the richest black man in the country.

I wanted to help slaves become free, but I knew that freedom wasn't enough; they needed an education too. I was upset that New Bedford didn't have a school for black children, so I had one built on my farm. I paid the teachers' salaries out of my pocket. I was also aware that many people who were free didn't want to live in America. Some folks felt we would never receive racial equality in this country and that we should return to Africa. I agreed with this for three reasons. First, I was a devout Quaker. I wanted our people to return to Africa to help spread Christianity. Second, as a businessman, I saw this as an opportunity to open a new trading market. Third, I believed people should be able to choose where they wanted to live. In 1811 I sailed my ship, the *Traveler*, to Sierra Leone and founded the Friendly Society for Emigration of Free Negroes from America. I planned to take free blacks to the colony, but the War of 1812 delayed my trips. After the war, I resumed my voyages to Africa. In 1815 I transported thirty-eight people to Sierra Leone. It cost $4,000, and I paid all the expenses. I tried to use my wealth to help others. I believe that if you're blessed, you should use your blessings for unselfish purposes. I hope you feel the same way.

Sojourner Truth
(1797–1883)
Abolitionist, Preacher

Sojourner Truth

(SOJOURNER explains why she became a preacher and an abolitionist.)

SOJOURNER

I was born a slave in New York. Yes you heard me right, New York. Every state in the Union allowed slavery to exist at some point in time. And it didn't matter if you were in the North or the South, the life of a slave was hard and unpredictable. You never knew from day to day if you or somebody in your family would be sold, or if you would be beat so bad, you'd wish you were dead. I brought thirteen children into this world and saw nearly all of them sold into slavery. It didn't do me any good to cry out loud, because nobody listened but Jesus.

My faith in God is the only thing that helped me make it this far, and I know he wants me to go even farther. That's why I changed my name from Isabella Bomefree to Sojourner. A voice from heaven told me to take that name, because I was supposed to travel and tell people about their sins. I asked God to give me a second name. He told me to take the name Truth, because he wanted me to tell people the truth about slavery. I made that my life's purpose and for nearly thirty years I traveled, preaching and speaking about the evils of slavery. I was called a pilgrim of God.

Frederick Douglass
(1817–1895)
Abolitionist

Frederick Douglass

(FREDERICK *describes how life as a slave prompted him to become an abolitionist.*)

FREDERICK

My name is Frederick Douglass, and I was born a slave in Maryland.
I barely remember my mother, because my master Thomas Auld
separated me from her when I was a little boy. I was raised by my
grandmother. She died when I was eight years old. I was then sent to
work for a family in Baltimore, Maryland. While there, the mistress
of the house began teaching me to read and write. When my master
discovered I was learning, he became very angry and made his wife
stop teaching me.

I was sent back to the Auld plantation when I was about sixteen. Mr.
Auld was cruel, and he didn't like my defiant attitude. He sent me to a
man named Covey, who was known as a Negro breaker. That meant he
mistreated slaves and beat them into submission. He worked me twelve
to fourteen hours a day and beat me constantly. I became tired of this;
and one day as Covey tried to beat me, I hit him. My actions shocked
him, but he never laid a whip on me again. This was a psychological
victory for me.

Covey sent me back to Mr. Auld, and Auld hired me out to work on
another farm. I tried to escape but was caught and returned to him. This
time Auld sent me back to Baltimore to work as a hired hand in the
shipyard. While there, I was attacked by racists who nearly blinded me
in one eye. It was there in Baltimore that I met and fell in love with a
freeborn woman named Anna Murray. She helped me escape in 1838. I
stowed away aboard a ship sailing north. Anna and I later married.

I settled in New Bedford, Massachusetts, and changed my name
from Frederick Augustus Washington Bailey to Frederick Douglass.
I quickly became involved in the abolitionist movement. I was
admired for my speaking talents and attracted the attention of many
abolitionists, including the Massachusetts Anti-Slavery Society and one
of its founders, William Lloyd Garrison. In 1841 I became a lecturer

for the Massachusetts Anti-Slavery Society. I started speaking at engagements held throughout the North. It was dangerous work for me, because I was a fugitive slave. The more popular I became, the easier it was for me to be captured. Not all Northerners were against slavery.

In Pendleton, Indiana, I was attacked by a proslavery mob. They broke my arm and knocked me out. I was unconscious and left for dead. However, I continued to write and speak out against slavery in the South and discrimination in the North. I was known as an eloquent, powerful speaker. In fact, my orations were so eloquent that many people doubted that I was ever a slave. I decided to write an autobiography. I wanted to expose slavery for the evil it really was. I also wanted to disprove any doubts that I had ever been a slave. My book pointed to specific incidents and provided details. Because it was so specific, I had to leave the country and go into hiding in England to keep Mr. Auld from finding me. While there, some of my friends in America helped me purchase my freedom so that I could return.

Back in America, I moved to Rochester, New York, and started a newspaper called the *North Star.* My printing office also served as a station on the Underground Railroad. During this time, I continued my antislavery lectures. In 1851 I broke away from Garrison and the Anti-Slavery Society. I wanted to be more independent, and I realized that political intervention was a better way to abolish slavery; speaking and writing about slavery wasn't going to bring it to an end.

I recruited black soldiers, including my two sons, to fight in the Civil War when it erupted. After the war, I continued to pursue equal rights for Negroes. I spoke out against sharecropping and the convict lease system in the South. I also spoke out against the Supreme Court's anti-Negro rulings and the prevalence of lynching. In all my protests and fights for rights, I never asked for pity. All I asked for was what every man wanted, "Liberty, equality, and fraternity for all Americans without respect to color."

"The Meaning of July Fourth for the Negro"

(SPEAKER *recites an excerpt from Frederick Douglass's July 4, 1852 speech "The Meaning of July Fourth for the Negro."*)

SPEAKER

. . . Fellow citizens, pardon me, allow me to ask, why am I called upon to speak here today? What have I, or those I represent, to do with your national independence? Are the great principles of political freedom and of natural justice, embodied in that Declaration of Independence, extended to us? And am I, therefore, called upon to bring our humble offering to the national altar, and to confess the benefits and express devout gratitude for the blessings resulting from your independence to us?

. . . I say it with a sad sense of the disparity between us. I am not included within the pale of this glorious anniversary! Your high independence only reveals the immeasurable distance between us. The blessings in which you, this day, rejoice, are not enjoyed in common. The rich inheritance of justice, liberty, prosperity and independence, bequeathed by your fathers, is shared by you, not by me. The sunlight that brought light and healing to you, has brought stripes and death to me. The Fourth [of] July is yours not mine. You may rejoice, I must mourn. To drag a man in fetters into the grand illuminated temple of liberty, and call upon him to join you in joyous anthems, were inhuman mockery and sacrilegious irony. Do you mean, citizens, to mock me, by asking me to speak today? If so, there is a parallel to your conduct. And let me warn you that it is dangerous to copy the example of a nation whose crimes, towering up to heaven, were thrown down by the breath of the Almighty, burying that nation in irrevocable ruin! I can today take up the plaintive lament of a peeled and woe-smitten people!

. . . My subject, then, fellow citizens, is American slavery. I shall see this day and its popular characteristics from the slave's point of view. Standing there identified with the American bondman, making his wrongs mine, I do not hesitate to declare, with all my soul, that the character and conduct of this nation never looked blacker to me than on this Fourth of July! Whether we turn to the declarations of the past, or to the professions of the present, the conduct of the nation seems equally hideous and revolting. America is false to the past, false to the present, and solemnly binds herself to be false to the future. Standing with God and the crushed and bleeding slave on this occasion, I will, in the name of humanity which is outraged, in the name of liberty which is fettered, in the name of the constitution and the Bible which are disregarded and trampled upon, dare to call in question and to denounce, with all the emphasis I can command, everything that serves to perpetuate slavery—the great sin and shame of America!

Dred Scott
(ca. 1795–1858)
Judicial Protester

Dred Scott

(DRED explains how his U.S. Supreme Court case affected all slaves in the nation.)

DRED

My name is Dred Scott, and I'm the subject—or rather victim, as it turned out—of a U.S. Supreme Court case. An army surgeon named Dr. Emerson owned me. He was stationed in Missouri, which was a slave state. He was later transferred to the free state of Illinois then to the free territory of Wisconsin. He took me with him each time. When Dr. Emerson returned to Missouri, he brought me back too. When he died in 1843, I sued for my freedom. My case, *Scott v. Sanford*, went all the way to the U.S. Supreme Court.

On March 6, 1857, the Court ruled against me for three reasons. First, it said I was a black man; therefore, I wasn't a citizen and had no right to sue. Second, it declared that I was a resident of Missouri, so the laws in Illinois didn't apply to me. Third, I was labeled as property. The Court said people had the right to take their property anyplace they went and that Congress had no right to interfere.

My case not only affected me, it affected the whole country. The decision was a setback to the North and the abolitionists, because it nullified the Missouri Compromise of 1820. After the decision, no state could prevent slavery from coming into their region. The ruling made many abolitionists aware of the political and judicial systems' unreliability. It also became very clear that the only way slavery would end was through war.

Jermain Wesley Loguen
(1813–1872)
Abolitionist

(JERMAIN explains why he was committed to abolition.)

JERMAIN

My name is Jermain Wesley Loguen, and I was a runaway slave. When I was twenty-one, I escaped to Canada. After I gained my freedom, I became an abolitionist. I admired Frederick Douglass and worked with him to end slavery. I also wrote articles for his *North Star* newspaper. The power of the pen is effective, but action is often necessary too. That was the reason I became a conductor on the Underground Railroad. I aided approximately 1,500 runaways, including Harriet Tubman. I risked my life to help others, and I don't have any regrets.

Moses on the Freedom Trail

Characters:
HARRIET TUBMAN, *female, Underground Railroad conductor*
JORDAN, *male fictional character, slave*
JAMES, *male fictional character, slave*
LINDA, *female fictional character, slave*
Costumes:
Typical attire for slaves
Props:
Baby doll wrapped in a blanket

(HARRIET, JORDAN, JAMES, *and* LINDA *walk swiftly through the woods at night; the sound of dogs barking is audible in the distance.)*

HARRIET
Come on y'all, we have to hurry. The slave catchers are right behind us!
(Barking in the background gradually gets lower.)
We're almost there.

JORDAN
I'm scared! I think we're lost. We better turn back. We can't make it!
(Starts to turn around.)

HARRIET
(Grabs his arm.)
Don't nobody turn 'round when they travel on my train. I never lost
a passenger and my train don't run backwards! I made a promise
to myself that I would be free or I would be dead. I ain't gonna be
nobody's slave no more and neither are you!
(Calmly)
Just settle down, we're not lost. I may not be able to read or write, but
I know how to read the signs of God. You see that bright star up there?
That's the North Star. Long as we keep following it, we'll find our way
to freedom.
(Dogs stop barking.)

JAMES
I don't hear the dogs. What happened?

HARRIET
You don't hear them, because we're in a free state now.

LINDA
You mean we're truly free? That means my baby is going to grow up a
free man.
(Hugs the baby doll closer.)

(The group starts singing, dancing, and praising God.)

(End scene.)

The Richardson Family

Characters:
JOHN, *male fictional character, Underground Railroad conductor*
DELIA, *female fictional character,* JOHN's *wife*

MARTHA, *female fictional character,* JOHN *and* DELIA'*s daughter*
CLARENCE, *male fictional character,* JOHN *and* DELIA'*s son*
BILL, *male fictional character,* JOHN *and* DELIA'*s son*
EVA, *female fictional character,* JOHN *and* DELIA'*s daughter*
Costumes:
Casual attire of the mid-1800s
Props:
Table, six chairs

*(*JOHN, DELIA, MARTHA, CLARENCE, BILL, *and* EVA *explain how the Underground Railroad operates.)*

JOHN
Delia! Delia!

DELIA
(Enters)
I'm right here John; stop your shouting. What's all the excitement about?

JOHN
I just got word that two more slaves are coming. We have to feed them, hide them, and get them across the border as soon as possible. I hear that slave catchers are all around.

DELIA
Operating a station on the Underground Railroad is getting more and more risky. Ever since they passed the Fugitive Slave Law in 1850, those slave catchers have gotten worse. They know that making it to a free state doesn't make you free anymore. That Fugitive Slave Law allows slave catchers to go anywhere in America and return slaves to their masters. Now we have to get people out the country, which is more dangerous, because we have to extend the railroad a lot farther.

JOHN

It's a good thing that the Underground Railroad runs as far north as Canada, as far south as the Bahamas, and as far southwest as Mexico.

DELIA

That's why we have to keep our safe house open. Remember we were runaways too. We wouldn't have made it if we didn't have help, but we were luckier than a lot of people who escaped. We were able to work and buy our freedom. Many others have to keep running and looking over their shoulders every day.

JOHN

Call the children. I want them to know that we're expecting some important parcels.

DELIA

Martha, Clarence, Bill, Eva. Come quickly.
(Children enter.)

JOHN

I want you to stay near the house, we're expecting company.

CLARENCE

You mean some runaways?

DELIA

Hush! You know we don't use words like that. You never know who's listening.

JOHN

We can't afford to get careless. I want each of you to take a seat and tell me what you remember about the Underground Railroad.
(All sit.)

MARTHA

Spirituals are the main way we pass codes. "Swing low, sweet chariot coming to carry me home" means that a conductor is in the area, and an escape will be coming soon. "Wade in the water" means wade in the rivers and streams so the dogs can't pick up your scent. "Follow the drinking gourd" means look for the Little Dipper, because the North Star is in it. The North Star points the way to freedom.

CLARENCE

Quilts are another way we pass secret messages. Slaves will hang quilts like they are airing them. When the master and mistress see these quilts hanging on the fence, they don't give them a second thought. They never suspect codes are stitched in them. The lengths between stitches let runaways know about how far the distances are between plantations. The wagon wheel design tells you to pack all the things that can go into a wagon and be used on a trip. A tumbling-box-patterned quilt is usually the last quilt hung. It means it's time to pack up and move on.

BILL

The Underground Railroad also has its own secret definitions for words. An agent is the person who transports the runaways. They have the most dangerous job, because they can be charged with slave stealing. That's a serious crime. If caught, they can be beaten, imprisoned for a long time, tarred and feathered, or even killed. A conductor is someone who goes into slave territory to lead the slaves to freedom. Parcels are the passengers. Tracks are the trails or roads in the backcountry that are safe to use.

EVA

A depot or station is a safe house. Even the safe houses have their secrets. If the porch light is on, it means that it's safe to come inside. The stationmasters hide slaves in attics, basements, and sometimes behind hidden walls. Slaves never know how long they have to stay there. It could be overnight or several weeks. Some houses are watched by slave catchers, so the quicker the runaways get out, the better. Also, other slaves might be coming for protection any minute.

JOHN
We've helped twenty people make it to Canada. It takes a lot of courage to be a part of the Underground Railroad but even more courage to try to escape. With God's help, we'll keep doing it.

(End scene.)

William Still
(1821–1902)
Underground Railroad Safe House Operator

(WILLIAM explains his role on the Underground Railroad as a safe house operator.)

WILLIAM
My name is William Still. In 1844 I left my family's farm in New Jersey and moved to Philadelphia. I got a job with the Philadelphia Society for the Abolition of Slavery. Shortly afterward, I became a conductor on the Underground Railroad. I kept a safe house for runaways who passed through that city. I helped 649 people escape, including my brother.

I was different from the other conductors, because I kept a record of all the people I aided. I wanted to document the mistreatment that the slaves endured. This information was also vital, because it helped friends and families find their loved ones. But recording it was extremely dangerous. If my record got into the wrong hands, it would prove that I had been helping slaves escape. I could be charged with slave stealing, which was a serious crime. Also, if slave catchers or owners had access to my files, they could identify and locate their runaways. I kept my records well hidden, and with the help of God, no one found them. In 1872 I put these records and other accounts of slaves' bravery into a book called *The Underground Railroad*. I hoped to expose the hardships of slavery and the strength of the slave.

After the Civil War, I became openly involved in helping former slaves. I established an orphanage for black children and helped manage a home for elderly citizens. I also helped organize one of the first YMCAs for Negroes.

I took many risks in my life, but I considered it a worthwhile sacrifice to help slaves and former slaves gain the privileges that all Americans deserved.

Harriet Tubman
(ca. 1821–1913)
Underground Railroad Conductor

Harriet Tubman

(HARRIET, *now a senior citizen, reflects on how she led slaves to freedom on the Underground Railroad.*)

HARRIET
(*Looking at a poster.*)

Forty thousand dollars! That's a lot of money for one person. See this poster?

(Turns the poster toward the audience.)

That's how much money slave owners offered for my capture. They put out a lot of wanted posters too. One time I went to sleep on a bench where one was nailed right over my head. I never learned to read, so I didn't know what it said. The Lord helped me then, and he helped me all nineteen times I journeyed into slave territory. Moses of Her People, that is what black people called me, but slave owners called me everything but a child of God.

My name is Harriet Tubman. I was a conductor on the Underground Railroad. I always knew slavery was wrong for me and everybody else too, and I wanted to do something about it. When I was young, I received a blow to my head from an overseer when I tried to defend another slave. It caused me to black out and have seizures, even to this day. But I wouldn't let seizures and not knowing how to read stop me from leading slaves north to freedom. When I was twenty-eight, I made up my mind to run away. I escaped to Philadelphia. I couldn't read a map, but I could read the North Star in the sky. That was the only guide I needed. After that, I went back to free others.

I was able to lead about three hundred slaves to freedom. After the Fugitive Slave Law was passed, we had to go all the way to Canada. Between my trips, I would work as a cook and take in laundry. When I had enough money saved, I would disguise myself and head south. I made sure I was careful with my plans. I would prepare the slaves to escape on Saturday nights, because I knew it would be Monday before slave masters could get their posters made up. I would disguise myself to look old and would sing as I went along the roadside. When white people saw me, they thought I was just a harmless little old lady singing to Jesus. They didn't know I used spirituals to send secret messages, but my people knew what the songs meant. Before we started, I gave everybody these rules: (1) keep your mouth shut and tell nobody about the escape plans, (2) be on time, (3) do what I tell you to do, and (4) be prepared to die rather than go back. I always said that on my underground railroad I never ran a train off the track, and I never lost a passenger.

During the Civil War, I led a raid that freed 750 people. I worked as an army nurse, spy, and scout too. After the war, I established a home for former slaves who were penniless and too old and sickly to work. I dedicated my life to helping my people in any manner God led me.

Thoughts from a Slave to His Master

(SPEAKER reaffirms his inner strength despite his status as a slave.)

SPEAKER
I know when I was bought
You believed you could control my thoughts
I know you don't want to hear it
But I will never let you break my spirit
I know there will come a day
When these words you will hear me say:

You cannot enslave my mind
This I will always know
Oh, I will pick your cotton
And the other things you grow

You cannot steal my mind
In my mind I will always be free
Even though my body was sold
And you stole my history

My father was a king
My mother was a queen
I know it is true
I saw it in a dream

You did not buy me for my beauty
You bought me because I was strong
But if you think you can buy my spirit
Let me tell you, you are wrong!

You cannot tell me how to pray
For when my prayers come true
There will be a day of justice
And I will be treated the same as you

You cannot enslave my feelings
No matter how much you try
I'm going to hide my tears
I refuse to let you see me cry

My tears are for freedom
My soul cries for liberty
One day it will not be just a dream
One day I will be free!

Auction and Negro Sales, Whitehall Street

A slave auction

REVOLUTIONARY WAR PATRIOTS

The Revolutionary War

(SPEAKER 1, SPEAKER 2, *and* SPEAKER 3 *consecutively come to center stage and discuss the impact African Americans had on the Revolutionary War.)*

SPEAKER 1
African Americans fought for the freedom of the United States at a time when they themselves were not free. Black patriots proved on more than one occasion that they were men of valor. When the American Revolution began, the colonists were losing badly to the British. The British Army was better trained, and General George Washington had difficulty recruiting dependable soldiers. Despite this, Washington didn't want to enlist black soldiers. He didn't reconsider his position until June 1775, when Lord Dunmore—Virginia's loyalist governor—offered freedom to any slave who would fight for the British. In December 1775 Washington allowed African Americans to enlist.
(SPEAKER 1 moves to stage right.)

SPEAKER 2
Even with Washington lifting his ban on black recruitment, many African Americans were reluctant to join the army. They wanted to be guaranteed their freedom. Most slave owners wouldn't give them that assurance. The British took advantage of this and promised freedom to

all who would fight on their side. It is believed that as many as twenty to thirty thousand African Americans joined the British Army or aided them in some way.

(SPEAKER 2 moves to stage right.)

SPEAKER 3

Numerous enslaved and free blacks fought bravely for the United States. Most hoped if America became free, all men would be free. Some who were already free fought out of pure patriotism. Many were sailors, privateers, spies, or drummers and fifers on the battlefields. Most men served in integrated regiments. Rhode Island was an exception. Their colony didn't have enough men to meet their required quota, so they formed an all-black unit. From the first conflict with the British in Boston until the last battle at Yorktown, African Americans were active in the War for Independence.

(Speakers exit stage.)

Crispus Attucks
(1723–1770)
Patriot

Crispus Attucks

(SPEAKER explains why Crispus Attucks is considered a patriot.)

SPEAKER

Crispus Attucks was born in Framingham, Massachusetts. He was a runaway slave, so he knew how important it was to have freedom. He worked as a seaman out of the Boston port. The tensions were mounting everywhere, and colonists resented British occupation. At approximately 9:00 p.m. on March 6, 1770, several British soldiers marched down a Boston street after hearing a fellow soldier call for help. As the soldiers advanced, the colonists started throwing rocks and sticks at them. A shot was fired. Crispus Attucks and three other patriots lay dead. Attucks became a martyr. He was the first person to die in the protest, which led to the war that gained the colonists' independence from Britain.

Peter Salem
(ca. 1750–1816)
Patriot

(PETER explains why he is called an American patriot.)

PETER

My name is Peter Salem. I was a member of the First Massachusetts Regiment. I was one of the Negro soldiers at the Battle of Bunker Hill on June 17, 1775. Some of the other patriots with me were Salem Poor, who had been sent earlier to help fortify the area, and Prince Hall, who later founded the first black Masonic lodge in the colonies. Besides us, other Negro patriots were Seymour Burr, Pomp Fisk, Cuff Whittemore, Caesar Dickerson, Cuff Hayes, and Barzillai Lew, who was also a veteran of the French and Indian War.

Perhaps I'm a little better known than some of the other Negro soldiers of that battle, because I was credited with firing the shot that mortally wounded British officer Major John Pitcairn. I also took part in the

Battle of Saratoga in 1777. I remained in the Continental Army for seven years.

Prince Whipple
(?–1796)
Patriot

(PRINCE explains why he is called an American patriot.)

PRINCE

I am Prince Whipple, and I was one of George Washington's bodyguards. I was also in the boat with him on December 25, 1776, when he crossed the Delaware River to lead a surprise attack on the German Hessian soldiers at Trenton, New Jersey.

Oliver Cromwell
(ca. 1753–1853)
Patriot

(OLIVER describes his military service during the American Revolution.)

OLIVER

I'm Oliver Cromwell. I was one of the 2,400 men that George Washington handpicked to go with him to attack the Hessian soldiers. They were quartered for the winter in a British garrison in Trenton, New Jersey. Washington needed brave, dependable men. He had become frustrated with trying to build an army. As he put it, "They leave you at the last critical moment." I was in the boat with him when he crossed the Delaware River on that bitter, cold Christmas night. Our surprise attack was a victory.

I served for six years and nine months directly under General Washington's command. I participated in four key battles, including the last battle at Yorktown in 1781. After the war ended, I received an annual pension of $90 for my military service. With some of this money, I bought a small farm where my wife and I raised our family.

Pompey Lamb
(dates undetermined)
Patriot

(POMPEY describes his service as a spy for the colonists during the Revolutionary War.)

POMPEY

I am Pompey Lamb. In 1777 I helped the colonists recapture the fort at Stony Point, New York. I was a spy and got into the fort numerous times by carrying a basket of strawberries and talking the sentry into letting me sell them to the British officers. He thought I was a comical, harmless black man and let me pass. The officers were glad to get the berries and allowed me to come night and day. On the tenth night some patriots came with me and overtook the sentry. Other soldiers scaled the wall and attacked the British. We were victorious.

James Armistead
(1760–1832)
Patriot

(JAMES describes his service as a spy during the American Revolution.)

JAMES

My name is James Armistead. I was born a slave in 1760. I was a young man when the Revolutionary War started. I wanted to help the colonists become independent of British control. I convinced my master to allow me to join General Lafayette, a French general who was one of George Washington's chief allies. I volunteered to act as a spy. I obtained a position as an aide to the British general Cornwallis. I was able to gain access to information that led to the colonists' victory at Yorktown. This was the last battle of the war. In 1786 I was granted my freedom and given an annual pension of $40.

SLAVE REBELLIONS

Rebels with a Cause

(SPEAKER describes the justifications given for slavery and the many ways in which slaves rebelled.)

SPEAKER
Slave owners had numerous explanations to justify the peculiar institution of slavery. Initially, slave traders and owners alleged that they kidnapped Africans, because they were heathens who needed to be converted to Christianity. Others rationalized that blacks were childlike and needed someone to take care of them. Another justification was that slaves were happy and well taken care of and that they didn't really desire to be free. Perhaps there were a few enslaved people who were treated reasonably well. Those few were usually the mistresses or children of slave owners, but these situations of kind treatment weren't the norm.

Almost every person enslaved desired to be free. Many rebelled against slavery in their own way. Slaves were known to break work tools, pretend to be too sick to work, slow down their work, or attempt to escape. There have even been accounts where some slaves poisoned their owners. There were also slave rebellions throughout the nation in the North and the South. Some Africans even committed mutiny aboard the slave ships before they reached land. There were individual martyrs, conductors on the Underground Railroad, and those who protested by becoming abolitionists. These brave protesters and rebels proved to the world that slaves weren't childlike, happy individuals. They were human beings who wanted to be free!

Major Slave Rebellions

(SPEAKER *tells of the six major slave rebellions in the United States.*)

SPEAKER
There were six major slave rebellions in the nation: (1) the New York Slave Rebellion in 1712; (2) the Stono, South Carolina Rebellion in 1739; (3) the Gabriel Prosser Conspiracy in 1800; (4) the Louisiana Rebellion in 1811; (5) the Denmark Vesey Conspiracy in 1822; and (6) the Nat Turner Rebellion in 1831. Many African Americans felt the same as American patriot Patrick Henry who declared, "Give me liberty, or give me death!"

The New York Slave Rebellion of 1712

(SPEAKER *briefly recounts the events of the New York Slave Rebellion of 1712 and its impact on slave importation.*)

SPEAKER
The New York Slave Rebellion of 1712 was the first major slave uprising in America. Although there was no identified leader, the rebellion was planned by one or more individuals. The strategy was to take advantage of the fight between the British and the French. The slaves sought to use the tensions between the colonists and the Iroquois Indians as well. Once the rebellion started, the soldiers were summoned and the rebellion was quashed. Twenty-five to thirty slaves and nine whites were killed, and six more were wounded in the aftermath. More than seventy African Americans were jailed, and twenty-one were executed. This rebellion had an impact throughout the country.

Massachusetts, for example, passed legislation the following year that put a ban on slave importation into its colony.

Jemmy
(dates undetermined)
Slave Insurrectionist

(SPEAKER *describes the events that led to Jemmy's revolt in 1739.*)

SPEAKER
There were several factors that contributed to the rebellion of 1739. First, the weakened economy caused many slave owners to reduce costs by feeding slaves less, which led to hunger. Second, in an effort to get more money, owners began to sell more of their slaves, thereby breaking up slave families. Third, the hostility among the Native Americans toward the white population presented an advantage and potential ally for those who wanted to escape.

In the midst of this climate a slave named Jemmy led a revolt in Stono, South Carolina, just several miles southwest of Charleston on September 9, 1739. Jemmy initially had twenty followers, who were called saltwater slaves because they were born in Africa. Their goal was to make it to Spanish Florida or Puerto Rico, which promised freedom to any runaway who could reach their borders. These men fought with the military strategies used in the African country Angola. The rebels killed two guards who were posted at a warehouse then proceeded to take guns and ammunition. At least sixty others followed. They killed more whites on their march to Florida. The militia was called out before the rebels could reach their destination. Approximately twenty-five whites and fifty blacks were killed during the revolt and its aftermath. Most of the rebels were tracked down and jailed.

Very little is known about Jemmy, except that he was probably born in Angola. Nothing indicates whether he was captured or if he escaped; however, one thing is certain. He chose to risk his life for the sake of freedom.

Gabriel Prosser
(1776–1800)
Slave Insurrectionist

(SPEAKER describes Gabriel Prosser's attempt to free more than one thousand slaves.)

SPEAKER

In 1800, when he was twenty-four years old, Gabriel Prosser led a rebellion known as the Great Gabriel Conspiracy. Gabriel, his brothers Solomon and Martin, and more than one thousand enslaved followers plotted to take over Richmond, Virginia. The revolt failed because a terrible storm hit the area on the Saturday night that they were supposed to meet. The swamp flooded, and bridges and roads were demolished, which made travel impossible. Two slaves became scared and told about the plot.

Governor Monroe, who later became the fifth president of the United States, sent troops to capture Prosser and his coconspirators. During the next few weeks, about forty people were executed. Some of them weren't even involved in the conspiracy. When authorities apprehended Prosser, they beat him over and over again trying to force him to reveal the others involved in the uprising. He refused to name anyone, despite being tortured. He was condemned to hang. On October 7, 1800, Gabriel Prosser went to his death with dignity and in silence.

Charles Deslondes
(?–1811)
Slave Insurrectionist

(SPEAKER describes the revolt along the Mississippi River led by Charles Deslondes.)

SPEAKER

On January 8, 1811, a year before Louisiana became a state, a black man named Charles Deslondes led one of the largest slave rebellions in the history of America. Deslondes was born in Haiti but was a slave driver on a plantation north of New Orleans. He organized and led between two hundred to five hundred slaves on a rampage through St. Charles and St. John the Baptist parishes by way of the Mississippi River. Their quest was to reach New Orleans. On their way to that city, they killed at least two people, burned crops and plantations, and took ammunition.

They were stopped just west of New Orleans by a militia of planters. Thirty-six slaves were killed. Deslondes and twenty of his rebels were captured, tried, and sentenced to die. After they were shot, their heads were decapitated and placed on poles along the Red River as a warning to other slaves who might have thought of joining a revolt in the future.

Garcia
(?–1816)
Runaway Slave, Soldier

(SPEAKER recounts Garcia's protection and surrender of Fort Negro.)

SPEAKER

Before Florida became a state, it was a territory that belonged to Spain. Runaway slaves would form settlements there under the protection and brotherhood of the Native American Seminoles. Runaways and Seminoles would band together and raid plantations in Georgia to attempt to free relatives and friends.

About three hundred black men, women, and children lived in Fort Negro, which was an abandoned British fort. The fort was under the command and protection of a runaway slave named Garcia. It was located in northwest Florida, sixty miles from the border of Georgia. It was a haven for escapees and a threat to Georgian slave owners. The slave owners pressured the American government to attack the fort, which was in Spanish territory. An invasion would have been considered an attack on a foreign country, but the government ignored that fact.

On July 27, 1816, General Jackson—who later became president of the United States—led the assault on Fort Negro. When Garcia refused to surrender, Jackson attacked the well-built fort with cannonballs. One of the cannonballs hit a powder house and caused an explosion. The blast killed and wounded more than two hundred people. The sixty-three survivors were returned to slavery. Garcia was captured and shot before a firing squad. Garcia was an example of another rebel who chose to die rather than give up his freedom.

Denmark Vesey
(1767–1822)
Slave Insurrectionist

(SPEAKER recounts Denmark Vesey's attempts to lead a revolt in South Carolina.)

SPEAKER
Denmark Vesey was born enslaved and lived in Charleston, South Carolina. His life changed when he won $1,500 with a lottery ticket.

He took $600 of it to buy his freedom. He opened a carpentry shop and became wealthy. He fearlessly spoke out against slavery and encouraged free blacks to speak up for equal rights and privileges.

In 1821 he believed the time had come for slaves to gain their freedom by force. Vesey planned a massive rebellion. He picked his leaders carefully and included an enslaved couple who worked for the governor of South Carolina. He expected to have about nine thousand followers. Midnight Sunday July 14, 1822 was the time scheduled to attack several key parts of the city.

Unfortunately, a house servant who was asked to join them revealed the plot. Once alerted, Charleston city officials acted swiftly. When Vesey learned that he had been deceived, he changed the rebellion date to June 16. Again he was betrayed by another slave. This time the slave confessed everything to authorities, because he was afraid of capture.

Vesey went into hiding but was found five days later. He was tried and given the death sentence. On July 2, 1822, Vesey and five of his followers were hanged. Denmark Vesey should not only be remembered for his bravery, but he should also be remembered as a man who gave up his personal freedom, his wealth, and his life so that others could also be free.

Nat Turner
(1800–1831)
Slave Insurrectionist

Nat Turner

(SPEAKER recounts Nat Turner's slave revolt in Virginia in 1831.)

SPEAKER

Nat Turner said, "I would never be of any service to anyone as a
slave." Turner was a deeply religious man. He preached on Sundays
and was greatly admired by blacks and whites. What would make
such a God fearing man lead a revolt in Virginia that would kill nearly
sixty slave holders and their families? Turner believed that he was
called by God to free slaves. When an eclipse of the sun occurred on
February 12, 1831, he interpreted it as a sign from the Lord that it was
time to prepare himself to slay his enemies with their own weapons.
He planned the rebellion for the Fourth of July. However, he became
ill and had to cancel his plans. On August 13 there appeared a bluish
green haze that covered the sun. This was the sign Turner was waiting
to see. He and six of his trusted followers made their final plans.
August 22 was the date set for the uprising.

Once the revolt started, it continued for forty hours. Between sixty and
eighty slaves joined in the attack. At least fifty-seven slave holders
and their families were killed. The rebels only spared poor whites who

didn't own slaves. By the time word spread about the revolt, hundreds of white men were riding the countryside in search of Nat Turner and his followers. Dozens of the men were caught or killed. Turner avoided capture for two months. On October 30, 1831, the Virginia militia found him in a little cave near his former home. On November 5, 1831, he went before the court, was tried and convicted, and received the death sentence. On November 11, 1831, he was hanged. He predicted on the day of his death that God would refuse to let the sun shine as a sign that slavery was evil. Though the sun didn't refuse to shine, a severe thunderstorm occurred. Thunderstorms were rare for that time of year. This made some people believe his words.

Joseph Cinque
(1817–1879)
Mutineer

Joseph Cinque

(SPEAKER recounts the events of Joseph Cinque's mutiny of Amistad.)

SPEAKER
"Give us free! Give us free!" Joseph Cinque didn't know many English words, but he could pronounce and understood these. Cinque was the leader of the most famous slave mutiny aboard a slave ship; the ship was the *Amistad.*

Cinque was kidnapped in 1839 and sold to the owner of a slave factory on the coast of Africa. From there, he and other captives were forced aboard the *Amistad.* Two weeks after the ship set sail, Cinque managed to pry a nail from the side of the ship, free himself, and unfasten the chains of the other fifty-one captives. The Africans proceeded to sneak onto the deck and overtake the crew and ship; however, they didn't know anything about sailing. They ordered the helmsman to sail east back to Africa, but they were tricked. The helmsman changed the course a little each night hoping to reach one of the Southern states where slavery was legal. Instead the *Amistad* landed in New York. The U.S. Coast Guard arrested Cinque and some of his followers when they went ashore to get food and supplies. They were charged with mutiny and murder.

Their fight for their right to return to Africa went all the way to the U.S. Supreme Court. Former president John Quincy Adams came out of retirement as a lawyer to represent Cinque and his followers. On March 3, 1841, the African mutineers were ordered to be freed without delay. They were returned to Africa and settled in Sierra Leone.

Madison Washington
(dates undetermined)
Slave Insurrectionist, Mutineer

(SPEAKER describes Madison Washington's mutiny of the slave ship Creole.)

SPEAKER
On October 27, 1841, the slave ship *Creole* carried 135 slaves from Hampton Roads, Virginia, to New Orleans, Louisiana. Madison Washington was one of the captives aboard the ship. He escaped to Canada a year earlier but returned in hopes of freeing his wife Susan.

He was caught, returned to his owner, and forced back aboard the *Creole.*

Washington was a smart man and took precautions in case he was captured. He sewed small files, saws, and other tools into the lining of his garments. He was chained to the floor of the ship and was watched carefully, because he was a runaway; but nobody checked his clothes. He waited for the right opportunity to make his move. Nine days later, the crew had to keep busy on deck because of bad weather. This gave Washington enough time to free himself and the other slaves. That night, he and eighteen others made their way onto the deck. They overtook the captain and crew and made them prisoners. Washington and his followers forced them to sail to a British colony where slavery was outlawed. On November 9, 1841, the *Creole* reached Nassau in the Bahamas. The British government gave the enslaved mutineers sanctuary. Slavery supporters in the United States demanded their return and wanted the mutiny leaders tried for murder. The British refused to send the former slaves back to America, and to Washington's surprise, his wife Susan was aboard the *Creole.* He didn't even know it at the time of the mutiny.

John Anthony Copeland Jr.
(1836–1859)
Conspirator

(SPEAKER describes John Anthony Copeland's involvement in the conspiracy to attack a federal arsenal.)

SPEAKER
John Copeland Jr. was born a free man in Raleigh, North Carolina, but he couldn't enjoy his freedom. He knew that thousands of other black people were being sold and brutalized by their masters. When he was a young man in Ohio, he was thrown in jail for helping a runaway

hide from slave catchers. While in prison, he concluded that slavery couldn't be brought to an end peacefully. When he was released, he and his uncle joined John Brown, the radical white abolitionist who was recruiting followers to attack the federal arsenal in Harpers Ferry, which at the time was a part of the state of Virginia.

On October 16, 1859, Copeland and four other African Americans were among Brown's twenty-one coconspirators. Word of the raid quickly spread, and soon a troop of Virginian militia surrounded them. That evening, General Lee led a trainload of marines to Harpers Ferry. The battle lasted two days. Nine of the conspirators were killed, and four others—including Copeland—attempted to escape but were captured. When Copeland went to court, he was found guilty of murder and treason. His final words were written in a letter. He wrote, "I am not terrified of the gallows . . . upon which I am to soon stand and suffer death for what George Washington was made a hero for doing. I am dying for freedom. I could not die for a better cause."

Osborne Perry Anderson
(1830–1872)
Conspirator

(SPEAKER describes Osborne Perry Anderson's role in the attack on Harper's Ferry.)

SPEAKER
Osborne Perry Anderson was born in the free state of Pennsylvania. He moved to Chatham, Canada in the early 1850s, because free African Americans were losing their rights in the United States. Once in Chatham, he settled in a community of fugitive slaves and emigrants. He was a member of the May 8, 1858 convention, which conspirators John Brown and Martin Delany convened. The purpose of the meeting was to make plans to free slaves by militant actions; however, the

plans were delayed. Members of the convention felt going to the South to free slaves would not be possible without the abolitionists' commitment, support, or funds. Anderson was the only delegate to meet John Brown near Harpers Ferry.

He accompanied John Brown to the raid on Harpers Ferry. Most of Brown's followers were killed during the attack. Brown and several others were hanged. Anderson was the only survivor of the raid. He managed to elude authorities with the help of friends. He later served as a recruiter for the U.S. Colored Troops in Indiana and Arkansas. It is also reported that Anderson served in the Civil War under an assumed name.

INVENTORS AND SCIENTISTS

The Mind Is a Wonderful Thing to Use

(SPEAKER recalls the lost inventions of African Americans.)

SPEAKER

No one knows for certain how many inventions African Americans actually made. Prior to the end of the Civil War, it was illegal in the South for slaves to get patents for their inventions. Some of their ideas were stolen, some were sold for little or no money, and some were never recorded. African Americans made thousands of devices, or improved existing discoveries in medicine, transportation, science, and health technology.

Benjamin Banneker
(1731–1806)
Inventor, Mathematician, Surveyor

(BENJAMIN explains his contributions to the United States as an inventor and a surveyor.)

BENJAMIN

My name is Benjamin Banneker. I was born near Baltimore, Maryland. I was born free, because my mother and grandmother were free women. My grandmother Molly Welsh used the Bible to teach me to read and write. When I was twelve, I attended a Quaker school that was nearby. I became interested in mathematics. I loved working with numbers so much that I would make up problems just for fun and solve them. When I was nineteen, I met a traveling salesman who showed me a pocket watch. I was so fascinated that I immediately started drawing plans for a clock. It took me two years to build, and it was made entirely of wood. It kept perfect time for over forty years and was the first clock built entirely in America.

Astronomy was another one of my loves. I predicted that a solar eclipse would occur on April 14, 1789. Two leading astronomers said I was wrong. Sure enough, on the date I predicted, an eclipse occurred. In 1792 I published my second almanac. Some of the things I included were facts about the weather, medical information, eclipse predictions, the hours of the sunrise and sunset, poetry, and antislavery essays. Even though I was busy with my research involving astronomy and mathematics, I was equally concerned about the treatment of my race. I was offended by whites who thought black people had limited intelligence. In 1791 I wrote a letter to the secretary of state, Thomas Jefferson, in response to his statement that blacks were inferior to whites in reason and imagination. I also included a copy of my almanac. It made Mr. Jefferson change his opinion in a hurry. He was so impressed with the almanac that he sent a copy to the French Academy of Sciences in Paris.

When the nation's capital was relocated from Philadelphia to Washington, D.C., Thomas Jefferson recommended that I become a member of the chief engineering team that was designing the city. I helped determine locations for a number of public buildings, including the White House, the Capitol, and the Department of the Treasury. I was proud to serve my country, but I was just as proud to represent my race. I proved that Negroes were intellectually equal to any other race of people.

Thomas Jennings
(1801–1859)
Inventor, Abolitionist

(THOMAS describes how he became the first African American to receive a patent.)

THOMAS

That's what I like, nice clean clothes. Hello, my name is Thomas Jennings. I was the first black person in America to receive a patent. On March 3, 1821, I was awarded a patent for a dry cleaning solution. Although I was the first Negro to receive a patent, I may or may not have been the first of my race to invent something. Nobody knows for sure, because it was illegal for slaves to get patents for their inventions. We will never know how many inventions we did not get credit for. I was lucky. I was a free man living in New York City. That's why I became an active abolitionist. I wanted others to be able to get credit for their contributions and to become freemen too.

Lewis Temple
(1800–1854)
Inventor

(LEWIS explains how he improved the harpoon's design.)

LEWIS

I'm Lewis Temple. Many of you may not have heard of me, because my invention is not used today. However, if you lived in the whaling town of New Bedford, Massachusetts when I lived there, you definitely would've known me. I was born into slavery but was freed in 1829 and moved north. I opened a blacksmith shop in New Bedford. The men on the whaling ships complained that their long spears, called harpoons, didn't work very well. When they tried to stick them into the whales, the harpoons would fall off and the whales would escape. I invented a much more effective one that could catch more whales. I never got a patent for my harpoon, so many others copied my idea and reaped the financial rewards.

Norbert Rillieux
(1806–1894)
Inventor, Scientist

(NORBERT recalls what led him to develop a method to extract water from sugarcane juice.)

NORBERT
My name is Norbert Rillieux. I was born in New Orleans, Louisiana. My mother was a black woman, and my father was a wealthy white plantation owner. The better schools in New Orleans wouldn't accept me, because I was black. My father decided to send me to Paris, France, because he wanted me to have a good education. As a boy, I saw slaves pour boiling sugarcane juice from one large pot into another. It was dangerous, and many workers were scalded. Unfortunately, it was the only way known to speed up the evaporation of the water in the juice.

While living in Paris, I developed a method of extracting the water from the juice. It was safer, cheaper, faster, and produced better quality sugar. My invention made me rich, but it also caused me personal problems. My sugar refining system increased the demand for slave labor, and many whites resented my wealth and success. Racial tensions were growing in New Orleans, and laws were passed to restrict the rights of all black people—enslaved and free. Blacks couldn't attend city-run schools, couldn't visit a white person without a formal invitation, and couldn't walk down the streets without a pass.

I became frustrated with racism in the United States and returned to France, where I lived for the rest of my life.

George Crum
(1822–1914)
Inventor

(GEORGE recounts what led him to create potato chips.)

GEORGE
(Sitting at a table eating potato chips.)
Potato chips, potato chips, yum, yum, yum! I invented them, my name is George Crum.
(Looks at the audience and offers some.)
Have a few. They're good. I made them myself.

I still remember the day I first made a potato chip. In 1853 I was working in Saratoga Springs, New York, at the Moon Lake Resort as a chef. Most of the guests loved fried potatoes, and I made them just right. One day we had a guest come in, and he complained that the potatoes were cut too thick. I knew they weren't, but I cut some thinner and sent them to him. He still complained. I decided to fix him. I cut them so thin he couldn't pick them up with a fork. He had to use his fingers. I was sure I wouldn't hear any more from him, but guess what happened? He loved them! And that's how I invented potato chips.
(Starts eating again.)

Elijah McCoy
(1841–1929)
Inventor, Engineer

(ELIJAH explains how he created an efficient way to lubricate train parts.)

ELIJAH

My name is Elijah McCoy. Have you ever heard the term "the real McCoy?" It came from my inventions, which were considered to be the best. I was born in Canada, because my parents were runaway slaves from Kentucky. When slavery ended in the United States, they returned and settled in Michigan. Because racism prevented me from getting the quality education I needed, my parents encouraged me to go to Scotland. I was able to get a job as an apprentice to a mechanical engineer while there. However, when I returned to America, no one would hire me because of my color.

I ended up taking a boring job on the railroad, where I oiled moving parts on trains. As the parts on the train moved, they would rub together and catch fire from the heat if they weren't oiled frequently. This was dangerous, time-consuming, and inconvenient. I invented a way for the train to automatically lubricate itself and patented my idea in 1872. Railroad companies around the country quickly adopted my invention. I continued to perfect my lubricating cup and worked on other inventions. I amassed over forty patents. Because my lubricating inventions were so simple, a lot of others tried to duplicate what I had done. Unfortunately for them, their duplicates were never able to reach the same high quality of performance as my machines. Most people only wanted the products I made, that's why they always asked if it was the real McCoy.

Lewis Howard Latimer
(1848–1928)
Inventor

(LEWIS describes his inventions in science and engineering.)

LEWIS

My name is Lewis Latimer. I was born in Massachusetts to parents who were runaway slaves. Abolitionists Frederick Douglass and William Lloyd Garrison raised money to buy my parents' freedom. I had to quit school when I was ten, because my father deserted our family. I had to work to help out. When I was sixteen, I joined the Union Navy and served aboard a warship during the Civil War. After the war, I returned to Boston and worked in a law firm that specialized in patents. During this period, inventors were required to submit detailed drawings of their inventions along with in-depth written descriptions. Companies were looking for people with those skills. I was hired by a firm and became an expert draftsman. My drawings were done so well that Alexander Graham Bell asked me to illustrate the drawings of his new invention, the telephone.

In 1874 I received my first patent. It was for improving the toilet on passenger trains. I devised a flushing mechanism that kept sewage from backing up. In 1880 I started working on more of my own inventions. I was always fascinated with any breakthroughs in science. In 1881 Joseph Nichols and I invented the Latimer lamp. Shortly afterward, I was hired to supervise the installation of electrical plants in New York City. In 1882 I received a patent for creating carbon filaments. In 1884 I began working for Thomas Edison. I became a primary member of Edison's elite scientific team known as the Edison Pioneers. A lot of people never knew a black man was a member of Edison's team, because most text books and Hollywood movies didn't reveal that fact. However, I too had an important role in that part of American history. Even though Edison employed me, I continued to work on my inventions. It gave me a deeper sense of independence and pride.

Andrew Beard
(1849–1921)
Inventor

(ANDREW *explains the tragic job that inspired him to invent the train coupler.*)

ANDREW

My name is Andrew Beard. I invented what is called a coupler. A coupler is a pin that connects two railroad cars. Before my invention, the pin had to be dropped manually. This was dangerous, because the men had to climb on top of a freight train, climb down between two cars, and drop the pin as the train came together. The locomotive would back up, and the two cars would crash together and become joined. I can't begin to tell you how many men lost their limbs and their lives on this dangerous job. I saw too many of these tragedies. I was determined to find a way for the trains to couple automatically. I finally discovered the solution. I invented a train car coupler and received a patent for it in 1897.

Sarah Goode
(1850–?)
Inventor

(SARAH *explains the invention that made her the first African American female to receive a patent.*)

SARAH

I'm Sarah Goode. I was born a slave in 1850, but when slavery ended, I moved to Chicago, Illinois. I became a businesswoman and opened a furniture store. Thousands of people were migrating north after the Civil War. Most of them came to the city with little or no money and had to live in small, overcrowded apartments. There was barely enough room for a bed, which took up most of the area. I saw this need for more space as a business opportunity. I designed a folding bed that could be converted into a rolltop desk with a stationery compartment when the bed wasn't in use. On July 14, 1885, I received a patent for my invention. I was the first black woman in the United States to receive a patent.

Grandville Woods
(1856–1910)
Inventor

(GRANDVILLE *describes how he improved safety on the railroad system.*)

GRANDVILLE

I'm Grandville Woods. I was nicknamed the Black Thomas Edison, because I had so many inventions. I'm rather proud of myself. I was one of those people who pulled themselves up by the bootstraps. My family was very poor. I had to quit school when I was ten years old. I didn't have the opportunities that you have now, but I was eager to learn and taught myself many things.

I received patents for over fifty inventions, including an incubator to help hatch eggs, a battery, and better electric lights for theaters. For streetcars, I devised a new kind of electric motor. However, most of my inventions were related to the locomotive, or what young children often call a choo-choo train. Have you ever ridden on a train? If so, you should thank me. I invented a telegraph system that kept trains informed of the locations of other locomotives. Prior to my invention, trains just ran up and down the tracks without knowing where another one was. Needless to say, there were many accidents and deaths. My telegraph system improved safety on the tracks, saved numerous lives, and perhaps saved the railroads.

George Washington Carver
(1864–1943)
Inventor, Scientist

George Washington Carver

(GEORGE describes his career as an inventor and a scientist.)

GEORGE

When I was a baby, my mother and I were kidnapped and taken to
Arkansas to be sold. My mother was never found, but I was returned
to the Carver plantation and exchanged for a racehorse. I was sickly as
a child and unable to do much work, so I spent hours studying flowers
and plants instead. I became known as the Plant Doctor. Neighbors
would bring me their sick plants to revitalize.

It was hard for me to get a formal education, because most schools
wouldn't accept black students. Many of the schools for black children
that were available didn't receive much funding, which limited what
they could offer. I had to leave home and move to Kansas on my own
to further my education. Upon graduating from high school, I received
a scholarship to college. But once the college discovered I was black,
they took back the scholarship. I then enrolled in Simpson College
in Iowa and graduated in 1894. I was offered a teaching position and
became the school's first black faculty member.

In 1896 Booker T. Washington, president of Tuskegee Institute, approached me. He asked me to accept a teaching assignment at his college. I agreed and left for Alabama to create a department of agriculture. When I arrived, I discovered that there was no laboratory. I had to make my own equipment. I taught my students and the local farmers too. For those who couldn't come to me, I went to them. I created the movable school. We traveled the countryside in a wagon. We taught farmers many new agricultural methods, including how to rotate crops for better production. I continued my research while teaching. I invented over 300 products from the peanut and 118 products from the sweet potato. I also discovered uses for the soybean. My discoveries helped save the South's economy by encouraging farmers to grow cash crops other than cotton.

Garrett Morgan
(1875–1963)
Inventor

(GARRET explains how his inventions saved human lives.)

GARRETT
Slow down! Why do you think that light is there? Sometimes I wonder if it did me any good to invent the traffic light. Don't they know by now red means stop?
(Points his finger at the audience.)
You would never run a red light would you? Of course not!

I'm Garrett Morgan. I invented the traffic light in 1923. I've always been interested in saving lives. I remember in 1916 there was a terrible explosion in Cleveland, Ohio. Workers were trapped in a tunnel over two hundred feet below Lake Erie. No one knew how to reach them, because the smoke and gas fumes were too strong. Someone recalled that I had invented a gas inhalator. I was summoned to try to save them.

I went into the tunnel with my brother Frank and several volunteers. I'll be honest with you; I'm no hero. I was scared, but I knew human lives were depending on us and my new invention. I'm glad to say we were able to save the men.

It didn't take long for word to spread of the rescue and the success of my inhalator. I started getting orders from all over the country. But I had to hire a white person to demonstrate my product in the South, because white companies and fire departments wouldn't buy it when they learned I was black. Seems to me they should have been more interested in how the invention would save lives rather than how the person looked who made it. I didn't let that bother me. I don't believe we should let ignorance stop progress. I hope you feel the same way.

Ernest Just
(1883–1941)
Scientist

(ERNEST *explains how his cellular discoveries advanced medicine.*)

ERNEST
I'm Ernest Just. I'm a researcher and marine biologist. My research included studies on fertilization, cell development, and cell division. My discoveries regarding the way cells work helped find ways to fight diseases and had an impact on medicine. I wrote two textbooks and authored more than sixty articles for scientific magazines.

Percy Lavon Julian
(1899–1975)
Inventor, Scientist

(PERCY *explains how his inventions advanced research and saved lives.*)

PERCY

My name is Percy Julian. I graduated from college with honors. I couldn't get accepted into any of the top graduate schools because I was black, so I went to Austria to study for my PhD. While there, I discovered a drug to fight the eye disease glaucoma, which is a disease that can cause blindness. I also discovered treatments to help people with arthritis. I later returned to the United States and became a researcher for a paint company. Within a year, my research helped their business turn a $35,000 loss into a $130,000 profit. I also experimented with soybeans and discovered many uses for them. One of the most important was AeroFoam. It could put out oil and gas fires. The navy used it to save the lives of thousands of pilots and sailors. Although I made many scientific discoveries, I was still interested in business and wanted to work for myself. I founded the Julian Laboratories in 1954. Six years later, I sold the company for over $2.3 million.

Lloyd Augustus Hall
(1894–1971)
Scientist

(LLOYD explains how his scientific discoveries advanced science and health.)

LLOYD

My name is Lloyd Augustus Hall. I've had an interest in chemistry ever since high school. After I finished college, I discovered ways to preserve meat and baked foods. My techniques proved very valuable during World War II, as they helped keep food supplies safe for our soldiers for long periods of time. I also found a way to kill bacteria. Hospitals still use my methods to sterilize bandages. I held patents for more than one hundred discoveries. I loved to research and find ways to help humanity.

Otis Boykin
(1920–1982)
Inventor, Scientist

(OTIS *explains how his inventions helped save lives.*)

OTIS

I'm Otis Boykin. I attended Fisk University, a historically black college in Nashville, Tennessee. After graduation, I worked in Chicago for a radio and TV corporation. I was very busy, because I was attending college and running my own business. I later worked as a research engineer, chemist, and international electronics consultant. I invented twenty-six electronic devices. One of my resistors is used in computers, radios, and television sets. But my invention that I'm most proud of is the control unit I made for the pacemaker. My unit used electrical impulses to maintain a regular heartbeat. I was glad to help save lives.

Other Significant Inventors

(NARRATOR, SPEAKER 1, SPEAKER 2, SPEAKER 3, SPEAKER 4, *and* SPEAKER 5 *consecutively come to center stage and discuss prominent scientists and inventors.*)

NARRATOR

There are numerous famous and unknown inventors and scientists whose discoveries made a significant impact on everyday life in the nation and the world. Here are some of these trailblazers and their noteworthy inventions.

(NARRATOR *exits stage.*)

SPEAKER 1

- Henry Blair received a patent for a mechanical seed planter in 1834 and another patent for a mechanical corn harvester in 1836. He was the second African American to receive a patent.
- Alexander Ashbourne received a patent for the biscuit cutter in 1875.
- In 1879 William Bailes received a patent for a ladder scaffold support.
- Charles Brooks received a patent for a street sweeper in 1890.
- William Davis received a patent for an improved horseback riding saddle in 1896.
- George Cook received a patent for the automatic fishing reel in 1899.
- In 1899 John Burr received a patent for an improved rotary blade lawn mower.
- Bessie Blount invented a device for helping disabled people eat. She received a patent for her invention in 1951.
- Marie Brown received a patent for a home video surveillance system in 1969.
- George Carruthers invented the ultraviolet camera spectrograph, which was used for the Apollo 16 trip to the moon in 1972.
- Phil Brooks received a patent for a disposable syringe in 1974.
- Dr. Patricia Bath received a patent for a laser eye technique in 1988. Her technique helped thousands with glaucoma.

(SPEAKER 1 *moves to stage right.*)

SPEAKER 2

- Furniture is much easier to move because of David Fisher. He received a patent for the furniture caster in 1876.
- In 1879 Thomas Elkins received a patent for an improved design of the refrigerator.
- In 1897 Lawrence Ray received a patent for an improvement to the dustpan. His invention had a tray attached to a short wooden

handle. This way no one had to get their hands dirty when sweeping up the trash.

- In 1899 George Grant received a patent for the golf tee.
- In 1925 Augustus Hall discovered ways to cure and preserve food with a method called flash drying. This method was used on the foods quickly, before they had a chance to spoil. Hall received over a hundred additional patents for food preservation methods.
- Philip Emagwai invented software for the supercomputer, which was said to be the fastest computer system in the world in 1989.

(SPEAKER 2 moves to stage right.)

SPEAKER 3

- Willie Johnson received a patent for the eggbeater in 1884.
- John Love received a patent for an improved pencil sharpener in 1895.
- Most know Jack Johnson as the first black heavyweight champion of the world, but I bet many don't know he was an inventor too. In 1922 Johnson received a patent for the tool known as the wrench.
- Marjorie Joyner was a cosmetologist. She worked in one of Madam C. J. Walker's beauty shops. In 1928 Ms. Joyner invented a permanent wave machine. It gave the hair longer, lasting curls. However, because she was Madam Walker's employee, she had no rights to the invention and was unable to fully profit from it.
- Lonnie Johnson and his partner Bruce D'Andrade helped make hot summers cooler and added a new level of fun to water-gun fights. They invented the Super Soaker. A patent was issued to them in 1991.

(SPEAKER 3 moves to stage right.)

SPEAKER 4

- Onesimus was a slave, but he still knew something about medicine. In 1721 Onesimus demonstrated a method to treat smallpox. During that time, smallpox was a deadly disease.

- In 1890 William Purvis patented his idea for an improved fountain pen. His pen had a built-in reservoir for storing ink. This made the use of an ink bottle unnecessary, and people could carry the pen in their pockets. He had patents for nineteen inventions in all.
- In 1887 Alexander Miles received a patent for improving the way elevator doors opened and closed.
- In 1898 Lydia Newman received a patent for an improved type of hairbrush that was more durable, easy to clean, and provided ventilation while brushing hair.
- In 1919 Alice Parker received a patent for an improved heating furnace that allowed central heating.

(SPEAKER 4 *moves to stage right.*)

SPEAKER 5

- Thomas White invented an improved lemon squeezer in 1893.
- Joseph Winters helped save the lives of people who lived in tall buildings. He invented the fire escape ladder. It could be transported, because it was mounted on a wagon. He received his patent in 1878.
- In 1906 Richard Spikes received his first patent. It was for the modern version of the railroad semaphore, which is a visual way of sending messages. He also had twelve additional patents for other inventions. Spikes's last patent was for an automatic safety brake. He lost his vision while working on this invention, but he refused to stop his work. As a result, he invented a drafting machine for the blind to help him complete the project.
- Paul Williams received a patent for improvements on the helicopter in 1962.
- Henry Sampson invented a type of cellular phone. He received a patent for it in 1971.

(*Speakers exit stage.*)

ENTREPRENEURS

John Merrick
(1859–1921)
Entrepreneur

(JOHN explains how he and his partners built one of the largest African American-owned insurance companies.)

JOHN

I'm John Merrick. I was a cofounder of one of the largest black-owned insurance companies in the United States. I was born in 1859 before slavery ended. When I became an adult, I developed an interest in business. I started my career as a bricklayer and a barber. I accumulated enough money to open five additional barbershops. In 1899 five other men and I founded the North Carolina Mutual Life Insurance Company. The office was set up in a spare room that belonged to Dr. A. M. Moore, one of the cofounders. It only had a desk and four chairs. The first year, business was so bad that five of the members quit. One of the reasons business was slow was because of the lack of confidence black people had in our insurance company. I could understand some of their skepticism. They weren't used to seeing successful black entrepreneurs. To promote sales, Moore and I hired C. C. Spaulding. He was our combination salesman, advertising agent, bookkeeper, and janitor.

When we finally sold our first policy, it literally proved very costly. The policy sold for sixty-five cents. The insured party died shortly afterward. We had to pay his estate $40. Moore and I contributed $39.71, and Spaulding paid the $0.29 balance. It nearly bankrupted our agency and left Spaulding flat broke. But we turned misfortune into a fortune. We used this incident to show prospective clients how we stood behind our policies and honored all claims. Within a year, we sold nearly $800 in premiums. The company continued to thrive. We are now one of the largest African American-owned businesses in the United States. The key to success is to always have faith in yourself and never let others convince you that your dream is foolish.

C. C. Spaulding
(1874–1952)
Entrepreneur, Philanthropist

(C. C. explains how he helped establish the North Carolina Mutual Insurance Company.)

C. C.
I'm C. C. Spaulding. I was the lone salesman for the North Carolina Mutual Insurance Company, which was established in 1899. I was hired by two of the founders of the company, John Merrick and Dr. A. M. Moore. The business had potential, because it was offering life insurance to black people when many white companies wouldn't issue us a policy. Most people never heard of a black-owned and operated company or a Negro salesman. I was often ridiculed, but I stayed focused on my mission, which was to sell policies. I was born in poverty, so I knew how to be thrifty and work hard. I had to work hard, because my income and travel expenses were dependent on my sales.

I created innovative marketing techniques. I was one of the first people to apply saturated advertising. I would pass out calendars, fans, pens, paperweights, and matchbooks to all the barbershops and beauty salons. I placed ads in the Negro newspapers. I hired schoolteachers as agents, because I knew they were highly respected in the community. I also believed they would create confidence in the company. My hard work and creativity paid off. In 1923 I was made president of the company. I became rich and admired in the communities where I was once ridiculed. I wanted to give back to the community. I donated time, energy, and money to numerous causes. I was shown gratitude in return. There have been schools, playgrounds, and parks named in my honor.

Maggie Lena Walker
(1867–1934)
Entrepreneur, Philanthropist

(MAGGIE explains how she established herself as an entrepreneur.)

MAGGIE
My name is Maggie Walker. I was born July 15, 1867 in Richmond, Virginia. My family didn't have much money, so I had to help my mother wash laundry for wealthy white families when I was a small child. After graduating from high school, I worked as a teacher for three years during the day and took business courses at night. I also met my husband during this time. Even though I was married and raising a family, I found time to become involved with the Independent Order of St. Luke. This was an organization that provided black people with health insurance. I was particularity supportive of St. Luke, because most white companies wouldn't insure Negroes.

In 1899 I was named the executive treasurer of St. Luke. My first year on the job, I doubled the number of clients and extended services to twenty-two states. In 1902 I published the *St. Luke Herald* newspaper. The paper kept members informed of the company's activities, and it gave advice on how to save and invest. I believed black people needed to learn how to manage money so they could earn power and respect in society. I continued to expand the company by helping to establish the St. Luke Penny Savings Bank. I served as bank president for twenty-five years. I was the first black female bank president in the United States. I also became one of the wealthiest black women in the country.

I not only worked with members of my race to teach them how to live better financially, I also donated time and money to improve the community. I was especially concerned about the difficulties faced by colored women. I helped found the Industrial School for Colored Girls and the Council of Women of the Darker Races. I also served on other committees that focused on educating black females. I supported Virginia Union College, worked with the Piedmont Tuberculosis Sanitarium for Negroes, and was a member of the NAACP. I might've accomplished much more if I hadn't become ill and confined to a wheelchair in 1928. However, I never considered myself handicapped, and I had a full life. My impact is felt all over the city of Richmond. A high school, a street, and a theater are named in my honor.

Madam C. J. Walker
(1867–1919)
Entrepreneur, Philanthropist

Madam C. J. Walker

Characters:

MADAM WALKER, *female, salon owner and beauty entrepreneur*

JANE, *female fictional character, client in* MADAM WALKER'*s salon*

Costumes:

Typical attire for a beautician and client of the early 1900s

Props:

Chair, straightening comb, mirror

*(*MADAM WALKER *explains to* JANE *how she built a successful business.)*

JANE

Ouch! Madam Walker, you burned my ear.

MADAM WALKER

No I didn't honey, that was just the heat from the comb.
(Blows JANE'*s ear.)*

JANE

(Looks up and rolls her eyes.)

That's okay Madam Walker. I don't mind a little burn—I mean a little "heat"—on my ear. It'll be worth it. I know I'll be looking real good when you're finished. When I move, I don't even have to worry about the upkeep of my hair. You have shops all over the country. Now colored ladies can go to beauty shops almost anywhere and get their hair done thanks to you. I admire you. How did you get started?

MADAM WALKER

When I was young, my hair began to fall out. I was going bald. Nothing I tried helped. Then one night a remedy came to me in a dream. I made a mixture from the herbs in my dream, and it worked! With only $1.50, I started my business. I sold my product door-to-door to other Negro women who had the same problem. It wasn't easy, but I learned that hard work and determination will bring success. So when people ask me how I got started, I tell them that "I got a start by giving myself a start."

JANE

You must've come from a wealthy family of businessmen.

MADAM WALKER

No, no. I was born December 23, 1867, on a cotton plantation in Louisiana. Needless to say, I grew up poor. My parents died by the time I was seven. I got married when I was only fourteen. My first husband died by the time I was twenty. I had to take in laundry to support myself and my daughter. But I never believed in feeling sorry for myself or making excuses.

JANE

Your early life was tough. But look at you now! You must make a lot of money.
(Looks up for a response from MADAM WALKER.*)*

MADAM WALKER

(Silence)

JANE

I'm not trying to get in your business, but they say you're probably the first black millionaire in America.

MADAM WALKER

I'm not boasting, but I am the first Negro to build a multimillion-dollar business. I can truly say I've been blessed, and I try to help others. I believe in what they say, when you have a blessing, pass it on.

JANE

I know that's true. I heard about how you paid to have a black YMCA built in Indianapolis. You gave the money to have Frederick Douglass's home in Washington, D.C., restored. You also donated $5,000 to the NAACP antilynching movement. You even went with some other black leaders with a petition to President Wilson to protest lynching. You do a lot that people don't even know about. All you hear is that you're rich.

MADAM WALKER

Blessings aren't meant for bragging. They're meant to be shared. I hope I will be an example to others by showing them that when we prosper, we should always reach out to help others.

(End scene.)

Arthur George Gaston
(1892–1996)
Entrepreneur, Philanthropist

(ARTHUR explains how he amassed a fortune as an entrepreneur.)

ARTHUR

My name is Arthur George Gaston, but you can call me A. G. I know you see me and think, "Look at that old man." I am an old man. I'm nearly 104 years old, and I'm an old man with old money.
(Pulls a wad of money from his pocket and raises it toward the audience.)
I was one of the first black millionaires in the United States. My business and personal philosophy is, "Success is founded on seeing and satisfying the needs of people." This is how I made my fortune. It was important to me to service black people, because many white establishments wouldn't do business with us or offer us opportunities. I'm the owner of numerous enterprises in Birmingham, Alabama. My enterprises include an insurance company, a realty and investment corporation, a business college, motels, a housing development, a large farm, fourteen funeral homes, and a cemetery. My business assets alone total more than $20 million.

I was born in 1892 and my early life wasn't filled with luxury. My father died when I was young and we were very poor. I always had a head for business, even as a little boy. When I was growing up, I had to live with my grandmother while my mother worked. I had a swing set in my yard. I would charge the other children admission. They would have to pay me pins and buttons to come inside and play. I quit school after eighth grade and started working for a coal, iron, and steel company. I only made $3.10 per day. To supplement my pay, I sold peanuts and loaned money to my coworkers who weren't as thrifty as me for $0.25 on the dollar.

In 1921, when I was around twenty-nine years old, I realized the need for a burial society. I convinced my father-in-law to become my partner. We started the business with $35. The burial society grew into an insurance company. I also saw a need for Negro housing and supplied it. That venture led to a savings and loan association. In

1923 I founded a business college, because I wanted to be able to get the quality clerks and typists I needed. But it wasn't all about me. I wanted to provide opportunities for Negroes, and help my community. I organized the Smith and Gaston Kiddie Club. It had over eleven thousand members. In 1945 I sponsored the Gaston Statewide Spelling Bee for Negro students. I was convinced that black people were capable of achieving any goal they set in life. I wanted others to be convinced too.

Reginald Lewis
(1942–1993)
Entrepreneur, Philanthropist

(SPEAKER *shares how Reginald Lewis built a billion-dollar business.*)

SPEAKER
Reginald Lewis was an entrepreneur. He was born and raised in Baltimore, Maryland, and attended Virginia State University. His junior year he took a course in securities law and wrote a paper on takeovers. This really sparked his interest. He graduated in 1965 then obtained a degree from Harvard Law School in 1968. After graduating from Harvard, he practiced as an attorney for one of the top law firms in New York City. Two years later, he started a firm and worked as a corporate lawyer for fifteen years. In 1983 Lewis started a capital venture company called TLC Group LP. A venture capital company is one that makes high-risk business deals. The outcome may turn you into a millionaire or a pauper.

Lewis's first major deal was the purchase of McCall Pattern Company in 1984 for $22 million. Three years later, he sold the McCall Company for $95 million. His personal profit was over $50 million. In 1987 he bought Beatrice International Foods for $985 million. He renamed the company TLC Beatrice International. It was a conglomerate of a snack food, grocery store, and beverage business. That same year his company's earnings were $1.8 billion. It was the first African American-owned and operated company to have more than $1 billion in annual sales. In 1996 TLC International Holdings Inc. was number 512 on *Fortune* magazine's list of the 1,000 largest companies. In 1992 *Forbes* magazine listed Reginald Lewis among the 400 richest Americans. He had a net worth of $400 million. He was also the first black man to build a billion-dollar business.

Success didn't stop Lewis from giving back to others. He also donated to Virginia Union University, Howard University, and Harvard University. The city of Baltimore has named a high school after him and erected a museum in his honor. The Reginald F. Lewis Museum in downtown Baltimore exhibits the history and contributions of Maryland's African Americans. It is the largest museum of its kind on the East Coast. Life wasn't always easy for him. He had many setbacks, but he conquered those obstacles by applying his personal philosophy, "Keep going no matter what."

POLITICIANS AND OFFICE HOLDERS

POLITICS THROUGH THE EARLY 1900S

The Early Years

*(*SPEAKER *chronicles African Americans' involvement in politics through 1929.)*

SPEAKER
African Americans weren't visible in politics until 1836, when Alexander Twilight became the first to serve in a state legislature. For the next thirty-four years African Americans' role in government seemed to come to a halt. However, Reconstruction set the stage for unprecedented political advancements. First, the Union was reorganizing politics in the nation and removing former Confederate office holders in the South. This left many state and federal congressional seats unfilled. Second, the Fifteenth Amendment was ratified in 1870, which gave black males the right to vote. Although political seats were vacant and black men were exercising the Fifteenth Amendment, some of them were afraid or reluctant to run for political office. They feared it would only make relations between whites and blacks in the South worse. However, as Republicans began to take control of Congress, African American men stepped to the forefront of politics and secured important jobs in government.

Beginning in 1870, twenty-one black men served in the U.S. House of Representatives and two served in the U.S. Senate. On the state level, almost eight hundred served as state senators and representatives; six served as lieutenant governors. All African American politicians were Republicans. This political success, however, was short lived. When Reconstruction ended in 1877, Southern white Democrats regained political power. Black Americans throughout the South were disenfranchised through state laws or intimidated to the point where they were afraid to vote. George White was the last African American to serve in Congress before Southern whites fully regained power. Twenty-eight years passed before Oscar Stanton De Priest, from Illinois, became the next black man to hold a seat in Congress, which was in 1929.

Alexander Twilight
(1795–1857)
Vermont State House Representative

(ALEXANDER recalls being the first African American to be elected to a public office.)

ALEXANDER

My name is Alexander Twilight. I was more fortunate than most black people living during this early period of our nation's history. I was born in Vermont to free parents. I graduated from Middlebury College in Vermont in 1823. I was the first Negro to graduate from a college in America. I was a licensed Presbyterian minister and a school principal. In 1836 I was elected to the Vermont House of Representatives. I was the first Negro elected to a public office and the first to serve in a state legislature.

John Willis Menard
(1838–1893)
U.S. House Representative for Louisiana

John Willis Menard

(JOHN recounts his election to Congress, which was overturned.)

JOHN
My name is John Willis Menard. I was the first black man to be elected to the U.S. Congress. I was elected in 1868 by the state of Louisiana, but I was denied my seat when my opponent challenged the election results. I moved to Florida, where I remained active in politics. I served in the Florida State House of Representatives in 1874. In 1874 and 1877, I was elected justice of the peace for Duval County.

Ebenezer D. Bassett
(1832–1908)
U.S. Ambassador

(EBENEZER explains how he became an ambassador to Haiti.)

EBENEZER
My name is Ebenezer D. Bassett. I was the first black ambassador in our country. I was born in Connecticut and lived most of my life in the North. I was a principal at the Institute for Colored Youth in Philadelphia. President Grant appointed me as minister resident

of Haiti. This came at a very tense time, because Haiti had strong anti-American feelings. But the Haitians accepted me; they had more confidence in me than my white predecessors. I served as a diplomat there from 1869 to 1877.

I returned to Haiti as a private citizen in 1888. I studied the culture and collected materials, which were published in a handbook. My work earned me recognition in the American Geographical Society and the Connecticut Historical Society.

Hiram Revels
(1822–1901)
U.S. Senator for Mississippi

Hiram Revels

(HIRAM describes his commitment to serving the public through politics and education.)

HIRAM

My name is Hiram Revels. I was a U.S. senator from Mississippi and represented the Republican Party. I was the first black man to actually serve in the U.S. Congress. I completed the term of Jefferson Davis, the former president of the Confederate States of America. My term in office was from February 2, 1870, to March 3, 1871.

Prior to serving in the U.S. Senate, I was a state senator in Mississippi. I was also a minister in the Methodist Episcopal Church. In 1863 and 1864, I taught school in St. Louis. Later, I became president of Alcorn University in Mississippi. Throughout my life, I was always interested in religion and education. I had a challenging but wonderful life, because I was able to serve the public in capacities that I enjoyed.

Alonzo Jacob Ransier
(1834–1883)
U.S. House Representative for South Carolina

Alonzo Jacob Ransier

(ALONZO recounts his career in state and federal politics for South Carolina.)

ALONZO

My name is Alonzo Jacob Ransier. I was a Republican congressman from South Carolina. When people looked for an honest politician, they looked for me. I prided myself on my reputation for honesty. I was fortunate enough to be born free in the South, while slavery was still legal in our country. In adult life, I worked as a shipping clerk until I was appointed state registrar of elections in 1865. From 1868 to 1869, I served in the South Carolina State House of Representatives. During that time, I was also a member of the State Constitutional Convention. In 1870 I became South Carolina's first black lieutenant governor.

In 1873 I was elected to the U.S. House of Representatives. I served from March 1873 to March 1875. As a congressman, I fought for a civil rights bill. I supported high tariffs and opposed a federal salary increase. I supported legislation for a six-year presidential term and campaigned for President Grant. After I left Congress, I worked as a tax collector for the Department of Internal Revenue.

Joseph Hayne Rainey
(1832–1887)
U.S. House Representative for South Carolina

Joseph Hayne Rainey

*(*JOSEPH *recounts his service as a congressman for South Carolina.)*

JOSEPH

I'm Joseph Rainey. I was the first Negro to be directly elected to Congress, as opposed to being appointed as my black predecessors were. I was also the first black man to preside over the U.S. House of Representatives. Both my parents were slaves, but my father was a successful barber. Shortly after I was born, he saved enough money to purchase our family's freedom. When the Civil War erupted in 1861, I was drafted by the Confederate government and forced to work on fortifications in Charleston, South Carolina. I also had to work as a laborer on blockade-runner ships. In 1862 I managed to escape to Bermuda with my wife. We remained there until the war ended.

We returned to South Carolina in 1866. Shortly afterward, I became active in politics and joined the state Republican Party. In 1868 I was a delegate to the convention that wrote the new constitution for the state. In 1870 I was elected to the South Carolina State Senate. I was also elected by the Republican Party to fill a vacancy for South Carolina in the U.S. House of Representatives. I became the longest-serving Negro congressman. I was reelected four times and served from December 1870 to March 1879. A Democrat named Richardson challenged my 1876 election. He alleged the results were invalid, because voters were intimidated by federal soldiers and black militias. He was unsuccessful. However, he defeated me two years later and Democrats regained control of politics in South Carolina. During my tenure as a congressman, I supported legislation to protect the civil rights of Southern Negroes. Following my retirement from Congress, I was appointed internal revenue agent of South Carolina. Two years later, I began a career in private commerce.

Jefferson Long
(1836–1900)
U.S. House Representative for Georgia

Jefferson Long

(JEFFERSON describes his efforts as a congressman for Georgia.)

JEFFERSON

My name is Jefferson Long. I was a congressman from the state of
Georgia. It's ironic that my name is Long, because my term in the U.S.
House of Representatives wasn't very long. I served from January 1871
to March 1871, a total of three months. After the Civil War, many new
congressmen were elected or appointed to finish the remaining terms
of former Confederate government officials. Many white people in
Georgia weren't ready to accept a black man representing their state.
On the day I was elected, seven black people were lynched. Many
others throughout the state were intimidated and beaten by white
protesters.

I was the first black person to make an address before the House of
Representatives. My address was a speech against a bill that would
have removed the restrictions on the Confederates' ability to participate
in politics. I knew if restrictions were lifted, the Southern politicians
would use their votes to bring back white supremacy. My speech
also stressed providing protection for qualified Negro voters. My
experience in Congress really discouraged me. I decided not to seek
reelection. I returned to Macon, where I had a successful tailoring
business. However, I remained active with the Republican Party and
was a mentor to other Negro and white Republicans.

Robert Carlos De Large
(1842–1874)
U.S. House Representative for South Carolina

Robert Carlos De Large

*(*ROBERT *recounts his tenure as a congressman for South Carolina.)*

ROBERT

I'm Robert Carlos De Large, and I was a congressman for South
Carolina. I was considered well educated, because I graduated from
high school, which was something few Negroes were able to do. Prior
to my service as a U.S. congressman, I was a delegate to the State
Constitutional Convention in 1868. From 1868 to 1870, I served in
the South Carolina State House of Representatives. I was considered a
conservative Republican while in the state house, because I lobbied to
remove political restrictions on former Confederates. I took this view,
because I was afraid that if the Republicans were too harsh on whites,
black people would suffer violence and abuse.

I was more of a radical when I became a U.S. congressman. I addressed
the House to support the Fourteenth Amendment and demanded that
black Americans be protected from violent groups like the Ku Klux
Klan. Unfortunately, my participation in the House was limited,
because my seat was challenged by my opponent from the 1870
election. Due to the turmoil surrounding this challenge, the House

committee declared my seat vacant in 1873. However, I held my political position from March 4, 1871, to January 24, 1873.

Although I was no longer a U.S. representative, I still held the Republican Party accountable for the welfare of the Negro population. In 1874 I raised the question, "Why is it that we colored men have become identified with the Republican Party?" I answered, "We joined this party because it professed equal rights and privileges to all . . . We thought on the grounds of expediency we must do nothing to offend them, but some impudent scoundrels in the party now say: 'You want too much, you want everything!' We elected them and by our votes we made them our masters. We now propose to change this thing a little, and let them vote for us. It is no more than reasonable that they should do so." I ended my public life by serving as a local magistrate.

Benjamin Sterling Turner
(1825–1894)
U.S. House Representative for Alabama

Benjamin Sterling Turner

(BENJAMIN recalls his service as a congressman for Alabama.)

BENJAMIN
My name is Benjamin Turner. I was a Republican congressman from Alabama. I was born to enslaved parents in North Carolina but was

taken to Alabama when I was five. I remained enslaved until President Lincoln issued the Emancipation Proclamation in 1863. As an adult, I set up a livery stable in Selma, Alabama.

I began my career in elected offices in 1867, when I was elected tax collector of Dallas County, Alabama. In 1869 I was a councilman for the city of Selma. I was elected to serve in the U.S. House of Representatives in 1871. I served from March 4, 1871, to March 3, 1873. As a congressman, I advocated to restore political and legal rights to former Confederates. I fought to have the cotton tax repealed, because I believed the tax hurt poor black farmers. In 1872 I received the Republican nomination for my district again, but another black person ran as an independent against me. This caused a split in the vote for a Republican candidate, and a white delegate from another party won the seat in Congress. For a while, I remained active in politics. In 1880 I was a delegate to the Republican National Convention. When I retired from politics, I remained in Alabama and became a farmer.

Robert Elliott
(1842–1884)
U.S. House Representative for South Carolina

(ROBERT *describes his agenda during his tenure as a congressman for South Carolina.)*

ROBERT
I'm Robert Elliott. I was born in England and moved to South Carolina in 1867. I was a member of the State Constitutional Convention in 1868 and served in the state legislature from 1868 to 1870. Following my term in the South Carolina legislature, I served in the U.S. House of Representatives from 1871 to 1874. My priority in Washington was to fight the Amnesty Bill, which would restore political rights to former Confederates. I also aimed to weaken the Ku Klux Klan's power

in the South and to establish civil rights for black Americans. After leaving Congress, I attempted to become the attorney general of South Carolina, but I didn't get the position. Shortly afterward, I moved to New Orleans and resumed my law practice.

Josiah Thomas Walls
(1842–1905)
U.S. House Representative for Florida

Josiah Thomas Walls

(JOSIAH recalls his service as a congressman for Florida.)

JOSIAH

My name is Josiah Walls. I was born enslaved in Virginia in 1842. When our country was fighting the Civil War, I was forced to join the Confederate Army. I was captured in 1862 in Yorktown. I voluntarily joined the Union Army with the U.S. Colored Troops in 1863. When I was discharged, I settled in Florida and got involved in politics. In 1871 I became the first black man to represent Florida in the U.S. Congress. While I was in Congress, I introduced a bill to establish a fund for national education and aid to pensioners of the Seminole War. Unfortunately, however, my opponent contested my election, and I was unseated two years into my term. But I didn't give up. I ran again in 1872 and was reelected for the 1873 through 1875 term.

In 1874 I ran for reelection and won. I served from 1875 to 1876. I was unable to serve the full term, because my Democratic opponent challenged the election and won. I was unseated in 1876. This final unseating brought an end to my political ambitions. After politics, I returned to Florida and engaged in agricultural interests.

Pinckney Benton Stewart "P. B. S." Pinchback
(1837–1920)
Governor of Louisiana

(P. B. S. shares his efforts to fight injustice against African Americans through politics.)

P. B. S.

I'm Pinckney Benton Stewart Pinchback, but I'm more commonly known as P. B. S. Pinchback. I was born in 1837 in Mississippi, but my mother's master—who was also my father—freed us. We moved to Ohio, where I worked as a cabin boy on the Ohio and Missouri Rivers. I felt early on that black Americans should have equal rights and privileges and decided to fight for those rights. In 1861, shortly after the Civil War started, I traveled to Louisiana and enlisted in the Union Army. I was appointed recruiting officer for Negro volunteers. As recruiting officer, I argued that black men should not be drafted if they could not vote. I also didn't agree with the mistreatment of black soldiers in the army and decided to resign.

In 1867 I was able to voice my concerns politically. I was selected as a delegate to the Louisiana State Constitutional Convention. At the convention, I advocated for universal suffrage and tax-supported schools. In 1868 I was a delegate to the Republican National Convention in Chicago. In 1871 I became lieutenant governor when Oscar Dunn died during his term. Oscar was the first elected black lieutenant governor, which made me the second black man to serve in that position. On December 9, 1872, the state governor was impeached, and I became acting governor for forty-three days. This made me the first black man to serve as a governor in the United States.

I hoped to continue my political success and ran for a seat in Congress. In 1876 I was elected to the U.S. House of Representatives and to the U.S. Senate. However, both elections were challenged, and I was unable to take either seat. But I was awarded $16,666 out of the contingency fund from the U.S. Senate for the salary I would have earned up to the time I was officially denied my seat. After politics, I served on the Louisiana State Board of Education and helped establish Southern University, a college for Negroes. I finally settled in Washington, D.C., where I practiced law.

James Thomas Rapier
(1837–1883)
U.S. House Representative for Alabama

(JAMES recalls his service as a congressman for Alabama.)

JAMES

I'm James Rapier. I served the state of Alabama as a Republican congressman during the Reconstruction period. I was born free in Alabama prior to the Thirteenth Amendment, which freed Negroes in 1865. I was raised by my grandmother in Nashville, Tennessee, but moved to Canada when I was nineteen. I settled in Buxton, Ontario, which was a haven for runaway slaves. My uncle owned property there. I attended the Buxton Mission School. Later, I attended a school in Toronto, where I earned my teaching certificate. I decided to move back to Buxton and work as a teacher.

I returned to Nashville, Tennessee in 1864, where I bought two hundred acres of land and farmed cotton. I always believed that

Negroes should have rights equal to whites, including the right to vote; so in 1865 I gave the keynote speech at the Tennessee Negro Suffrage Convention. However, the state of politics in Tennessee became very discouraging for me, and I decided to move back to my birthplace—Florence, Alabama. Eighteen sixty-seven was a big year for Alabama: freedmen were finally allowed to vote, my county elected its first black registrar—my father, and I represented my county at the state Republican convention. I was also selected to be a delegate to the State Constitutional Convention. The purpose of the convention was to assist Alabama in reentering the Union.

In 1870 I ran for secretary of state. Although I lost the election, I helped pave the way for other Negroes, because I became the first black man to run for a state office in Alabama. In 1872 I started a newspaper called the *Republican State Sentinel* to publish my views. It was the first newspaper in my state to be owned by a black man. I also ran for a seat in Congress and won. I served from March 4, 1873, to March 3, 1875. As a congressman, I advocated for the passing of the Civil Rights Bill of 1875. The bill pushed for equal standards in lodging, transportation, and education for black Americans. I also served on the Committee on Education and Labor. In 1874 I began to campaign for reelection, but threats from Democrats and violence by the Ku Klux Klan caused me to lose the election. At one voting site, over one hundred Negroes were murdered. I attempted to run again for the following election but ran against another black man, Jeremiah Haralson. Because we split the black vote, the Democrats won the election. I retired from politics as a collector for the Internal Revenue Service in 1878.

John R. Lynch
(1847–1939)
U.S. House Representative for Mississippi

(JOHN recounts his political service for Mississippi.)

JOHN

I'm John Lynch. I represented Mississippi in the U.S. House of Representatives. I'm a self-educated man and very motivated. Politicians began to notice me and one of them appointed me justice of the peace for Natchez County, Mississippi. In 1869 I was elected to the Mississippi State House of Representatives.

In 1873 I was elected as a Republican to the U.S. House of Representatives. I was reelected in 1875 and served through 1877. I ran again in 1877 but lost, because my state was rezoned by Democrats, who had regained control of politics in Mississippi. I ran again in 1880 but lost to a Democrat. This time I fought for my seat. I contested the election on the grounds of misconduct by my opponent. I won my case, and in 1882 I was reseated. I then served from 1882 through 1883. It was near the end of Reconstruction, and black people throughout the South were losing their rights in all aspects of life. I ran three more times in the midst of this turmoil, but lost each time to a Democrat.

Despite these losses, I remained active in politics. In 1884 I became the first black man to give the keynote address at the Mississippi Republican National Convention. After retiring from politics, I practiced law and wrote two books. I also became a public speaker and advocated for the rights of members of my race.

Blanche K. Bruce
(1841–1898)
U.S. House Representative for Mississippi

Blanche K. Bruce

(BLANCHE recounts how he fought for equality as a congressman for Mississippi.)

BLANCHE
My name is Blanche K. Bruce. In 1875 I represented the state of Mississippi in the U.S. Senate. I was the first black person to be elected to a full term in the Senate. When you're elected, it's traditional congressional protocol for the senior senator from your home state to escort you to the rostrum to be sworn in. My senior senator pretended to be busy reading the newspaper. He didn't even look up when it was his turn to escort me. I was halfway up the isle when a senator from New York asked me if he could be my escort.

I served from 1875 to 1881. I campaigned against the Chinese Exclusion Act of 1878 on the grounds that it was racially discriminatory. I fought to integrate the military, and I called for an investigation into the treatment of John Whittaker, a West Point cadet who was beaten by his fellow cadets. I also recommended federal support for the Negroes migrating to Kansas, who were known as the Exodusters.

John Adams Hyman
(1840–1891)
U.S. House Representative for North Carolina

(JOHN shares his service as a congressman in the U.S. House of Representatives.)

JOHN

I'm John Adams Hyman. I was born enslaved in North Carolina in 1840. In 1861 I was sold to a new master as punishment for trying to learn to read. During my twenty-five years of enslavement, I was sold at least eight times for attempting to educate myself. When the Civil War ended, I returned to North Carolina and studied elementary-level schoolwork. I was determined to obtain at least a basic education.

I decided to become active in politics. In 1865 I was a delegate to the North Carolina State Convention. In 1868 I was elected to the North Carolina Senate. I served there from 1868 to 1874. In 1874 I was elected as a Republican to serve in the U.S. House of Representatives. I was the first Negro from North Carolina to serve in the U.S. House of Representatives. I served one term, from March 4, 1875, to March 3, 1877. I was unsuccessful in my 1876 bid for reelection. After losing the election, I returned to North Carolina and served as the special deputy collector of internal revenue for my district for a year. I later moved to Washington, D.C., and worked for the U.S. Postal Service and the Department of Agriculture.

Jeremiah Haralson
(1846–1916)
U.S. House Representative for Alabama

Jeremiah Haralson

(JEREMIAH describes his service to the state and federal government for Alabama.)

JEREMIAH

My name is Jeremiah Haralson. I was active in state politics for several years. In 1870 I was a member of the Alabama State House of Representatives. In 1872 I served in the state senate. From March 4, 1875, to March 3, 1877, I served in the U.S. House of Representatives as a Republican for Alabama. As a U.S. congressman, I supported amnesty for former Confederates. I felt amnesty would help bridge harmony between blacks and whites. In 1876 I ran for reelection but lost to another black man. I lost in part because my congressional district was rezoned. I ran again in 1878, but I faced political maneuvers again. During the election period, more than two thousand black men had been disenfranchised since the last election. This shortage in my voting base partially attributed to my defeat. It was also a sign of the end of Reconstruction. Following my career in politics, I was appointed to the U.S. Customhouse in Baltimore, Maryland. Later, I was a clerk in the Department of Interior and the Pension Bureau in

Washington, D.C. I resigned from the Bureau in 1884. I later moved to Colorado where I worked as a coal miner.

Charles Edmund Nash
(1844–1913)
U.S. House Representative for Louisiana

Charles Edmund Nash

(CHARLES chronicles his service as a congressman for Louisiana.)

CHARLES

My name is Charles Edmund Nash. Prior to my political career, I was a bricklayer. In 1863 after the Civil War broke out, I enlisted as a private in the 82nd Regiment U.S. Volunteers and later achieved the rank of sergeant major. At the end of the war in 1865, I was appointed night inspector of customs. My interest grew in politics, and I was later elected to the 44th Congress as a Republican. I represented Louisiana in the U.S. House of Representatives from March 4, 1875, to March 3, 1877. I fought for the Thirteenth, Fourteenth, and Fifteenth Amendments to be upheld in the South, which was becoming increasingly violent against Negroes. Unfortunately, however, Democrats controlled the House and often denied my attempts to voice my concerns for public record. My bid for reelection in 1876 was unsuccessful. I retired from politics and became a postmaster in a Louisiana parish.

Robert Smalls
(1839–1915)
U.S. House Representative for South Carolina

Robert Smalls

(ROBERT recalls how he advocated for African Americans' rights as a congressman for South Carolina.)

ROBERT

I'm Robert Smalls. Some of you may know me as a Civil War hero. I was a seaman aboard a Confederate ship named the *Planter*. On May 13, 1862, the black crew was left alone on the ship. I smuggled my wife and six slaves aboard. We successfully sailed the *Planter* out of the Charleston harbor and all the way to the Union Navy. The Union forces made me a naval captain and gave me command of the *Planter*.

After the war ended, I became a politician. From 1870 to 1874, I was a member of the South Carolina State Senate. In 1874 I decided to run for a seat in the U.S. House of Representatives and won. I served from 1875 to 1879, from 1882 to 1883, and from 1884 to 1887. While in office, I advocated for legislation to integrate the military and to protect black Americans from brutal violence in the South. My main accomplishment was my introduction of legislation to support the immediate passing of the Civil Rights Bill of 1875. It was to guarantee free men the right to own property, make contracts, and have the full protection of the law.

I continued to do my part even after I retired from politics. For example, when I was seventy-three, I single-handedly prevented a black man from being lynched by a mob. Regardless of my age, I never let fear prevent me from doing whatever was necessary to help myself and other black people obtain freedom and justice.

James Edward O'Hara
(1844–1905)
U.S. House Representative for North Carolina

(JAMES chronicles his state and federal political career in North Carolina.)

JAMES

I'm James Edward O'Hara. I represented North Carolina in the U.S. House of Representatives from 1883 to 1887. I was born in New York City. Unlike most of my Negro peers in Congress, I was born in the North. I studied law at Howard University. I was admitted to the bar in North Carolina and began a law practice.

I became active in state politics. In 1868 I served as a clerk for the state convention that drafted North Carolina's new constitution to reenter the Union. In 1873 I was elected to the board of county commissioners for Halifax County. It wasn't until 1874 that I decided to run for a seat in the U.S. House of Representatives. That campaign lasted nine years, and in 1883 I was elected as a Republican to the U.S. House of Representatives. In 1885 I was fortunate enough to be reelected. I continued my efforts to restore the liberties that Negroes had lost since Democrats regained control of the South. My bid for reelection in

1886 was unsuccessful. I retired from politics and returned to my law practice.

Henry P. Cheatham
(1857–1935)
U.S. House Representative for North Carolina

Henry P. Cheatham

*(*HENRY *describes his efforts as a congressman for North Carolina.)*

HENRY
My name is Henry Cheatham. I was born a slave in 1857 in North Carolina. I attended public school and graduated from Shaw University in 1883. Prior to my political career, I was a school principal. My interest in politics grew. I was elected county registrar of deeds one year later. In 1888 I won a narrow victory for our state's congressional seat. I defeated my white Democratic opponent who wanted to take away black citizens' rights. When I was sworn in, I was the only black man in Congress. This lack of diversity was evidence of the power Democrats had regained in the South.

I served in the U.S. Congress from March 1889 to March 1893. While in Congress, I advocated for federal support for education and to protect black American's voting rights. Unfortunately, I didn't get enough support to pass my bills. I was reelected in 1890, but lost in 1892. One of the reasons I lost was because the North Carolina legislature changed my district's boundaries. I ran again in 1894 but wasn't reelected. In 1896 I was defeated by my brother-in-law George Henry White. In 1897 I was appointed recorder of deeds for the District of Columbia by President McKinley's administration. I remained in Washington for four years then returned to North Carolina. In 1907 I served as the superintendent of the Colored Orphan Asylum, which I cofounded in 1883. I remained in this position for twenty-eight years.

John Mercer Langston
(1829–1897)
U.S. House Representative for Virginia

(JOHN recounts his career in politics for the state of Virginia.)

JOHN

I'm John Mercer Langston. I was the first black congressman for Virginia. I was born free in 1829 and was able to receive a formal education. I received a bachelor's degree in 1849 and a master's degree in 1852. I wanted to attend law school but was denied entrance because I was black. But I was determined to receive an education to become a jurist, so I studied privately with abolitionists. I was admitted to the Ohio bar in 1854.

Before I entered the U.S. House of Representatives, I had nearly forty years of experience in a variety of public service jobs. I was also one of the founders of Howard University's law department, a minister resident to Haiti, and president of Virginia Normal Collegiate Institute. In 1865 I was president of the National Equal Rights League, and in 1870 I helped found the Negro National Labor Union.

In 1888 I ran for a seat in the U.S. House of Representatives but lost. However, I challenged the election and eventually won my case. In September 1890 I was sworn in. I only served seven months, but I made the most of my time in Congress. I fought for legislation to protect American goods from competing foreign countries. I also pressured the House to investigate lawsuits citing the disenfranchisement of black Americans. Unfortunately, my pleas were ignored and violation of black people's rights in the South continued.

I decided not to run in the following election but remained committed to helping my race politically and socially. Although my career in Congress was short, I'm proud that I was able to make some impact on political and economic benefits for black Americans.

Thomas Ezekiel Miller
(1849–1938)
U.S. House Representative for South Carolina

(THOMAS recalls his service as a state and federal politician for South Carolina.)

THOMAS

I'm Thomas Miller, and I was a Republican U.S. congressman for South Carolina. I was born in South Carolina and attended school in Charleston. I was fortunate enough to receive a college education and graduated from Lincoln University in Pennsylvania. In 1872 I moved back to my home state and served as a county school commissioner. I studied law and was admitted to the bar in 1875.

Prior to coming to the U.S. Congress, I was heavily involved in state politics. I was a member of the South Carolina House of Representatives from 1874 to 1880, from 1886 to 1887, and from 1894 to 1896. I also served in the state senate in 1880, and in 1895 I became a member of the State Constitutional Convention.

My service in the U.S. House of Representatives was not without problems. I had to contest the election when I was declared the loser. Unlike many other Negroes who lost their congressional seats because of a challenge by a losing opponent, I successfully won my case. I served from 1890 until 1891. Even though I was only able to serve for five months, I made my limited time useful. I gave two important speeches before the House. One speech supported federal oversight of elections and emphasized the need for voter protection. In my other address, I attacked the accusation that Negroes caused the South's economic problems. I ran again in 1890 for the 1891 through 1893 term, but lost to another black candidate. I tried again to regain my seat in 1894 but was unsuccessful. After politics, I focused more on education. I became president of the state college in Orangeburg, South Carolina, from 1896 to 1911. Following my tenure as a college president, I fully retired.

George W. Murray
(1853–1926)
U.S. House Representative for South Carolina

(GEORGE discusses his term in Congress after Democrats regained power in the South.

GEORGE

My name is George W. Murray. I was born enslaved in South Carolina. I received what was considered a good education for a black person during that time. I graduated from high school and attended college for two years. I became a schoolteacher for fifteen years. From 1890 to 1892, I was a customs inspector at the port of Charleston, South Carolina.

I was chairman of the Republican Party in Sumter County and was known as the Republican Black Eagle. I was a delegate at several

Republican National Conventions and lectured for the Colored Farmers Alliance. I was elected to the U.S. House of Representatives as a Republican for South Carolina in 1892. My term was from March 4, 1893, to March 3, 1895. I ran for reelection in 1894; however, I had to run against another black man because of redistricting. I lost the popular vote but successfully contested the election and was able to win the congressional seat. I served from June 4, 1896, to March 3, 1897.

I was the only black congressman during both my terms. I fought to protect black voters at voting polls and to overturn legislation that made it practically impossible for former slaves to vote. I also petitioned President Cleveland to pursue more black representation in Congress. Unfortunately, our nation's government was strongly Democratic and my pleas fell on deaf ears. That was my last term as a representative for South Carolina in the House. After my terms in Congress, I moved to Chicago in 1905 and became active in the Illinois Republican Party.

George Henry White
(1852–1918)
U.S. House Representative for North Carolina

(GEORGE recalls his efforts during his tenure as a congressman for North Carolina.)

GEORGE

My name is George Henry White. I was a Republican in the U.S. House of Representatives for North Carolina. Although the Reconstruction period officially ended before my election, I'm considered the last black congressman of that era. Southern Democrats regained power; they used voter intimidation and violence to dissuade black men from voting. They created state laws that disenfranchised blacks. This made it difficult, if not impossible, for black Americans to get elected. However, because the Populist and Republican parties fused between 1894 and 1900, blacks in North Carolina were able to have a brief period of political success.

I was educated in North Carolina's public schools after the Civil War. I graduated in 1877 from Howard University in Washington, D.C. Following graduation, I studied law privately and was admitted to the North Carolina bar in 1879. I practiced law, taught school, and was a principal at one of the state normal schools. I quickly became interested in politics, and in 1880 I was elected to the North Carolina State House of Representatives. I was also elected for one term in the North Carolina State Senate in 1884.

I decided to run for a seat in Congress against my brother-in-law Henry Cheatham. I defeated him, and in 1897 I was elected to the U.S. House of Representatives. I served two terms, from 1897 to 1899, and again from 1899 to 1901. During my time in office, I was able to arrange for a number of black people to be appointed postmasters throughout my district. I chose not to run a third term because of the political turmoil that Democrats were causing. Although I was no longer in the U.S. Congress, I continued my efforts to fight for equality. I was an officer in the newly created National Afro-American Council, a nationwide civil rights organization founded in 1898. I moved to Philadelphia, Pennsylvania, in 1906. When the council dissolved in 1908, I joined the National Association for the Advancement of Colored People. I also founded Whitesboro, New Jersey, a town I established as a real estate development.

I often think back to my days in Congress when I delivered my last address before the House on January 29, 1901. I felt I spoke the sentiments of black Americans in our country. I said, "This is perhaps the Negroes' temporary farewell to the American Congress, but let me say, Phoenix-like he will rise up some day and come again. These parting words are in behalf of an outraged, heart-broken, bruised and bleeding, but God-fearing people; faithful, industrious, loyal, rising people—full of potential force." I have been out of the U.S. House of Representatives for seventeen years and have not seen another black person in Congress. But I have faith in my people and my country. One day we will rise like the phoenix and regain a place in American politics.

RISE LIKE THE PHOENIX: AFRICAN AMERICANS REEMERGE IN POLITICS

Modern Era Politics

(SPEAKER *briefly cites African Americans' involvement in politics since 1929.*)

SPEAKER
During the Great Migration, which was from 1910 to 1940, African Americans from the rural South migrated to the urban North, creating black-majority congressional districts in Northern cities. Oscar De Priest was elected to the First Congressional District of Illinois from the South Side of Chicago in 1928. He became the first black congressman in the modern era. He was also the last African American Republican in the House of Representatives for fifty-six years.

African Americans switched to the Democratic Party with the election of Franklin D. Roosevelt in 1932. This was due primarily to Roosevelt's proposed economic programs in the New Deal. From 1940 to 1970, almost 5 million African Americans moved to the North and West, especially to California. Southern states continued their efforts to disenfranchise black voters. It wasn't until the Voting Rights Act of 1965 that African Americans regained their full voting privileges in the former Confederate states.

Until 1992 most black members serving in the U.S. House of Representatives were elected from inner-city districts in the West and the North. From 1929 to 2008, there were ninety-six African Americans elected to the House. Winning the U.S. Senate race, however, is much more difficult for black politicians as there are only two representatives from each state. The Great Migration resulted in no state having a black majority population. Thus African American politicians couldn't solely rely on the black vote. They had to reach a cross section of racially diverse voters. However, from 1929 to 2008, there have been three African American senators: Edward Brooke from Massachusetts, and Carol Moseley Braun and Barack Obama from Illinois.

Oscar De Priest
(1871–1951)
U.S. House Representative for Illinois

(SPEAKER highlights Oscar De Priest's service in the U.S. House of Representatives.)

SPEAKER
In 1929 Oscar De Priest, a Republican from Illinois, became the first African American to be elected to Congress since George Henry White, whose term ended in 1901. De Priest's career in politics began in Chicago in 1904 when he served on the Cook County Board of Commissioners. In 1915 he became alderman to Chicago, making him the city's first African American to fill this position. In 1929 he was elected to the U.S. House of Representatives for the state of Illinois. He served from 1929 to 1935, a total of three terms in the House.

De Priest's tenure in Congress focused on creating equality for African Americans. He fought for pensions for former slaves, limited seats in Congress for states that disenfranchised black voters, and legislation that would force states to prevent lynching. Although most of his bills were unsuccessful, his presence reinserted the African American voice in Congress. His tenure gave renewed hope to members of his race in that they could again have a significant role in politics on the national level.

Arthur Mitchell
(1883–1968)
U.S. House Representative for Illinois

*(*SPEAKER *highlights Arthur Mitchell's career in the U.S. House of Representatives.)*

SPEAKER
In 1935 Arthur Mitchell became the first African American to be elected to Congress as a Democrat. Arthur Mitchell was born in 1883 in Alabama to parents who were former slaves. He attended college at Tuskegee Institute, where he served as an assistant to Booker T. Washington. He later attended both Harvard and Columbia universities, and subsequently practiced law in Washington, D.C. In 1929 Mitchell moved to Chicago where he became active in politics. Although Mitchell was originally a Republican, he changed his party affiliation to Democrat after the success of President Roosevelt's New Deal program.

Mitchell ran for a seat to represent Illinois in the U.S. House of Representatives in 1934 and won. He served four terms, from 1935 to 1943. His career as a representative was not easy. Similar to other

African American members of Congress in the past, he was pressured to answer the needs of the entire black race. However, Mitchell made very clear that his intentions were to serve all races within his district and not to solely focus on black American issues. Mitchell did, however, pursue some special needs of African Americans. He advocated for legislation that would provide blacks positions within civil service, transportation, and the military. He also fought to overturn the poll tax, which prevented many blacks from voting. Mitchell retired from Congress in 1943. He moved to Virginia where he continued to help African Americans improve their status in the United States through the Southern Regional Council.

Adam Clayton Powell Jr.
(1908–1972)
U.S. House Representative for New York

(SPEAKER *highlights Adam Clayton Powell Jr.'s contributions to the U.S. House of Representatives.*)

SPEAKER
Adam Clayton Powell Jr. was a flamboyant Democrat who represented New York's Harlem district and was an associate minister at Abyssinian Baptist Church, which was the largest church in the borough of Manhattan. He used his ministerial position to bring about changes in Harlem, which had a majority African American population. Many of his political colleagues considered him radical and agitating, but that didn't faze Powell. He continued to be an outspoken leader in the fight for African American civil rights. Powell served a total of twelve terms. He held office from 1945 to 1967 and from 1967 to 1971.

Ralph Bunche
(1904–1971)
U.S. Ambassador

Ralph Bunche

(RALPH *recalls his tenure as a U.S. ambassador.*)

RALPH
My name is Ralph Bunche. I was the first African American to win
the Nobel Peace Prize. I served in the Office of Strategic Services
during World War II. The military used my expertise on African
affairs to prepare for the invasion of that continent. In 1944 I joined
the State Department, where I became acting chief of the Division
of Dependent Area Affairs. Following the war, I was assigned to the
United Nations, where I was the under-secretary-general in 1968.
Under-secretary-general was the highest position in the UN to be held
by an African American. I also served as director of the Division of
Trusteeship and Non-Self-Governing Territories. This office dealt with
the rights of people living under colonial rule.

I was awarded the Nobel Peace Prize in 1950 for my efforts to resolve
the conflict between Israel and the Arab states. I was involved in other
diplomatic activities, including attempts to end fighting on Cyprus and
supervising peacekeeping troops at the Suez Canal. I also worked to
settle the dispute between India and Pakistan.

Charles Diggs
(1922–1998)
U.S. House Representative for Michigan

(SPEAKER highlights Charles Diggs's contributions to the U.S. House of Representatives.)

SPEAKER

Charles Diggs represented the state of Michigan in the House of Representatives from 1955 to 1980. He was one of the dominate forces in the creation of the Congressional Black Caucus. He was an avid supporter of African American civil rights and fought for increased aid to African countries.

Augustus Freeman "Gus" Hawkins
(1907–2007)
U.S. House Representative for California

(SPEAKER describes Gus Freeman's career as a U.S. congressman.)

SPEAKER

Gus Hawkins, a Democrat from California, became the first African American west of the Mississippi to serve in the House of Representatives. He was deliberately low-key but very effective. He was called the Silent Warrior by the other members of the Congressional Black Caucus. Hawkins said, "The leadership belongs not to the loudest, not to those who beat the drums or blow the trumpets, but to those who have the stamina to persist and remain dedicated." Gus Hawkins was a living example of his own philosophy as he served in Congress twenty-eight consecutive years. His primary focuses were decreasing unemployment, increasing minimum wage, protecting the jobs of minorities and women, and increasing funding for public education. He was in office from 1963 to 1991.

John Conyers Jr.
(1929–)
U.S. House Representative for Michigan

(SPEAKER *notes John Conyers Jr.'s achievements as a U.S. Congressman.)*

SPEAKER
John Conyers Jr. is the second longest serving congressman in the House of Representatives. He has served for over forty years. He began his career in 1965 and his reelection in November 2010 allowed him to continue representing his Michigan district for a twenty-third consecutive term. His tenure as a senior member of Congress has allowed him to be very influential and to be a member and chair of some of the most powerful committees. From 1989 to 1994 he was chairman of the House Committee on Government Operations, later renamed the Committee on Oversight and Government Reform.
In 2006 Conyers's congressional peers elected him as chairman of the House Committee on the Judiciary. It is one of the most vitally important committees in the U.S. government. The Judiciary Committee oversees the Department of Justice, which includes the FBI and the Federal Courts. Civil rights, constitutional issues, consumer protection, and copyrights all fall under the jurisdiction of the Judiciary Committee. Congressman Conyers was a member of this committee in 1974 during the impeachment proceedings of President Nixon and the 1998 impeachment hearings of President Clinton. Conyers was the only person on the Judiciary Committee who was a panel member of the impeachment process for both presidents.

Conyers is on record for being a champion for civil rights and civil liberties of all Americans. In 1994 he was the primary sponsor of the Violence Against Women Act, or VAWA; he introduced the Hate

Crimes Prevention Act in 2001; and was the key advocate of the End Racial Profiling Act in 2004. He also coauthored legislation for election reform, which included termination of discriminatory practices in elections and making polling places accessible to person with disabilities.

Representative Conyers's success in Congress has been acknowledged with numerous honorary degrees from colleges and universities and many leadership awards.

Edward Brooke III
(1919–)
U.S. Senator for Massachusetts

(SPEAKER highlights Edward Brooke's career in the U.S. Senate.)

SPEAKER
Edward Brooke was a Republican from Massachusetts who added to the political pages of African American history firsts. He was the first to be elected to the Senate in nearly one hundred years, the first African American senator from the North, and the first to be elected by popular vote. Senator Brooke served two full terms, from 1967 to 1979. He fought for low income housing, racial equality in the South, increased minimum wage, and improvements in mass transportation and the commuter rail systems. In 2004 Senator Brooke received the highly distinguished honor of being awarded the Presidential Medal of Freedom in a White House ceremony.

Shirley Chisholm
(1924–2005)
U.S. House Representative for New York

Shirley Chisholm

(SPEAKER *explains the impetus behind Shirley Chisholm's campaign for the U.S. presidency.*)

SPEAKER

Shirley Chisholm represented New York in the U.S. House of Representatives. She was the first African American woman ever elected to the House. She served from 1969 until she retired in 1982. In 1972 Chisholm ran for the Democratic nomination for president of the United States. She was the first black person to run for the office of president. She knew the odds were against her. However, at the Democratic National Convention she did receive about 5 percent of the party's vote.

When people asked her why she ran knowing she didn't have much chance, she replied, "I ran because someone had to do it first . . . in this country everybody is supposed to be able to run for president, but that's never been really true. I ran because most people think the country is not ready for a black candidate, not ready for a woman candidate. The next time a woman runs, or a black, a Jew, or anyone from a group that the country is 'not ready' to elect to its highest office, I believe he or she will be taken seriously from the start. The door is not open yet, but it is ajar." It seems today, many years later, that Shirley Chisholm had an eye into the future.

Louis Stokes
(1925–)
U.S. House Representative for Ohio

(SPEAKER highlights Louis Stokes's career as a U.S. House Representative for Ohio.)

SPEAKER

Louis Stokes, a Democrat from Ohio, served in the House of Representatives from 1969 to 1999. He was the first African American to win a seat on the House Appropriations Committee. It is one of the most powerful Committees in Congress. He later became the committee's subchair or "cardinal." This position gave him both the opportunity and obligation to oversee a $90 billion federal budget. Through this budget he was able to control how money was allocated to Housing and Urban Development, or HUD, Veteran Affairs, and Independent Agencies.

Barbara Charline Jordan
(1936–1996)
U.S. House Representative for Texas

Barbara Jordan

*(SPEAKER recounts Barbara Jordan's contributions to the United
States as a congresswoman for Texas.)*

SPEAKER
Barbara Jordan graduated from Texas Southern University in 1956.
In 1959 she received a law degree from Boston University. After law
school, she returned to Texas and worked as an administrative assistant
to the county judge of Harris County. She remained in that position
until 1966, when she was elected to the Texas Senate. Jordan was the
first African American elected to this position since 1883. In 1972
she was elected president pro tempore of the state senate. Following
the tradition of the state senate, she served as governor for a day. This
made her the first black woman to serve as governor in our country.

Jordan was also the first African American from Texas to be elected to
the U.S. House of Representatives. She served from 1973 until 1979.
She was a member of several important committees during her tenure
in Washington. In 1976 she became the first black female to deliver a
keynote address. She delivered the address at the Democratic National
Convention. She nominated Bill Clinton for president of the United

States. Jordan retired from national politics at the end of her term, but remained active and vocal regarding important issues facing all Americans.

Andrew Young
(1932–)
U.S. House Representative for Georgia, U.S. Ambassador

(SPEAKER highlights Andrew Young's career as a politician.)

SPEAKER

Andrew Young, a Democrat from Georgia, served in the House of Representatives from 1973 to 1977. He was the first African American appointed to the House Rules Committee. Prior to his political career, he was active in the civil rights movement and worked closely with Dr. Martin Luther King Jr. and the Southern Christian Leadership Conference, or SCLC. In 1970 he resigned from the SCLC and entered the political arena, because he wanted Dr. King's goal to be both national and global.

In 1972 Young was elected to the House of Representatives for the state of Georgia. He came to Congress as a civil rights advocate. His main objectives were to improve the lives of African Americans by upgrading and extending public transportation, increasing opportunities for fair and quality education, and ensuring that African Americans had adequate housing. He also spoke before the House to extend the Voting Rights Act of 1965, which ensured that blacks wouldn't be denied their right to vote.

Andrew Young was dedicated to helping other countries as well. He extended his efforts to Latin America, Asia, and Africa. His dedication was given credence when President Carter asked him to become U.S. Ambassador to the United Nations. Young decided to decline a third term in Congress in order to take this position. As ambassador, he fought for equality and against apartheid for three years on behalf of the Carter administration.

His retirement from the United Nations was not the end of his career in government. In 1982 he became Atlanta's mayor and held the position for eight years. Today, Andrew Young continues to help the underprivileged in the United States, Africa, and the Caribbean.

Maxine Waters
(1938–)
U.S. House Representative for California

*(*SPEAKER *highlights Maxine Waters's achievements as a U.S. congresswoman.)*

SPEAKER
Maxine Waters has been a member of the House of Representatives since 1990. She has a history of advocating for her grassroots constituents. This outspoken Democrat from California has been a leader in the fight for women, minorities, children, and the poor. She has been a member of the Democratic National Committee and has played a key role in five presidential campaigns. Congresswoman Waters was influential in attaining $10 billion in loan guarantees for economic and infrastructural development in cities and for expanding debt relief for Africa and other developing nations.

Lawrence Douglas Wilder
(1931–)
Governor of Virginia

Characters:

JULIAN, *male fictional character, undergraduate political science major,* CAMERON's *roommate*

CAMERON, *male fictional character, undergraduate business major*

Costumes:

Present-day casual attire

Props:

Two desks, two chairs

(JULIAN and CAMERON discuss why Lawrence Wilder is an inspiration to African Americans.)

JULIAN

What are your plans after graduation, Cameron?

CAMERON

I have several job interviews lined up. I'll probably take a job with one of those companies and make six figures. Later, I'll establish my own business and become a multimillionaire like Reginald Lewis. What are you going to do?

JULIAN

I plan to go into politics. I want to make a difference in our country, especially in my home state. I want to get involved at the ground level and do a lot of community service.

CAMERON

Well you do it your way, I'll do it mine. I'm going to give back to the community too by creating jobs. What made you decide to go into politics?

JULIAN

I was influenced by Douglas Wilder, former governor of Virginia. I've been reading a lot about him, and I admire his accomplishments. Check this out. Wilder was born in Richmond, Virginia, in 1931 and raised there. He was named after poet Paul Laurence Dunbar and abolitionist Frederick Douglass. He attended public schools in the city, which were segregated at that time. He graduated from Virginia Union University. Later, he served in the Korean War and received the Bronze Star for heroism in combat. Wilder used the GI Bill of Rights to attend law school. He wanted to attend in Virginia but was denied admission because of his race. He didn't let that discourage him. Instead he traveled to Washington, D.C., and enrolled at Howard University. After graduation, he returned to Virginia and established a law firm. It was one of the few minority-owned businesses in the state.

Wilder entered the political arena in 1969, when he won a state senatorial seat in a special election. He became the first African American state senator from Virginia since Reconstruction. He served ten years in the General Assembly too. In 1985 he was elected as Virginia's lieutenant governor. Later, he successfully ran for the state's highest office. In 1990 Wilder became the first elected African American governor in the United States. He couldn't run for reelection, because Virginia had a mandatory term limit on the position of governor. I guess you could say he's one of those people that folks like to say pulled himself up by the bootstraps. His grandparents were enslaved in Virginia, and he had to go to segregated public schools. He couldn't attend a law school in Virginia, yet he rose above all this adversity and became its governor. He didn't even have hostility. In his inaugural speech he said, "The force I represent is Virginia's new mainstream. It looks forward, not backward. It tries to unify people not divide them."

CAMERON

I read that he easily won the election for mayor of Richmond in 2004. He must really be dedicated. He was over seventy years old when he took that office. A lot of people his age just chill and enjoy their retirement.

JULIAN

Not Governor Wilder. He told CNN in an interview in November 2004 that he was just hitting his stride. He's a true warrior. He said, "I was elected mayor of Richmond. I will continue to fight to accomplish worthwhile goals . . . I did not leave the ease of retirement to succumb to the fatigue of failure."

CAMERON

All I can say is, if you had to pick a political role model, you picked yourself a good one.

(End scene.)

Carol Moseley-Braun
(1947–)
U.S. Senator for Illinois

(SPEAKER highlights Carol Moseley-Braun's career as a U.S. Senator.)

SPEAKER

Carol Moseley-Braun was the first African American female elected to the U.S. Senate. She served from 1993 to 1999 and represented the state of Illinois. She was motivated to run for office, because she felt most politicians were not relating to the average American. She felt that "the Senate absolutely needed a healthy dose of democracy," and more diversity. She referred to her senatorial role as a "symbol of hope and change." Some of her legislative accomplishments and key roles include the Multiethnic Placement Act, the Child Support Orders Act, and the Improving America's Schools Act. She also supported affirmative action, women's rights, and the rights of African Americans. She sponsored legislation that called for the creation of the Sacagawea coin, which honored women of color.

She served as ambassador to New Zealand and Samoa from 1999 to 2001. She also sought the office of president as a Democrat in 2004.

Yes, We Can

(SPEAKER recalls the struggles that laid the foundation for President Obama's election.)

SPEAKER
When the first African American males were given the right to vote by the Fifteenth Amendment in 1870, I'm sure they asked each other in wonderful disbelief, "Does this mean we can really vote?" I'm sure the answer was, "Yes, we can."

When the first African American congressmen tried to pass legislation to protect the rights of black men in the South, I'm sure they were told, "Not many of your fellow congressmen support you, black voters are disenfranchised or too scared to vote, you don't have enough political experience; do you really think you can make a difference?" I'm sure they responded, "Yes, we can."

When Fannie Lou Hamer and others were beaten, forced off their jobs, and arrested for trying to vote, I'm sure when asked, "Is it worth it? Do you think you can persevere?" I'm sure they answered, "Yes, we can."

Today, when little boys and girls plan their careers, they can dream without limitations. If asked, "Do you think you could ever be elected president of the United States of America?" They can finally answer with certainty, "Yes, we can."

LEADERS AND SPOKESPERSONS

Booker Taliaferro Washington
(1856–1915)
Spokesperson, Educator

Booker T. Washington

(BOOKER explains why he was a controversial spokesman for African American equality.)

BOOKER

I'm Booker T. Washington. I founded Tuskegee Institute in Tuskegee, Alabama. Not only was I an educator, but I was also considered the premier spokesman for the black race for years. This especially became the case after I delivered my "Atlanta compromise" speech at the 1895 Atlanta Exposition. I shared my philosophy on Negro and white relationships. I assured white Americans that the Negro was no threat to them. I stated that "in all things that are purely social, we can be as separate as fingers, yet one as the hand in all things essential to mutual progress." I apologized for the errors my race had made by seeking careers in politics instead of developing skills in industry and real estate. I encouraged my race to stay in the South and learn skills in agriculture, mechanics, and domestic service. I felt that if we proved ourselves successful citizens, that we could get the respect of the white race and eventually make political and social gains.

I received a lot of criticism from many black leaders like W. E. B. Du Bois. They believed that I was encouraging Negroes to accept segregation and forget about political rights. This wasn't my purpose. My goal was to see that the Negro survived in a climate of unforgotten hate. It was easy for Du Bois and others to criticize me, since they were living safely in the North. I lived in a section of America where Negroes had their homes burned, were lynched for little or no reason, or were evicted from their place of work for trying to vote. I've seen Negroes placed in chain gangs because they couldn't pay a fine for a misdemeanor, or simply because they didn't have a job. I saw the effects of Jim Crow laws every day, whereas they only read about them.

What many people didn't know was that I fought for civil rights behind the scenes. I used my influence to persuade the Republican Party to aid Negroes. I paid the legal fees of several lawyers to work to overturn discriminatory laws. Although I may have been guilty of encouraging the Negro to accept a position of accommodation and conciliation, my primary objective was the welfare, safety, and uplifting of my people.

William Edward Burghardt "W. E. B." Du Bois
(1868–1963)
Spokesperson

W.E.B. Du Bois

(W. E. B. describes the adversity he faced as a spokesperson for African Americans.)

W. E. B.

I'm W. E. B. Du Bois. I played many roles in my struggle for the improvement of the black race's status in America. I graduated from Fisk University then attended Harvard University for graduate studies. I was the first Negro to receive a PhD from Harvard. I was a professor at Wilberforce University and Atlanta University, two historically black colleges. In 1903 I published my famous book *The Souls of Black Folk.* It was a series of fourteen essays. In the series I stressed voting rights protection for Negroes living in the South. I attacked Booker T. Washington for encouraging black people to give up their political and civil rights, and for opposing higher education beyond trade schools. I also included my theory that I called "the talented tenth." I believed that educated black people made up about one-tenth of the Negro population. I felt that they should be the ones to take the lead to advance the black race.

In 1905 I helped organize the Niagara movement, which was the forerunner of the NAACP. I was the editor for their magazine, the

Crisis. I was also a member of the pan-African conferences, where I demanded an end to colonialism in Africa. In 1934 I resigned my position in the NAACP for ten years. When I returned, I worked for the organization as the director of special research.

I was an outspoken person, and as a result the government indicted me as a foreign agent in an effort to silence me. The charges were later thrown out by a judge. The government retaliated by revoking my passport from 1951 to 1958. During these seven years, they intimidated my friends and tampered with my mail. I eventually moved to Ghana in Africa and never returned to the United States.

Marcus Garvey
(1887–1940)
Black Nationalist

Marcus Garvey

(MARCUS *explains how he promoted black pride in the United States.*)

MARCUS
My name is Marcus Garvey. I was born in Jamaica. Before coming to the United States, I lived in London, England, where I became interested in African independence. When I returned to Jamaica in 1914, I established the Universal Negro Improvement and

Conservation Association and African Communities League, also known as the UNIA. The goal of the UNIA was to unite black people throughout the world. In 1916 I came to the United States to establish a UNIA chapter. I planned to get support for the organization by emphasizing black pride.

I made my headquarters in New York City. I began by publishing the *Negro World* newspaper in 1918. It was widely accepted instantly. I followed up by establishing a steamship company called the Black Star. I also established the Negro Factories Corporation, the Black Cross Nurses, the African Legion, and the Black Eagle Flying Corps. I sold stock at $5 per share to raise money.

I was deliberately flamboyant. I would hold huge parades down the streets of Harlem. I would lead the parades dressed in a military-style uniform, usually purple colored with gold epaulets. Scores of people would parade with me or watch the procession. In 1920 I held a month-long convention in Harlem. There were thousands of black people from around the world. We voted to create a free republic in Africa, and I was elected president. We sent UNIA delegates to Liberia, but it wasn't long before the British and French pressured the Liberian government to expel the delegates.

Not only was I a threat to foreign countries, I was also a threat to many black leaders in the United States. A lot of Negroes still believed that black leaders should be light complexioned. Light skin meant that they were probably decedents of a slave master, which brought black people status. They wanted to forget about everything that reminded them of slavery. They called anyone who reflected images of slavery or who wasn't refined, according to their definition, "no class." I reminded them of all the things they resented. I'm a large dark-skinned flashy man and I spoke about black pride and going back to Africa. I didn't care that they said I didn't have class; I was doing things in the community that the government and the black middle-class leaders and citizens wouldn't or couldn't do.

I was convicted of mail fraud by the government when my Black Star Line failed in 1923. I was fined $1,000 and sentenced to five years in prison. In 1925 I was incarcerated in the Atlanta Penitentiary, but in 1927 President Coolidge commuted my sentence. I was deported back to Jamaica. Although I never returned to the United States, people remember me for a couple reasons: I made the African liberation flag—with the symbolic red, black, and green colors—famous; I also showed the world that black people could accomplish things by working together and having pride in themselves.

Elijah Muhammad
(1875–1975)
Nation of Islam Leader

Elijah Muhammad

(SPEAKER explains how Elijah Muhammad and the Nation of Islam influenced the black community.)

SPEAKER

Many African Americans lacked faith in traditional black religions. People began to seek other religious groups and leaders. Elijah Muhammad and the Nation of Islam became the voice of the black population that was looking for a more radical approach on social issues and faith.

Elijah Muhammad took over the Nation of Islam in 1934 after the founder, Fard Muhammad, mysteriously disappeared. In 1942 Elijah Muhammad was arrested for inciting his members to refuse the military draft. He was imprisoned for four years in Milan, Michigan. He moved to Chicago, Illinois, when he was released in 1946 and began to broaden his religious movement.

The Nation of Islam combined secular issues with sacred beliefs. The religion focused on instilling a sense of affirmation and identity. The Nation of Islam taught that blacks who lived in the Nile Valley were the first human inhabitants of Earth. This emphasis on black awareness and self-respect appealed to many African Americans. The Nation of Islam continues to be a highly visible religion in the American community and an influence within the black race. Fard Muhammad is recognized as Allah, and Elijah Muhammad is known as the prophet and messenger of Allah.

Malcolm X
(1925–1965)
Militant African American Leader

Malcolm X

(SPEAKER recounts Malcolm X's growth into a major leader in the black community.)

SPEAKER

Malcolm Little was born in Omaha, Nebraska, on May 19, 1925. His father, an outspoken black advocate, was murdered by a mob of angry whites in 1931. Shortly after his father's death, his mother moved the family to Detroit, Michigan. Malcolm dropped out of school when he was fifteen. When he turned sixteen, he moved to Boston to live with relatives. He subsequently became involved in crime. By the time he was twenty-one, he had been incarcerated for burglary and sentenced to a ten-year prison term. While in prison, he learned of the teachings of Elijah Muhammad and the Nation of Islam movement. Upon his release, he became active in the Nation community. In 1953 he changed his name from Malcolm Little to Malcolm X and became the assistant minister at the Nation mosque in Detroit. Elijah transferred him to Philadelphia, and later, Malcolm was assigned to Mosque Number 7 in Harlem. It emerged into the most successful mosque in the Nation of Islam. He became the voice of northern urban blacks and young civil rights workers who were not in favor of the more pacific attitude of established black leaders. Malcolm dismissed the goal of racial integration. By the early 1960s, his popularity attracted thousands of followers.

In 1963 he attempted to establish his own group, the Organization of Afro-American Unity. This action caused him to be suspended from the New York mosque as a minister. He began to have conflicts with Elijah Muhammad. In March 1964 he broke from the Nation of Islam and established his own organization, the Muslim Mosque Inc. He made a pilgrimage to Mecca that same year. He traveled through the Middle East and Africa. These journeys increased his optimism regarding unity between blacks and whites. He changed his name to El-Hajj Malik El-Shabazz. As his popularity continued to grow, so did his list of enemies. He feared for his life. On February 21, 1965, he was assassinated in the Audubon Ballroom in New York. The legacy Malcolm X left behind was his love for his African American brothers and sisters. He taught them to believe in themselves, understand, and embrace their connection to their roots in Africa.

Martin Luther King Jr.
(1929–1968)
Nonviolent Civil Rights Leader

Martin Luther King Jr.

(SPEAKER gives a brief history of the life and work of Martin Luther King Jr.)

SPEAKER

Martin Luther King Jr. was born in Atlanta, Georgia, in 1929. He followed in his father's footsteps by becoming a Baptist preacher. In 1954 he became pastor of Dexter Baptist Church in Montgomery, Alabama. He rose to the forefront of the civil rights movement in 1955 during the Montgomery bus boycott, which was inspired by Mrs. Rosa Parks's arrest.

King was influenced by the nonviolent methods of Mohandas Gandhi. He applied those same techniques in his protests. It's ironic, because he was the victim of violence and unjustified arrests on many occasions. His home was bombed, and he was stabbed and stoned. He was arrested more than thirty times. Despite all this, he still told all who would listen, "Let no man drag us so low as to hate."

On January 9, 1957, he and a group of young ministers founded the Southern Christian Leadership Conference. It was a Christian-based organization established to fight racism in the South. On August 28, 1963, he delivered his famous "I have a dream" speech at the March on Washington. Dr. King was the recipient of the Nobel Peace Prize in 1964. He donated the $54,000 cash prize to the SCLC. He gave most of the money he earned from his writings and lectures to various civil rights organizations.

Dr. King faced danger every day of his life. He and his wife never knew when they would see each other for the last time. Two months before his death, he described what he wanted to be said at his funeral. He told his congregation, "I'd like somebody to mention that day Martin Luther King Jr. tried to give his life saving others and he wanted you to say that I tried to love and serve." Martin Luther King Jr. was assassinated April 4, 1968.

The Congressional Black Caucus paved the way for the passage of Martin Luther King Jr. Day to become a national holiday. On November 3, 1983, President Reagan signed the bill into law. Our country has also honored him on a United States postage stamp.

Warith Deen Mohammed
(1933–2008)
Muslim Leader

(SPEAKER describes Warith Deen Mohammad's conversion to Islam.)

SPEAKER
Imam Warith Deen Mohammed was born Wallace Dean Muhammad. He was the son of the Nation of Islam leader Elijah Muhammad. In 1975, while facing a continuous decline in health, Elijah Muhammad appointed his son to be the new leader of the organization. This was

a surprise to many because Warith sided with Malcolm X against Muhammad, was excommunicated for several years, and believed his father's teachings to be heresy. Wallace believed that his father's black-separatist theology was incorrect after he studied the Qur'an and the life of the Islamic prophet Muhammad. He changed the spelling of his name when he began his reforms within the religion. He accepted whites into the fold of Muslim worshippers. He also attempted to network with mainstream Muslim communities. His goal for implementing changes was to bring the Nation closer to traditional Islamic teachings. This new philosophy caused a split in the denomination. In 1981 those who rejected these changes followed Louis Farrakhan, who revived the name of the Nation of Islam.

Warith Mohammed was the first Muslim to give an invocation in the U.S. Senate. He also rendered an Islamic prayer during President Clinton's 1993 and 1997 inaugural interfaith prayer services. In February 2000 he and Louis Farrakhan publicly announced their reconciliation at the annual Savior's Day convention.

Louis Abdul Farrakhan
(1933–)
Leader of the Nation of Islam

(SPEAKER gives a brief history of Farrakhan's work for the African American community.)

SPEAKER
Louis Farrakhan is the charismatic leader of the Nation of Islam. In 1981 he led a faction of members who withdrew from the Nation of Islam while it was under Warith Mohammed's leadership. They were dissatisfied with the reforms that Mohammed was implementing. Farrakhan revived the name of the Nation of Islam and continued in the tradition of Elijah Muhammad.

Louis Farrakhan was born Louis Eugene Walcott. He was born and raised in Massachusetts and was a devout Episcopalian. He was a multitalented student who was a standout in academics, sports, and music. His first encounter with direct racism occurred after he enrolled at Winston-Salem Teachers College in North Carolina in 1950. However, the incident that had the most impact on him followed the death of a close friend who was killed in the Korean War. Farrakhan had gone to a theater in Washington, D.C. and was refused admittance because he was black. He said, "At that point I was very, very, angry with America." He started writing a song called "Why America Is No Democracy."

Later, he dropped out of college and became a calypso singer. He named himself the Charmer. His religious life was also taking a turn. He began to question the alleged virtues of Christianity. He couldn't understand why there was so much hate by white Christians toward black Christians. In 1955 while playing at a club in Chicago, he encountered some old friends who had joined the Nation of Islam. He accepted their invitation to visit the mosque to hear Elijah Muhammad speak. He was impressed and filled out a membership application that same evening. When he heard Malcolm X speak, he was further convinced that he wanted to join the Nation of Islam. He became Malcolm's best student. When Malcolm broke ties with the Black Muslims in 1964, Farrakhan remained loyal to Elijah Muhammad.

Before the end of December 1965, Farrakhan became minister of Harlem Mosque Number 7, where Malcolm X had been the minister. He set about to restore the Nation of Islam's original tenets. He engaged in building the Nation's economy and ideologies. In 1984, however, he broke the Nation's policy of not getting involved in politics by registering to vote and supporting Jesse Jackson for president of the United States.

Farrakhan's audience grew from only small rooms of people to crowds of up to ten thousand. He became a national figure. Even those who weren't supporters of the Nation of Islam felt he was the only black man who was bold enough to challenge white America. His affirmation of black pride is his main appeal to African Americans. His million man march in 1995 was proof of this. He was the driving force behind the success of the historic event. The million man march drew support from a broad range of political and religious groups within the black community. The march didn't have a political purpose like the March on Washington in 1963. It was a symbol of unity, black pride, encouragement, and recognition of the African American male.

CIVIL RIGHTS

Activists

Ida B. Wells
(1862–1932)
Civil Rights Activist, Newspaper Editor

Ida B. Wells

(IDA explains how she used writing as a means to expose unjust conditions in the South.)

IDA

I think this article is ready for press. I hate writing about things like this, but someone has to tell the real truth about these crimes against Negroes.
(Looks up at the audience.)
Please excuse me. I get so caught up and angry about the murders of my people in the South that sometimes I forget my manners. I'm Ida B. Wells, and I'm pleased to meet you. I've been researching and

documenting all the lynchings of Negroes in the United States. I'm going to publish my findings in a book and call it *The Red Record.* But I'm not going to stop there. I'm going to meet with the president and let him know that something must be done to stop these terrible killings of innocent people.

I used to have my own newspaper office in Memphis, Tennessee. In 1892 three Negro men in that city were lynched simply because their grocery store was taking customers away from white merchants. Me and my big mouth! I wrote about it in my paper. That wasn't the first time I'd gotten into trouble for standing up for what was right. In 1884 I was forced off a train, because I wouldn't move from my seat and go to a segregated section. I also used to be a teacher in Memphis. That didn't last long, because I was fired when I wrote an article protesting the unfair conditions of the Negro schools.

My newspaper was a threat to the white community but a blessing to me. It allowed me the opportunity to expose the evil that was going on. One time I had to go out of town and some whites in the city destroyed my office. I was warned that I would be killed if I returned. Now I write for a paper in New York. They should know by now that running me out of town isn't going to stop me from running my mouth. I'm going to keep speaking out and using the power of the press no matter where I am until my people's freedom is protected.

Mary Eliza Church Terrell
(1863–1954)
Civil Rights Activist, Writer

Mary Church Terrell

(MARY explains how she became a prominent civil rights activist.)

MARY

My name is Mary Church Terrell. I was born in Memphis, Tennessee, in 1863. I was blessed because the Civil War ended two years after I was born, and because my parents were prosperous. I graduated from Oberlin College in 1884 and accepted a teaching position at Wilberforce College in Ohio. My father was really upset about this, because he didn't believe women should work. In fact he was so angry that he disinherited me and refused to write to me for a year. He told me that "no man would want to marry a woman who studied mathematics." I responded by telling him, "I'll take a chance and run the risk." But Daddy was wrong. I took a teaching job in Washington, D.C. in 1887. It was in D.C. that I met my husband Robert, an attorney.

Neither marriage nor working would stop me from being a civil rights activist and a fighter for women's rights. In 1892 I united with Frederick Douglass in an unsuccessful attempt to convince President Harrison to condemn lynching. When I was appointed to the Board of Education in Washington, D.C. in 1895, I became the first black woman to hold that position. In 1896 I founded the National

Association of Colored Women, also called the NACW. The purpose of the organization was to form kindergartens, to teach home economics, and to provide programs in self-help and parenting education. I delivered a speech in German in 1904 at the International Congress of Women in Berlin. In 1906 I publicly protested the dismissal of black soldiers following the Brownsville, Texas Affair. In 1909 I became one of the cofounders of the National Association for the Advancement of Colored People, or the NAACP.

I also worked with Susan B. Anthony and other feminists to get the right to vote. I wrote articles about lynching and discrimination throughout my life. However, one of my greatest joys came when I was ninety years old. I wasn't able to move around as well as I used to, but I grabbed my cane and walked to the head of the picket line that successfully forced restaurants in Washington, D.C. to integrate. I spent most of my life on the battlefield, but I didn't mind because I was a willing warrior.

Asa Philip Randolph
(1889–1979)
Civil Rights Activist, Union Organizer, Magazine Editor

A. Philip Randolph

(A. PHILIP explains how he became one of America's most prominent civil rights activists.)

A. PHILIP

My first name is Asa, but most people know me as A. Philip Randolph.
I'm a labor leader, union organizer, civil rights activist, and publisher.
That may be the reason some people have dubbed me the Prophet of
the Civil Rights Movement. I spent the majority of my life organizing
my people and protesting injustices in our county. I began protesting
early in life. I was born in Crescent City, Florida, and raised in
Jacksonville, Florida. When I lived in Jacksonville, the city's streetcars
were segregated. My father, who was a Methodist minister, refused to
allow his sons to ride the streetcars. We protested by walking wherever
we had to go.

When I turned twenty-two, I moved to Harlem. Even though it was
called the Negro Capital of the World, it didn't take long for me to
realize that racism didn't stop south of the Mason-Dixon Line. I
attended the City College of New York and met other Negroes who
shared my views on racism in America. We formed a militant group
called the Harlem Radicals. Some of us combined socialism with
race radicalism. I later included the trade union as one of my issues
of concern. I believed racism could be overcome by the integration of
the labor movement. For a short period, I joined the Socialist Party.
I separated from them in the early 1920s, because the party failed to
push for black people to be included in labor unions.

In 1917 my friend Chandler Owen and I founded the *Messenger*
magazine. Our subtitle was, "the Only Radical Magazine Published by
Negroes." We spoke out about lynching in the South. In the summer
of 1919 there were twenty-five race riots. At least seventy-six Negroes
were lynched and others were shot or beaten. That summer was called
Red Summer. After this atrocity, we encouraged blacks to defend
themselves. We attacked the American Federation of Labor, or AFL,
for its racist union policies. We criticized the Republican Party for not
having any black candidates. We even denounced our black leaders

for supporting America during World War I. We wrote that rather than make the world safe for democracy, it would be preferable to make Georgia safe for the Negro. We also encouraged blacks to resist the military draft. Needless to say, it didn't take long to capture the attention of the federal government. In 1918 the postmaster general revoked our magazine's second-class mailing privileges. In 1919 the justice department ordered an investigative report. The attorney general's conclusion was that the *Messenger* was, "by long odds the most able and most dangerous of the Negro publications."

I continued advocating for economic progress. In 1925 several black delegates from the Pullman porters asked me to help them organize in their struggle against the Pullman Company. The company provided railroad cars with sleeping berths. It was the largest employer of Negroes in the country. We formed the Brotherhood of Sleeping Car Porters union. Our fight with the Pullman Company lasted ten years before they officially recognized us. In 1937 we were successful in negotiating our first contract with them.

My opposition to the government's racial policies continued into World War II. I led protests, because the weapons industry refused to hire Negroes. I began organizing people and informed President Franklin Roosevelt that I would lead over 100,000 black people on a march to Washington. This pressured him to ban discrimination in industries that had government contracts. In 1948, with the help of other leaders, we persuaded President Truman to end segregation in the armed forces. In 1955 the AFL merged with the Council of Industrial Organization, or the CIO. I became their vice president and held that office for thirteen years. In 1963 I asked my deputy director, Bayard Rustin, to help me organize a March on Washington. This historic event was attended by over 250,000 peaceful protesters. It was the rally where Martin Luther King Jr. delivered his famous "I have a dream" speech. This demonstration was also directly responsible for the passing of the Civil

Rights Act of 1964. This same year President Johnson awarded me the Presidential Medal of Freedom. It is the highest honor given to a civilian.

I want to leave you with this personal message: "Salvation for a race, nation, or class must come from within. Freedom is never granted; it is won. Justice is never given; it is exacted. Freedom and justice must be struggled for by the oppressed of all lands and races, and the struggle must be continuous."

Daisy Lee Gaston Bates
(1920–1990)
NAACP Chapter President, Newspaper Editor

Daisy Lee Gaston Bates

(DAISY recounts her struggles to achieve integration at Central High in Little Rock, Arkansas.)

DAISY

My name is Daisy Bates. When people talk about strong black women, I have to be counted in that number. I wasn't strong because I wanted to be strong; life made me a fighter almost from the time I was born. When I was a baby, my mother was murdered by three white men who attacked her. Following her death, my father arranged for me to be raised by friends, then he left town. I married Louis Bates after I became an adult, and we moved to Little Rock, which is the capital of Arkansas.

In 1941 my husband and I started a weekly newspaper called the *State Press*. At first the paper was going along pretty well, but after we ran a story about a colored soldier being killed by a local policeman, we lost a lot of advertisers. Later, an antiunion judge had me arrested, because I ran a story criticizing him. He sentenced three black men to a year in prison for walking in a picket line when another striker was murdered.

Life was especially rough for black people in Little Rock and other parts of the South. That's why we had to stick together to make a change. It's the reason I joined the NAACP. In 1954, following the U.S. Supreme Court's ruling to end segregation in public schools, the Little Rock school board drew up a plan to integrate Central High School for the 1957 fall term. I was president of the local chapter of the NAACP. Our chapter organized the nine black children who would be attending the school. These students became known throughout the country as the Little Rock Nine. On August 8, two weeks before school was to start, someone threw a rock through my living room window. The rock had a note on it that read, "Stone this time, dynamite next." Most of the white people in town were doing everything they could to keep the black students from attending Central High. Even Governor Faubus, a known segregationist, added to the problem. He sent the National Guard troops to prevent the Little Rock Nine from going into the school. Things got so bad that President Eisenhower had to send the 101st Airborne Division to protect the teenagers.

It's hard to describe all the pressure I was going through, but I had to stay strong for those nine children. I had to provide emotional support for them and their families. Our newspaper, which we ran for eighteen years, was forced to close. Members of the NAACP and I were harassed by city officials in an effort to intimidate us. They demanded information about us and the NAACP's finances. When the NAACP refused, other leaders and I were arrested. The Supreme Court later overturned our convictions. In addition to all of this, two crosses were burned on my front lawn, and two firebombs were tossed at my home. My husband and several others had to become armed guards on our premises. We had to keep guns available throughout the house at all times. We endured it all. God knows it wasn't easy for any of us, especially the Little Rock Nine. I'm proud of the way they were able to stick it out. Central High School became integrated and blacks were able to get an equal education.

Bayard Rustin
(1910–1987)
Civil Rights Activist

Bayard Rustin

(BAYARD describes the injustices that prompted him to become a civil rights activist.)

BAYARD
I'm Bayard Rustin. I was born in West Chester, Pennsylvania. Even though I was born and raised in the North, I had some painful experiences with Southern racism. When I was on a field trip with my high school, I was thrown out of a restaurant because I was black. When I was in Tennessee in 1942, I was brutally beaten by police, because I refused to move to the back of the bus. During World War II, I spent twenty-eight months in prison as a conscientious objector.

In 1947 I was sentenced to twenty-two days on a chain gang for participating in a freedom ride. The chain gang prison system was brutal, inhumane, and racist. Two years after I was released from prison, I published my account of the brutality that went on during my confinement. My documented account led to North Carolina abolishing their chain gang prison system.

I participated with other black leaders in persuading President Truman to end segregation in the military. I led protests against British colonization in India and was active against apartheid in South Africa. I worked with A. Philip Randolph as a youth organizer on the proposed initial March on Washington during World War II. The intent of this proposed march was to protest hiring discrimination in the defense plants. The threatened protest forced President Franklin Roosevelt to issue an executive order banning discrimination in companies receiving government contracts. I continued to work with Randolph and helped him plan the 1963 March on Washington. Years later, I met Martin Luther King Jr. and became one of his advisors. I assisted him with the bus boycott in Montgomery, Alabama.

When I look back over my life, I guess I was always fighting against injustice. There's nothing wrong with that, because sometimes that's the only way to bring about change. More of you need to speak up to make a positive change in the world. Just remember that there's a difference between an activist and a troublemaker. In other words, before you start your fight, make sure you're on the right battlefield.

The Two before Rosa

(SPEAKER *introduces teenage activists Claudette Colvin and Mary Louise Smith.*)

SPEAKER
Less than a year before Rosa Parks
Gave the civil rights movement its needed sparks
Two brave teenagers not as well known to us
Also refused to move from their seats on a Montgomery bus
Like Rosa, their story is very true
So let me talk a little about them to you

Claudette Colvin
(1939–)
Teen Activist

(SPEAKER *recounts Claudette Colvin's protest against segregation on Montgomery buses.*)

SPEAKER
On March 2, 1955, fifteen-year-old Claudette Colvin was riding the Montgomery city bus. She and three other African Americans were sitting in the no-man's-land section. That's the section near the middle of the bus where black people were allowed to sit if no white people needed a seat. The bus became crowded, and they were ordered to let the white passengers who had just boarded have their seats. An elderly black lady and Colvin refused to get up. Colvin told the driver, "I done paid my dime. I ain't got no reason to move." The other two black people got up when told. When the driver left to call the police, the older lady got up and sneaked off the bus before the police arrived. Colvin knew she would get into trouble but decided that she wasn't going to get up for white people anymore.

The police dragged her off the bus and handcuffed her. She was mad, screaming, fighting, and crying all the way to the squad car. When Colvin went to court, she was charged with violating the city's segregation law; she was also charged with assault and disorderly conduct. She was represented by the NAACP. Her lawyer was able to get all the charges dropped, except the assault, and she had to pay a fine. Claudette Colvin was only fifteen but old enough to know right from wrong. She knew that the ordinance was wrong and that she was right for protesting an unjust law.

Mary Louise Smith
(1939–)
Teen Activist

(SPEAKER describes how Mary Louise Smith resisted bus segregation in Montgomery.)

SPEAKER
It was October 1955. Mary Louise Smith was on the city bus minding her own business when a white woman wanted her seat. Since Smith didn't get up when she saw her coming, the woman told the driver to make her move. Smith told the driver, "No!" so he had her arrested. She was charged with breaking the law and had to pay a nine dollar fine.

Some people might have looked at Claudette Colvin and Mary Louise Smith and said, "Oh, they're just a couple of teenagers; they didn't know what they were doing." But I don't see it that way. I see them as two young people who were brave enough to do something that most adults feared doing. They too were civil rights heroes.

Rosa Parks
(1913–2005)
Civil Rights Activist

Rosa Parks

(ROSA reflects on the events that earned her the title Mother of the Civil Rights Movement.)

ROSA

It seems like the bus is running late again. It doesn't really matter. This time I know I can sit where I want and not have to give up my seat.

It wasn't that way on December 1, 1955, in Montgomery, Alabama. I will never forget that day. I had just gotten off my job as a seamstress at the Montgomery Fair Department Store. I walked a half block to the bus stop on Court Square. I boarded the bus through the front door, paid my fare, and went to the rear door with the rest of the black people to get my seat. That's the way it was back then. Black people couldn't go to their seats from the front of the bus. We had to pay our money to the driver, get off, and then go through the back door to get to our seats. We also had to sit in the back of the bus even if there was space in the white section up front.

The section between the front of the bus and the back of the bus was called no-man's-land. It was in no-man's-land that I got into trouble. We could sit in that section of the bus as long as a white person didn't need to sit down. It wasn't long before the bus was full, and a white man needed a seat in no-man's-land. The driver yelled, "Let me have those seats!" No one moved. He shouted again, "You better make it light on yourselves and get up!" The other two colored people, as we were called back then, got up. I refused to move and remained seated.

I was arrested, taken to jail, and fingerprinted like a hardened criminal. I had to go to court too. The judge found me guilty of violating the segregation law and fined me $10. When the black community learned what happened, a bus boycott was started. We were led by Dr. Martin Luther King Jr. You know the rest of the story. The boycott lasted 381 days and resulted in a U.S. Supreme Court case. On November 13, 1956, the Court ruled that segregation on buses was unconstitutional.

By now, I'm sure you know who I am. I'm Rosa Parks. Some people call me a martyr. Many call me the Mother of the Civil Rights Movement. I wasn't trying to be a martyr. I didn't plan what happened. Many people think I didn't give up my seat because I was tired from working on my $0.75 per hour job. I was tired, but not from working. I was tired from being pushed around. I had to sit down in order to stand up for what was right.

Fannie Lou Hamer
(1917–1977)
Voter Rights Advocate

Fannie Lou Hamer

Characters:
FANNIE LOU HAMER, *female, voter rights advocate*
ELECTION WORKER, *male or female fictional character,*
nonspeaking role
Costumes:
Casual attire of the mid-1900s
Props:
Table, ballot box

(FANNIE *explains the struggles she endured so that African Americans*
would be able to vote.)

FANNIE

I want to introduce myself before I vote. I'm Fannie Lou Hamer.
I may not be as well-known as some of the people who fought for
civil rights, but there were many unknown people like me who risked
everything—including our lives—to fight injustice.

I was born into poverty. I was the youngest of twenty children. My
parents were sharecroppers in Mississippi. I suffered from a serious
leg injury when I was a baby, but my family was too poor to get me
the medical help I needed. I limped for the rest of my life. I started
working in the cotton fields when I was only six years old. When I
was young, my daddy saved enough money to buy three mules. This
allowed him to work his own land. It wasn't long before some angry
whites poisoned his mules. They were mad about his minor success.

I may have been poor and only able to go to school for six years,
but I knew the value of voting. I was encouraged when two civil
rights organizations came to Mississippi to register black people to
vote. Would you believe that as late as 1962, out of a population of
13,524 eligible black voters in Sunflower, Mississippi, only 155 were
registered to vote? People were scared. They had good cause to be. I

remember on August 31, 1962, eighteen of us rented a bus. We went to sign up to vote but were denied, because we couldn't pass the literacy test. On the way home, we were arrested. The police said our yellow bus looked too much like a school bus. To make matters worse, when I got home, I was kicked off the plantation where I had worked for eighteen years. I had to stay with a lady I knew. A few nights later, gunshots were fired into her house.

Things kept getting worse for me. In 1963 several of us, including a fifteen-year-old girl, were returning from a voter's education training. We were arrested and beaten. I was beaten so badly that I received permanent damage to my eye and kidneys. Because I was so determined and refused to back down, my husband was fired and no one would hire him. We had to live off a ten-dollar-a-week handout from the local civil rights organization.

Later, when I was asked about the beatings, I told the world, "We're tired of these beatings; we're tired of taking this. It's been a hundred years and we're still being beaten and shot at, crosses are still being burned, because we want to vote. But I'm going to stay in Mississippi and if they shoot me down, I'll be buried here." I became famous for saying, "I'm sick and tired of being sick and tired." Y'all, when you're tired, you have to dig deep within yourself and pull out your inner strength.

My strength and determination paid off. On August 5, 1965, President Johnson signed the Voting Rights Act into law. I knew it was worth the fight when he said, "The vote is the most powerful instrument ever devised by man for the breakdown in injustice." I'm glad we don't have that problem today. Be powerful! Exercise your right to vote. *(Walks to the table where* ELECTION WORKER *is sitting.)*
I'm Fannie Lou Hamer, and I'm here to vote.

Coretta's Dream

Dr. King and Coretta Scott King

Characters:
MRS. KING, *female, Martin Luther King Jr.'s widow and civil rights activist*
LADARIUS, *male fictional character, TV reporter*
Costumes:
Typical attire for a reporter and interviewee of the early 2000s
Props:
Two chairs, microphone

(LADARIUS interviews MRS. KING about her life and contributions to the civil rights movement.)

LADARIUS
Good morning. This is Ladarius Swan reporting to you live from our studio. I have a very special guest today, Mrs. Coretta Scott King, the widow of the late Dr. Martin Luther King. Thank you for being with us Mrs. King. We know a lot about your husband, Dr. King, but we would like to know more about you. Please tell us something about your life, starting with your childhood.

MRS. KING
I was born April 27, 1927, in Heiberger, Alabama, near the rural farming community of Marion. I had an older sister and a younger brother. My family owned a farm that had been in the family since the

Civil War. Each morning before we went to school we had to complete our chores. Afterward we walked five miles each way to and from school, because the black students didn't have buses. The schools were segregated, and our black school consisted of only one room for everybody.

Even though my family didn't have to sharecrop, we weren't rich by any means. When the Depression hit the United States, my siblings and I had to pick cotton to make ends meet. But my parents were motivated. They bought a country store and my father bought a truck. He was the only black man in the area to own one. By the early 1940s, his truck farming business had become quite successful.

LADARIUS
I'm sure this was considered somewhat of a milestone for a black man in the South.

MRS. KING
It was an accomplishment, but our success angered a lot of local whites. Some of them began to harass my father. In 1942 our home was destroyed by fire.

LADARIUS
Did the police find out who did it?

MRS. KING
No one was arrested, but we suspected that it was some of the men who had been harassing my father.

LADARIUS
Tell me about your mother. What was she like?

MRS. KING

My mother was a strong-willed person, and a good mother. She made her children's education her priority. When we finished elementary school, we were going to have to attend high school in another town. The closest black high school was nine miles away. It was too far for us to walk and our mother didn't want me and my sister to have to be out of town during the week. They were also concerned about the other black students. So guess how we got to school?

LADARIUS

I have no idea, tell me.

MRS. KING

My parents furnished a bus and my mother drove it. She was our unofficial school bus driver. My parents wanted to make sure every black child who wanted to go to high school had the opportunity to go.

LADARIUS

You came from a very unselfish family that was concerned about everyone. No wonder you were attracted to Dr. King.

MRS. KING

Well, I wasn't that attracted to Martin at first. I met him when I was in college in Boston. He asked me to marry him many times before I said yes. I wanted to become an opera singer. He wanted a wife who would put her family first. I finally agreed. Despite all that happened, I never regretted marrying him.

LADRIUS

I know that in addition to raising a family, you were active in the civil rights movement. You helped Dr. King with the bus boycott after the arrest of Mrs. Rosa Parks in Montgomery, Alabama. You marched with him in Birmingham and gave many freedom concerts to tell people about civil rights. In 1962 you were a delegate to the Women's Strike for Peace in Geneva, Switzerland. I admire you for so many things. However, I think my greatest admiration came when you displayed so much strength after your husband was assassinated in Memphis, Tennessee, on April 4, 1968. Four days after your husband's death, you took his place to carry out his commitment to the sanitation workers by leading their protest march in that city. In 1969 you and Ralph Abernathy led a demonstration for hospital workers in Charleston, South Carolina. They were protesting discrimination and racism in that city. Dr. King's death certainly didn't stop you from continuing to fight for change.

MRS. KING
Martin had a dream. I have a dream too. It is my dream that people will always remember him. My dream is that people will never forget Martin's work, his words, and the things for which he fought and died.

(End scene.)

MOVEMENTS AND PROTESTS

Niagara Movement

(Fictional character CAROLINE, who lives in the South, reads a letter from her cousin Irene, who describes the Niagara meeting's participants and goals.)

CAROLINE
Dear Cousin Caroline,

I hope this letter finds you and the rest of the family fine and in good health. I'm doing fine, in fact, more than fine. I'm truly excited about what's going on up this way. This year, 1905, should be the beginning of some long-overdue changes in our lives. A group of Negroes held a civil rights meeting on July 10 in Niagara Falls, Canada. Initially the group was supposed to meet in Niagara Falls, New York, but hotels on this side of the border refused to give them rooms. My neighbor found that insulting and ironic, because they were organizing to fight against such treatment.

My neighbor, who has a successful business, was impressed with the list of representatives who attended the meeting. He said there were doctors, teachers, ministers, businessmen, and lawyers. I wasn't surprised. The group was headed by Dr. W. E. B. Du Bois, and those are the kinds of intellectuals he believes should lead our race. Even though they're highbrow Negroes, they seem to understand the problems of all levels of our race.

He tells me the committee emphasized getting rid of the stereotype of colored people being inferior; and that we should no longer be apologetic after being insulted. They want to demand a vote for black men; it would've been nice if they remembered that women need to vote too. They condemned racial discrimination and talked about an end to segregation. They also talked about freedom of speech and equal economic and educational opportunities.

It all sounds good, but it's going to take more than talk to change the laws of our government and the hearts of some of the evil people in our country. My neighbor says they plan to meet annually, and he invited me to join them for the next meeting in 1906. I just might do that, providing they're not too stuck up. But it's important that we all stick together.

I'm going to close now. I just wanted to write to you about the Niagara movement. I'm sure you'll be hearing about it soon. But you know me; I like to be the first one to deliver news.

Love to all,
Cousin Irene

Sit-in Movement

(SPEAKER describes the impact that sit-ins had on the civil rights movement.)

SPEAKER
On February 1, 1960, four students from North Carolina Agricultural and Technical College sat down and ordered coffee at the F. W. Woolworth store in Greensboro, North Carolina. They were not surprised when they were refused service because they were African Americans. When service was denied, they refused to move. They returned the next day with sixteen other African American students. They were refused service again. On February 3 seventy students, including some whites, returned and began what became known as a sit-in. By the tenth day, sit-ins had spread to five other states. Cities began charging students with disorderly conduct and trespassing.

More than one hundred students were expelled from their colleges. Over seventy people, black and white, became involved in the sit-in movement. These tactics spread to similar protests. There were kneel-ins at segregated churches, read-ins at segregated libraries, and swim-ins at segregated pools. People were also protesting segregated seating at movie theaters and stores that wouldn't allow blacks to try on clothes prior to buying them. The sit-in movement was another example of young people fighting discriminatory practices.

Freedom Riders

Freedom Riders Board a Bus in Montgomery, Alabama

(SPEAKER recounts the brutality that the Freedom Riders endured.)

SPEAKER

Take the Bus and Leave the Beatings to Us. I bet you never heard
that saying. I made it up the other day when I was thinking about my
experiences as a Freedom Rider. It's ironic, because the Greyhound
bus company has the slogan Take the Bus and Leave the Driving to Us.
Those were the buses we used for our freedom rides to promote our
civil rights campaign. Let me take you back to the beginning so you'll
understand. In 1961 CORE, which stands for the Council for Racial
Equality, decided to implement strategies to integrate interstate buses
and public facilities. CORE recruited a group of its members to ride the
buses into the South to challenge Jim Crow laws. In 1946 and 1960 the
Supreme Court ruled that segregation on interstate buses and terminals
was illegal. In the South, however, black people were still forced to
sit in the back of the bus or stand if all the seats were taken, even if
the front had empty seats. They were also forced to use separate ticket
counters, waiting rooms, and dressing rooms.

On May 4, 1961, thirteen of us—seven blacks and six whites—boarded
two buses in Washington, D.C. Our goal was to reach New Orleans,
Louisiana, in time for the anniversary of the *Brown v. Board of
Education* decision. I'm not superstitious, but the number thirteen
proved to be unlucky for us. When we reached Anniston, Alabama,

everything went up in flames. An angry white mob met the buses and forced us to stop. They slashed the tires and set fire to the bus I was on. It burned so badly it couldn't move. At first they refused to let us off while it was burning. The driver on the second bus must've panicked, because he let the mob get on. They immediately attacked us with chains and baseball bats. We were beaten, burned, and bruised, but we continued. When we arrived in Birmingham, Alabama, we were attacked again. The police just watched while the mob beat us. We had to stop, because we were injured too badly to continue.

But that wasn't the end of our protest. The Student Nonviolent Coordinating Committee, which we called Snick for short, sent volunteers to finish the trip. When the new group of Freedom Riders reached Montgomery, Alabama, they were attacked and beaten too. Reverend Martin Luther King Jr. flew to Montgomery to head a protest rally. U.S. Attorney General Robert Kennedy was so infuriated by the violence and lack of protection for us that he sent six hundred federal marshals to Montgomery for our safety. That cut down on the violence, but that didn't stop the harassment.

We kept the freedom rides going throughout the summer. Hundreds of us were arrested and charged with disorderly conduct and trespassing. Southern racists saw that we wouldn't be stopped, and the federal government was forced to do the right thing. On December 1, 1961, the Interstate Commerce Commission banned discrimination on interstate travel.

Vietnam Veteran

(Fictional character JOSHUA, a Vietnam veteran, recalls Dr. Martin Luther King Jr.'s views on the Vietnam War.)

JOSHUA

My name is Joshua, and just like Joshua in the battle of Jericho, I was involved in a mighty battle too—the Vietnam War. I was drafted into the army when I was only eighteen years old. I'm not ashamed to tell you that I was scared. But what was worse was that I didn't understand why we Americans were fighting.

Dr. Martin Luther King didn't understand either. When he started speaking out against the war, a lot of people criticized him. They said he was a leader looking for a cause. He wasn't looking for a cause; he was looking at the future. He knew that crime, drugs, and violence would increase as a result of the war. He knew those who were lucky enough to return home would probably have problems with employment and readjustment. Not all Vietnam veterans had problems though. Many are happy and successful. But thousands of soldiers lost their lives, limbs, sanity, and pride.

(He hangs his head for several seconds.)

It was bold of him to criticize the government, but Dr. King was a bold man and wasn't afraid to speak the truth. Like my fellow soldiers who gave their lives, he gave his life too.

(Takes a handkerchief from his pocket and wipes a tear from his eye.)

Two Walkers

Characters:

SALLY, *female fictional character, ANN's childhood friend, and a participant in the children's crusade in Birmingham, Alabama*

ANN, *female fictional character, participant in the children's crusade in Birmingham, Alabama*

Costumes:

Present-day exercise attire

Props:

Bench

(SALLY and ANN sit on a park bench after exercising and recall the brutality that occurred during the children's crusade in 1963.)

SALLY
Walking is good, isn't it?

ANN
Not according to my feet. My dogs are barking.
(They sit on the bench.)

SALLY
Stop complaining and enjoy this beautiful day.

ANN
Yeah you're right. But speaking of dogs, do you know what today is?

SALLY
May 3. So?

ANN
So! Is that all you have to say? How could you forget what happened on this day in 1963?

SALLY
It's your birthday?
(Laughs)
I'm just kidding. It was over forty years ago, but I'll never forget that nightmare.

ANN
Humph, the children's crusade in Birmingham, Alabama. How could anyone forget that?
(Shakes her head.)

You know, we never really went into detail about what we went through that day. The Southern Christian Leadership Conference and Dr. King took a big risk when they organized us school children to protest discrimination in Birmingham.

SALLY

Yeah, Dr. King got a lot of criticism for including us, but he didn't have much choice. Many of the adult protesters were in jail or couldn't afford another arrest. He also knew the movement in Birmingham was losing momentum, and he recognized how important it was to keep the protest alive.

ANN

That's right. I remember that his critics were challenging him for involving us. But he let them know that we had to live with discrimination every day and that our safety had to be risked to ensure our freedom.

SALLY

There were thousands of us. I was ten and my little cousin was only six.

ANN

I never told you this Sally, but I almost didn't make it. My parents were scared. They said I couldn't protest and that I had to stay home where it was safe. I told them everybody else was going, and I wanted to go too. They told me, "We don't care about everybody else; we only care about you." I never argued with them before, but I told them that was the problem. I said, "We have to care about each other and we have to fight together. "You're not going!" Daddy said. It was the first time in my life that I was ashamed of my parents. I'd never defied them before, but I told them softly, "I'm going. You can spank me if you want to, but I'm going." The next morning, I got up early to slip out the house. I heard my parents' door open. I just knew it was Daddy coming out with a strap, but instead he had a small Bible in his hand. I could tell Mama had been crying. They walked over to me, and Daddy put the Bible in my hand. "Take this. It will protect you," he told me. We joined hands and prayed. We hugged and cried as I went out the door. I had to run down the street before I changed my mind.

SALLY

My parents were different. They were proud that I wanted to participate. Both of them had been arrested for protesting, and they worked closely with the civil rights workers. They told me about some of the things that might happen and asked me if I wanted to change my mind. I told them no. I was glad to be going, until I got there. That's when reality set in. It was horrible.

ANN

Yeah, it was terrifying. It wasn't long before I kind of wished I had listened to my parents and let them talk me out of it. Somehow, I became brave and joined the others. I knew it was important. I didn't want to spend the rest of my life living in a place that refused to change. When we started our peaceful protest, Sheriff Bull Connor let his policemen beat us with nightsticks and let their dogs attack us. I still have the teeth prints from when the dogs bit me right here.
(Pats her stomach.)
It would've been worse, but he bit part of the Bible my daddy gave me. I had it tucked in my clothes. He was right, it did protect me.

SALLY

I was holding my little cousin's hand, trying to protect him, but they turned the fire hoses on us. We got separated as we slid down the sidewalk. My skin was cut and my blouse was nearly torn off my back. They arrested about 950 of us. Some of the parents got real angry when they saw what happened. They started fighting back. Things got violent. It would've turned into a major riot if wasn't for Dr. King and some other black leaders. I think it was worth it all, though. Don't you?

ANN
I know it was worth it. The white businessmen were afraid they would lose money, so a week later they agreed to hire black workers and integrate the facilities downtown. Today is a beautiful day.

SALLY
Yes, it certainly is.

(End scene.)

March on Washington

March on Washington

(SPEAKER describes how the March on Washington was planned.)

SPEAKER
The brainchild for the March on Washington was that of civil rights activist Bayard Rustin. Rustin was an advisor and close friend of A. Philip Randolph, who had been active in civil rights activities for nearly fifty years. Randolph had also laid the groundwork for a similar march to Washington during World War II to protest discrimination in hiring in the defense plants. That march was called off, because

President Franklin Roosevelt agreed to ban discrimination in companies that received government contracts.

Rustin presented to Randolph the idea for a massive protest that would involve all the civil rights organizations. This protest would demand jobs, a higher minimum wage, and an income that was guaranteed. Randolph had already felt that the many protests and sit-ins in the South needed a national demonstration. He supported Rustin's plan after it was agreed that the demonstration would include a demand for full civil rights. Randolph met with other civil rights leaders and was chosen as the national director for the march. Rustin was to be his deputy director.

The demonstration took place on August 28, 1963. Hundreds of churches, businesses, civic groups, fraternities, sororities, and labor unions participated in organizing the event. There were movie stars, entertainers, civil rights leaders, and politicians. The day was filled with speakers, but the most memorable one was Dr. Martin Luther King. That was the day he gave his famous "I have a dream" speech. There was an estimated 250,000 people who came from all over the country and around the world. Ground transportation to Washington, D.C. included thirty special trains and two thousand chartered buses. It was the largest demonstration in the United States up to that date.

Four Voters

Characters:
AL, *male fictional character, voter*
CHARLES, *male fictional character, voter*
JOHNNY, *male fictional character, voter*
DAVID, *male fictional character, voter*
JOANN, *female fictional character, voter registrar*

Costumes:
Casual attire of the early 1900s
Props:
Table, chair, voting box, papers

(AL, CHARLES, JOHNNY, *and* DAVID *attempt to register to vote in the rural South prior to the Voting Rights Act of 1965.)*

JOANN
What y'all want?

AL
We want to register to vote.

JOANN
Just because you want to vote doesn't mean you're going to vote. You have to be qualified.

AL
What do you mean qualified? We're American citizens and the proper age, that makes us qualified.

JOANN
Not in this state it doesn't. Did your grandfather vote?

AL
No, ma'am. He was a slave. Slaves couldn't vote.

JOANN
Then neither can you!

AL
But why?

JOANN

We have a law called the Grandfather Clause. It means if your grandfather didn't vote, neither can you. Next!

AL

(Walks away with his head held low.)

CHARLES

Good morning, ma'am. I'm here to register to vote.

JOANN

Here.

(Hands him some papers.)

This is from the state constitution. Read it over and I'm going to give you a literacy test on it, and you must answer the questions to my satisfaction.

CHARLES

But I don't know how to read.

JOANN

If you don't know how to read, you don't know how to vote. It's the law. Next!

CHARLES

(Walks away with his head held low.)

JOHNNY

My name is Johnny, and I came to sign up to vote.

JOANN

Well, I hope you brought some money for the poll tax.

JOHNNY
How much is it?

JOANN
It's $2, cash.

JOHNNY
I don't have $2. I only make about $30 a month, and I have to take care of my family out of that. It's not fair that I should have to pay to vote.

JOANN
It may not seem fair, but it's the law. If you can't pay, you can't vote. Next!

JOHNNY
(*Walks away with his head held low.*)

DAVID
My name is David. My grandfather was a free man, and he voted. I have a college degree, so I can read and pass your literacy test, and here's the money for the poll tax. I'm qualified, and I have the right to vote. It's the law!

(*End scene.*)

The Black Power Movement

(SPEAKER *recounts the birth of the black power movement.*)

SPEAKER
The black power movement emerged from the civil rights movement of the 1950s and 1960s; it was in the mid-1960s that it gained its momentum. The movement derived its name from Stokely Carmichael

in 1965 during a rally in Greenwood, Mississippi. In his speech Carmichael let out the cry, "Black Power!" The term caught on immediately, especially with the younger generation and various new African American organizations. The black power movement demanded that black culture and contributions get proper recognition. It also emphasized black pride and economic and political control of black communities.

The movement influenced African Americans to take pride in their identity and to discover more about their history. Colleges and universities began to incorporate black studies into their curricula. African garments incorporated the colors red, black, and green. Red symbolized the blood that African Americans' ancestors shed, black symbolized the people, and green symbolized Africa—the mother country. Blaxploitation films and blacks in nontraditional roles in white movies were popular.

The phrase "black is beautiful" was a source of pride. Darker skin and kinkier hair brought more ethnic pride among the masses. Many historically black colleges chose dark-complexioned campus queens, a title that had traditionally been held by light-complexioned females with long, straight hair. The Afro was the hairstyle of choice and the black power sign of the upheld fist was the symbol of greeting and brotherhood.

The civil rights movement's goals were civil and political. The black power movement's objectives were racial pride and recognition and acceptance of black culture by all Americans. Both groups, however, advocated economic and political independence.

Memphis Protester

(Fictional character LUKE, *a sanitation worker, recalls the pride Dr. Martin Luther King Jr. instilled in people of all professions.)*

LUKE

How y'all do? My name is Luke. I know a lot of people laugh at me, especially you young people. Many of you look at old Luke and say, "He's nothing but a garbageman picking up other people's trash." But that doesn't bother me. You see, I didn't have the chance to get a good education like you, but I don't mind, because I met a man named Martin Luther King Jr. He told all Americans that no matter what your job was, you should take pride in it and be the best at it. His words made me feel good. It made me realize that it didn't matter if people looked down on you, as long as you didn't look down on yourself. Dr. King never looked down on anyone. He believed that all people were equal, which meant that all people should be treated equally in every situation in life. That's why we sanitation workers asked him to return to Memphis to lead a peaceful protest march to help us get better wages and better job conditions.

On April 3, 1968, I attended a meeting at the Bishop Charles H. Mason Temple to hear Dr. King speak. I'll never forget his words. He said, "We've got some difficult days ahead. But it doesn't matter with me now. Because I've been to the mountaintop . . . And I've seen the promised land. I may not get there with you. But I want you to know tonight that we, as a people, will get to the promised land." He was supposed to lead our march, but never got the opportunity. The next evening he was shot down while standing on the balcony of the Lorraine Motel in front of room 306.

Martin Luther King Jr. gave his life for us. He gave us pride and encouragement. We have to continue his fight for better opportunities in the workplace and society. Please don't let his death be in vain.

CIVIL RIGHTS ORGANIZATIONS

The National Association for the Advancement of Colored People (NAACP)

Walter White for the NAACP

(Fictional character MS. BUDDY *explains to her grandson the history and importance of the NAACP.)*

MS. BUDDY
(Picks up the telephone and dials a number.)
Hello. Is this you, Punchie? This is Grandma Buddy.
(Pause)
What do you mean don't call you Punchie?
(Pause)
I don't care if you work out at the gym, and you aren't fat anymore; you'll always be Punchie to me. Besides, people still call me by my nickname Buddy, and I'm seventy-five years old. Some folks are going to always call you by your nickname no matter how old you get. Why didn't you return my calls? I called you at least three or four times

today, but your secretary kept telling me you were in meetings. She said she'd tell you I called.

(Pause)

Oh, you forgot. Um. Well, you know why I'm calling. You promised to send me a check for your membership to the NAACP.

(Pause)

Oh, you forgot that too.

(Pause)

You say you're going to make it out now so I can stop bugging you? Is that the only reason you're taking a membership?

(Pause)

You say you need to know what NAACP stands for so you can make out the check? Punchie, to be a man who's supposed to be so smart, you don't know nothing! NAACP stands for the National Association for the Advancement of Colored People.

(Pause)

You say you feel funny spending money on something that still says colored people? You need to feel funny about spending money on those songs that be calling you the N word!

(Pause)

And put something extra in that check for a donation. The organization needs support.

(Pause)

How's that? You'll be glad to, because you need a tax write-off? I hoped you would give the money because you wanted to help the NAACP.

(Pause)

What do you mean you don't hear that much about them anymore? Let me tell you something; the only reason you don't hear about the NAACP as much as you used to is because their members have already done most of the hard work. They have been fighting for us ever since they were founded back in 1909. They fought racism so people like you could sit behind a big desk in an air-conditioned office, making six figures. If it wasn't for organizations like the NAACP and a lot of brave people who put their lives on the line, you probably would've been a sharecropper just like me and your granddaddy.

The NAACP helped bring about the changes you young people seem to take for granted. You hear stories about police brutality now, huh, it isn't anything like it used to be. When the NAACP was formed, the primary concerns were illegal arrests, violence toward black people, and discrimination. They even had a member named Walter White who could pass for white. Isn't that funny? White went into the South and posed as a Caucasian man to check out the lynchings and antiblack riots. Our local leaders, like Daisy Bates, led the way to end school segregation in Little Rock, Arkansas.

We had some of the best attorneys in the world, like Thurgood Marshall, Charles Houston, Constance Baker Motley, and Fred Gray. It was these outstanding lawyers who not only represented blacks in our communities, but also the soldiers that the military discriminated against and accused of trumped up charges. The NAACP's legal defense attorneys even argued our cases before the U.S. Supreme Court.

The NAACP is still a civil rights advocate and is still needed. It's up to the rest of us to continue what they've started. So what about you? Are you ready to step up to the plate?
(Hangs up the phone.)

Congress of Racial Equality (CORE)

James Farmer for CORE

(SPEAKER explains CORE's role in the civil rights movement.)

SPEAKER
The Congress of Racial Equality, or CORE, was founded in 1942 by James Farmer. CORE's purpose was to integrate public places and restaurants in the South. It was established as a nonviolent organization that used the strategy of direct action and civil disobedience to fight racial segregation. As the sit-in movement gained strength throughout the South, CORE was asked to provide nonviolent training techniques. CORE led the way in sponsoring the Freedom Riders to integrate bus terminals and facilities. Despite their philosophy of nonviolence, three of their workers were murdered in Mississippi in 1964 during the Freedom Summer Project, in which they were to register black voters.

The Southern Christian Leadership Conference (SCLC)

(SPEAKER defines the SCLC's influence on the civil rights movement.)

SPEAKER
During the 1950s and 1960s, the civil rights movement was reaching its peak in the United States. African Americans of all ages were more

aggressively demanding their long-overdue rights. Thousands joined various protest organizations. Many of these organizations were calling for black power and more radical methods to bring about change. Martin Luther King Jr. and his followers believed that nonviolence was the best solution.

Dr. King and a group of young ministers, who had been working in the local civil rights protests throughout the South, believed church leaders and churches should be more politically active. He and these clergymen needed an organization that could coordinate their efforts. On February 14, 1957, Dr. King and over sixty ministers and activists formed the Southern Christian Leadership Conference, or the SCLC. Dr. King was named the SCLC's president.

The SCLC maintained a philosophy of nonviolence and Christian beliefs as it worked to organize the many protests throughout the South. One of its key endeavors was the Poor People's Campaign of 1968. The purpose of the Poor People's Campaign was to bring attention to poverty stricken Americans and to bring an end to economic inequality.

Although the SCLC had its own priorities, the organization embraced other civil rights groups. The SCLC supported the Student Nonviolent Coordinating Committee's restaurant sit-in movement. It also supported CORE's Freedom Riders in their campaign to integrate interstate bus terminals throughout the South. In addition, they participated in the Voter Education Project of 1962, in which the federal government assisted in registering and protecting African American voters in the South.

Student Nonviolent Coordinating Committee (SNCC)

H. Rap Brown for SNCC

(SPEAKER defines SNCC's role in organizing African Americans during the civil rights movement.)

SPEAKER

The Student Nonviolent Coordinating Committee, whose acronym is pronounced Snick, was formed in 1960 primarily through Ella Baker's efforts. The purpose of SNCC was to coordinate the student sit-in movement. The organization gained national attention when their volunteers finished the crusade that the Freedom Riders started. SNCC advocated participation in democracy and the need to develop local black leadership. In 1962 they played a major role in selecting which six counties in Mississippi would be targeted to promote black voter registration. Southern whites resisted by bombing, beating, incarcerating, and imposing economic threats. They even denied black citizens who tried to register to vote surplus food from the USDA.

In 1964 SNCC and the Council of Federated Organizations, or COFO, organized the Mississippi freedom summer. They recruited over one thousand volunteers, mostly white college students, to help African Americans register to vote. SNCC also helped establish freedom schools, which provided academic education and political training. The campaign received national attention when three of their workers—Michael Schwerner, Andrew Goodman, and James Chaney—disappeared and were later found murdered. The movie *Mississippi Burning* was based on this event. The disappearance forced the federal government to become involved by employing a federal task force. Despite these tragedies, the organizations managed to get a voter turnout of eighty-three thousand African Americans.

Council of Federated Organizations (COFO)

*(*SPEAKER *explains COFO's role in the civil rights movement.)*

SPEAKER
The Council of Federated Organizations, or COFO, was founded in 1961. Its objective was to coordinate the civil rights agencies operating in Mississippi. In 1963 COFO started its Freedom Ballot Campaign. The campaign was a drive to establish a mock election to educate African Americans about the voting process, encourage them to vote, and persuade the federal government to provide protection for civil rights workers.

WHITE SUPPORTERS, PROTESTERS, AND PHILANTHROPISTS

Prudence Crandall
(1803–1890)
Teacher

(PRUDENCE *describes the attacks she received for opening a school that accepted black children.*)

PRUDENCE

Good morning. I am Mrs. Prudence Crandall. I just finished a hot cup of tea, and I'm on my way to work. I'm a schoolteacher. I think every child should have the opportunity to receive an education, regardless of their skin color. But it's regrettable that not everyone feels the same way.

When I lived in Canterbury, Connecticut, I opened a private boarding school for girls in 1832. The parents were pleased and my school was very successful. However, things rapidly changed when I admitted one black girl. Her name was Sarah Harris. She came from a successful family, but that didn't matter to the local residents. White families started withdrawing their children. I received so many threats that I had to close the school.

In February 1833 I angered the townspeople even more. I opened a school solely for "young ladies and little misses of color." When well-to-do colored families learned of my school, parents from the east—mostly Boston and Philadelphia—began enrolling their daughters. I had between fifteen to twenty students.

The local residents were so angry that they boycotted us and would not sell us any goods and supplies. They even got waste from a slaughterhouse and dumped it on my porch. They would not allow us in their churches, and the doctors refused the girls medical care. They threw stones at us and even tried to enforce an outdated vagrancy law that would make it legal to give the girls ten lashes with a whip for attending my school.

In 1834 a local politician got a state law passed that made it illegal to board, harbor, or teach anyone of color who was not a resident of the state, unless the town gave preapproval. I was arrested and taken to jail, because I refused to obey the law. My arrest brought a lot of attention and controversy. My case went to court three times, because the jury could not make a decision. They later convicted me when a judge ruled that blacks were not United States citizens. I continued to fight the court system and won my case on appeal.

When the people of Canterbury got word that my conviction was reversed, a mob of whites set a fire to the school and did other damage. I finally had to close the school, because the girls were getting too many threats and were no longer safe. I left Canterbury and moved to northern Illinois. However, I didn't let that bad experience quench my desire to teach. I must go now. My students will be arriving soon.

William Lloyd Garrison
(1805–1879)
Abolitionist, Newspaperman

William Lloyd Garrison

(WILLIAM reflects on the hardships he faced as a result of speaking out against slavery.)

WILLIAM

My name is William Lloyd Garrison. I became involved in the abolitionist movement when I was in my early twenties. I started my own newspaper when I was twenty-six. I called it the *Liberator*. Most whites called me radical, because I called for immediate emancipation of slaves with no payment to slaveholders. Although I was white, a lot of members of my race hated me as much as they did black people. Even many in the North were against me. In 1835 a mob in Boston tied me to the end of a rope and dragged me through town. More of them turned against me when I attacked the government and the churches for not condemning slavery or taking a stand to bring slavery to an end.

My views were considered extreme, but I did not let threats or opinions deter me from voicing what I knew was right. In the *Liberator* I wrote the following: "I am aware that many object to the severity of my language, but is there not cause for severity? I will be as harsh as truth and as uncompromising as justice. On this subject [immediate emancipation], I do not wish to think or speak or write with moderation . . . I am in earnest—I will not equivocate—I will not excuse—I will not retreat a single inch—and I will be heard."

Richard Humphreys
(1750–1832)
Quaker, Philanthropist

(RICHARD explains how he started the first college in the United States for African Americans.)

RICHARD

My name is Richard Humphreys. I believe every person should have freedom and the opportunity to obtain an education. I donated money and land to build a school near Philadelphia for black children. I was concerned that black Americans would not be able to compete for jobs because of the large increase in white immigrants. I wanted people of African descent to have the opportunity to become teachers in order to help others. What began as a farm school in 1837 evolved into a college, later known as Cheyney College. It was the first college for black people in this country.

Levi Coffin
(1798–1877)
Underground Railroad Conductor

(LEVI describes how he helped thousands of slaves on the Underground Railroad.)

LEVI
My name is Levi Coffin. I'm a Quaker. Our religious order did not support slavery. Many of us were active in the Underground Railroad. I personally helped between two thousand and three thousand enslaved people escape. I was called the president of the Underground Railroad.

John Quincy Adams
(1767–1848)
U.S. President, Congressman, Lawyer

John Quincy Adams

(JOHN recalls how he intervened on behalf of the slaves aboard the Amistad.)

JOHN
I'm John Quincy Adams. I was the sixth president of the United States. During my lifetime, there were eleven presidents. My father, John Adams—who was the second president—and I were the only two presidents who didn't own slaves. After I retired from public life, I was asked by a group of abolitionists to represent the kidnapped Africans who were aboard the slave ship *Amistad*. I delivered an eight hour argument before the U.S. Supreme Court on their behalf. On March 9, 1841, the Court ruled in their favor. The victims were freed and returned to Sierra Leone, Africa.

Harriet Beecher Stowe
(1811–1896)
Writer, Reformer

Harriet Beecher Stowe

(HARRIET describes the impact her novel, Uncle Tom's Cabin, had on emancipation.)

HARRIET

I'm Harriet Beecher Stowe. My hatred for slavery grew when my family moved to Cincinnati, Ohio. I will always remember watching the boats from Kentucky filled with slaves being shipped to the slave markets.

I became famous when my book *Uncle Tom's Cabin* was published in 1852. My novel was an instant best seller. It sold three thousand copies in the first week. Although my book was based on fictional characters, it was effective because it highlighted the cruelties of slavery. I presented my enslaved characters as human beings with feelings. *Uncle Tom's Cabin* was successful in generating sympathy for those in bondage. My book showed that slavery was not only a moral issue, but a political one as well. After its publication, my novel was performed around the country in traveling shows. Some stage versions of *Uncle Tom's Cabin* even used live bloodhounds. I met with Abraham Lincoln during the Civil War. He looked at me and said, "So this is the little woman who started the Civil War." I did not start the war, but I was glad to do my part and help to promote emancipation.

John Brown
(1800–1859)
Abolitionist

John Brown

(JOHN describes the persecution he suffered in his attempts to free slaves.)

JOHN

Fanatic, insane, radical, extremist, crazy, zealot, insurrectionist. I've been called all these things, but nobody called me a hero. I would've been called a hero if I were fighting for the freedom of white men, like the patriots in the War for Independence. Instead, I was fighting for the freedom of black men. That is the reason I have been called all those negative things. But I don't care what I'm called. I received a message from God. He chose me to end slavery. I organized eighteen men—including three of my sons and five black men—into an army that would fight to bring an end to slavery. Our mission was to take the federal arsenal in Harpers Ferry, Virginia, distribute weapons to slaves, and to start a slave uprising.

On October 16, 1859, we attacked Harpers Ferry. The fight lasted two days. Eight of my men, including two of my sons, were killed. I was captured and wounded. The raid itself was a failure in that no slaves were freed. Those of us who were caught were tried, found guilty of treason, and sentenced to death by hanging. But the impact of the raid was a success, because it made the nation—North and South—take a serious look at how divided they really were over the issue of slavery. It also showed the country how men like me were willing to go to any extreme to end slavery. My actions terrified Southerners and motivated some Northerners to step up their efforts to abolish slavery. I'm to be executed on December 2, 1859. I'm not afraid to die. "To my executers I say, the Bible teaches me to remember them that are in bonds . . . I have endeavored to act up to that instruction . . . Now if it is deemed necessary that I should forfeit my life for the furtherance of justice . . . I say let it be done."

Anna T. Jeannes
(1822–1907)
Quaker, Philanthropist

(ANNA describes her commitment to ensure equal educational opportunities for African American children in the South.)

ANNA

I'm Anna Jeannes. I realized that Negroes had been free over forty years; however, they lacked the opportunity to receive even a basic education, especially in the South. I knew the only way they would ever be able to become independent was for them to be able to receive an education. To help, I started the Jeannes Teacher Program. I sponsored teachers who would go into the South and train other teachers. I focused mostly on improving education in small rural Southern schools for Negroes. In 1907 I transferred $1 million to the trusteeship of Booker T. Washington and Hollis B. Frisell. The endowment was to be known as the Fund for Rudimentary Schools for Southern Negroes. The money was primarily to be used for the elementary education of Negro children in the South.

Eleanor Roosevelt
(1884–1962)
First Lady of the United States

Eleanor Roosevelt

(ELEANOR describes how she proved her intolerance for racism.)

ELEANOR

I'm Eleanor Roosevelt. I was married to President Franklin D. Roosevelt, which made me the First Lady of the United States from 1933 to 1945. I wasn't the traditional first lady. I believed in getting out among the people and trying to make changes that were necessary for them to receive the respect and justice due them. I became directly involved with black Americans to further their pursuit for equal rights. Allow me to take a few minutes to give you three examples. In 1938 I attended a meeting in Birmingham, Alabama. It was the Southern Conference for Human Welfare. The group was integrated, but because of Jim Crow laws, blacks and whites had to sit in separate sections of the auditorium. I took it upon myself to sit in the center aisle to protest racism. This naturally brought national attention to the South's refusal to change.

In 1939 Marian Anderson was scheduled to give a performance at Constitution Hall in Washington, D.C. The Daughters of the American Revolution owned the building, and they refused to allow her to sing there because she was black. I immediately resigned my membership from their organization and arranged for Ms. Anderson to perform at the Lincoln Memorial instead.

When civil rights leaders fought to have the Tuskegee Airmen program instituted in 1941, many white congressmen and military personnel didn't believe these pilots were capable of flying complicated aircraft. The army was reluctant to deploy the airmen for overseas duty during World War II. I was confident that the airmen were highly skilled. To destroy the myth that they weren't competent, I went down to their training base in Tuskegee, Alabama, and had one of the pilots take me on a mini flight.

I love my country and want everyone to love it. The only way that can happen is if all of us reach out to each other and extend the hand of friendship. That's the start to equal opportunity and justice.

SPORTS

THE OLYMPICS

George Coleman Poage
(1880–1962)
Olympic Runner

(GEORGE recalls his success in the 1904 Summer Olympics.)

GEORGE
My name is George Poage. In 1904 I became the first black person to represent the United States in the Olympic Games. I received bronze medals in the 1904 Summer Olympics for the men's two-hundred- and four-hundred-meter hurdles.

Jesse Owens
(1913–1980)
Olympic Runner

Jesse Owens

(JESSE recalls his record-setting success at the 1936 Summer Olympics.)

JESSE

My name is Jesse Owens. I was born in Oakville, Alabama to poor sharecroppers. My parents had ten children. When I was seven, my family moved to Cleveland, Ohio, for a better life; but we were still poor. I had to work to help pay the bills.

I always loved to run and would race whenever I got the chance. When I was in high school, I set national records in the one-hundred- and two-hundred-yard dashes. The coach from Ohio State University convinced me to go to college. He promised to give my father a job. I attended the university but wasn't given a scholarship. I had to work and study in addition to running track.

In 1936 I ran in the Olympics in Berlin, Germany. Adolf Hitler was the leader of the Nazi party. He had been bragging to the world that the Aryan race was superior to any other race. I proved to everybody that he was wrong. I won four gold medals and set a record that lasted forty years. I believe that if anybody thinks they're superior to you, prove them wrong!

Alice Coachman
(1923–)
Olympic High Jumper

(SPEAKER recalls Alice Coachman's success in the 1948 Summer Olympics.)

SPEAKER

Alice Coachman competed in the 1948 Olympics. She won a gold medal in the high jump competition. She set an Olympic record in the women's high jump and became the first African American female gold medalist.

John Davis
(1921–1984)
Olympic Weight Lifter

(JOHN recalls his success as an Olympic weight lifter.)

JOHN

My name is John Davis. I'm a weight lifter. I began dominating this sport in 1938 when I was seventeen. I won two Olympic gold medals: one in 1948 and the other in 1952. I also won the world championship in 1946, 1947, 1949, 1950, and 1951. In 1952 I became the first amateur weight lifter to clean-and-jerk more than four hundred pounds. In 1989 I was inducted into the Olympic Hall of Fame.

Rafter Lewis Johnson
(1934–)
Olympic Decathlete

(Fictional character DONALD describes his aspirations to become an Olympic decathlete like Rafter Johnson.)

DONALD
(Jogs onto the stage and carries a large U.S. flag.)
My name is Donald, and I compete in the decathlon event for our high school. I'm practicing for the day that I'm going to carry the U.S. flag in the Olympics like my track and field hero, Rafter Johnson. In the 1956 Olympics, Rafter won a silver medal for the decathlon event. In 1960 he won a medal for the decathlon again, only this time it was the gold. Rafter carried the U.S. flag in the opening ceremony of the 1960 Olympics in Rome, Italy. He was the first African American to have that honor.

Wilma Rudolph
(1940–1994)
Olympic Runner

Wilma Rudolph

(WILMA recalls her record-setting success at the 1960 Summer Olympics.)

WILMA

My name is Wilma Rudolph. I was born in Bethlehem, Alabama, and was the twentieth of twenty-two children. When I was four, I was unable to walk. I had polio, pneumonia, and scarlet fever. But my family wouldn't accept doctors or anyone telling them that I would never walk again. They took turns massaging my legs. When I was nine, I was able to walk again.

In high school I played basketball and ran track. During my four years in high school, I never lost a race. In 1960 I ran in the Olympics in Rome, Italy. I won three gold medals and set a new world record in the one-hundred-meter sprint. I believe that people shouldn't make excuses for their handicaps. Instead, handicaps should be seen as obstacles to overcome. All things are possible if you believe in yourself.

Tommie Smith and John Wesley Carlos
(1944–) (1945–)
Olympic Runners

Characters:

BYRON, *male fictional character, collegiate track star*

BRENTON, *male fictional character, collegiate track star*

Costumes:

Present-day running attire

Props:

Two water bottles

(BYRON and BRENTON discuss John Wesley Carlos and Tommie Smith's success and bravery at the 1968 Summer Olympics.)

BYRON

Say Brenton, I heard you could've gone to almost any college you wanted. Why did you pick our school?

BRENTON

Yeah, I had a lot of scholarship offers, but I wanted to go to a historically black college like my dad. It's true I had choices, but he didn't. Back then, all African American students in the South had to go to black colleges no matter how smart or athletic they were.

BYRON

I heard it was really rough for black people back in the day. Even athletes who represented this country didn't get any respect when they returned home, especially in the South. They could've been dripping in medals and wearing red, white, and blue; but those Jim Crow laws only knew one color, and that was black. That had to be heartbreaking. Our government should've done something about the way they were treated.

BRENTON

The United States wanted to be seen by other countries as a haven for democracy, but two Olympic athletes made the world take a second look at our double-standard society. Tommie Smith and John Carlos upset the world at the 1968 Olympics in Mexico City. Tommie had won the gold medal for the two-hundred-meter track event and John had won the bronze for the same race. It was during the sixties, and the civil rights movement was at its peak. Tommie and John wanted to show their support for the movement in some way. When they got to the winners' podium and the U.S. national anthem was played, the men raised their black-gloved fists and lowered their heads, which was the symbol for black power. Their actions shocked everybody. Tommie and John loved our country, but they knew they would be hypocrites if they ignored the racism in the United States the way our government did.

BYRON

I read about them and saw their story on a TV special. They were exercising their right to freedom of speech, but white America didn't see it that way and was angry. African Americans understood, and most of them were proud. However, Tommie and John's actions really cost them, and they paid a high price for years. First, the United States stripped them of their medals, and they were expelled from the Olympics. But it didn't stop there. They were blackballed from decent employment. Some people said what they did was dumb, but Tommie and John weren't dumb. They were college educated and smart enough to bring global attention to the plight of black Americans.

BRENTON

I know their actions drew attention to our need for civil rights. They make me proud to be a black man, an athlete, and an American. (BYRON *and* BRENTON *lower their heads, raise their fists, then exit the stage.)*

(End scene.)

Debi Thomas
(1967–)
Olympic Figure Skater

(SPEAKER *recalls Debi Thomas's Olympic success as a figure skater.*)

SPEAKER

In 1984 Debi Thomas became the first African American figure skater to be on a world team. She won a bronze medal in the Winter Olympics held in Calgary, Canada, in 1988. That year she became the first African American to win an Olympic medal for ice skating.

Jacqueline "Jackie" Joyner-Kersee
(1962–)
Olympic Heptathlete

(*Fictional character* BRITTNEY *discusses her aspirations to make Olympic history like Jackie Joyner-Kersee.*)

BRITTNEY

Hi, I'm Brittney. I'm getting ready for track practice. I've been offered a college scholarship, and my coach says I have a good chance for an Olympic tryout. I know I'm pushing myself. I was sick this morning, but I came to practice anyway. Whenever I'm not feeling well, I look to Jackie Joyner-Kersee for motivation. She had asthma, but she didn't let that stop her from competing. I'm going to keep on pushing the way she did. I guess you know by now she's my role model.

Jackie is a natural athlete, especially when it comes to track and field. In 1988 she became the first woman from the United States to win the Olympic long jump. She was also the only athlete in sixty-four years to win both an individual and multievent in the Olympics. Jackie medaled twice in the Olympic heptathlon, which has seven events: the

100-meter hurdles, the high jump, the shot put, the 200-meter dash, the long jump, the javelin throw, and the 800-meter run. She won the gold in 1988 and the silver in 1984.

She's been called the world's fastest woman. In 1989 the Associated Press named her Female Athlete of the Year. She made her final Olympic appearance in 2000. She will always be an Olympic great.

Charles Lakes
(1965–)
Olympic Gymnast

(SPEAKER recalls Charles Lakes's success at the 1988 Summer Olympics.)

SPEAKER
In 1988 Charles Lakes was a member of the men's gymnastics team. He was the first African American male to compete in Olympic gymnastics.

Elizabeth "Betty" Okino
(1979–)
Olympic Gymnast

(SPEAKER cites Betty Okino as one of the first black women to compete as an Olympic gymnast.)

SPEAKER
In Barcelona, Spain, in 1992 Betty Okino and Dominique Dawes became the first African American female gymnasts to compete on an Olympic team.

Dominique Dawes
(1976–)
Olympic Gymnast

(SPEAKER recalls Dominique Dawes's success at the 1996 Summer Olympics.)

SPEAKER
Dominique Dawes and Betty Okino became the first African American females to compete on an Olympic gymnastics team in 1992 in Barcelona, Spain. Dawes was also a member of the 1996 and 2000 Olympic teams. In 1996 the U.S. team won a gold medal, and she won an individual bronze medal.

BASKETBALL

African Americans and Basketball

(SPEAKER gives a brief history of basketball in the African American community.)

SPEAKER
The game of basketball was invented by a white physical education instructor named Dr. James Naismith in 1891. As early as 1907, African Americans began playing basketball; however, they were restricted to all-black teams. Basketball was popularized in the black community primarily by Edwin B. Henderson. Henderson was a black physical education instructor at Harvard University. In 1905 he returned to Washington D.C., where he became physical education director for the African American D.C. schools. He introduced basketball to the high schools, clubs, and YMCAs. In 1909 Henderson was hired as an instructor at Howard University. In 1911 he established

a varsity program. He recruited most of his players from Washington's black YMCA. Other black colleges soon joined Howard by forming intramural and intercollegiate teams.

In 1916 Howard University, Lincoln University, Virginia Union University, Shaw University, and Hampton Institute—now Hampton University—formed the Central Interscholastic Athletic Association. In 1920 coaches from schools in the Deep South met at Morehouse College in Atlanta to form the Southeastern Athletic Conference. The growth of basketball programs continued on campuses, and by 1928 most of the black colleges below the Mason-Dixon Line were covered by four regional conferences.

Basketball was incorporated into the majority of African American high schools. The fact that it was cheaper to sponsor than football, and that it came at a more central time during the academic year than the baseball season, increased its popularity in the schools. In 1924 the West Virginia Black High School Athletic Associations sponsored the first state basketball tournament.

Robert Douglas
(1883–1979)
Professional Basketball Coach, Player, Team Founder

(ROBERT explains why he is considered the father of black professional basketball.)

ROBERT

What a shot! That's amazing. I love basketball. When my team—the Rens—was playing, couldn't nobody touch us, white or black. We were the number one black team during our time. The game has changed a lot since my day. All teams were segregated back then. Today the NBA has many African American players. That's good. I think everybody should have the opportunity to excel in all aspects of life.

We competed with some of the best white teams in the country and boasted years of winning records. One of our highlights was on March 30, 1932. We won the world professional championship by beating the Celtics. We continued to play into the 1940s. We ended our career with a record of 2,588 wins and only 529 losses. The men on my Rens team were the first African Americans to be inducted into the Basketball Hall of Fame.

The Harlem Globetrotters

Wilt Chamberlain for the Harlem Globetrotters

(Fictional character NIKKI *gives the history of the Harlem Globetrotters.)*

NIKKI

I can't wait until Grandpa James gets here. He's taking me to see the legendary Harlem Globetrotters. He took me last year too, but I don't care. I never get tired of going to their games. Grandpa James used to watch them when he was my age, and he still likes to watch them. He knows all about them too. He told me that the Globetrotters were formed in the late 1920s on the South Side of Chicago, where most of the players lived. In 1929 a white team owner named Abe Saperstein took over the team and named them the Globetrotters. Later he changed the name to the Harlem Globetrotters, because Harlem was the center of African American culture at the time.

Back in the day the Globetrotters played competitive ball. But like other black teams during that time, they mostly had to play each other. For years they and the Rens dominated the other teams. But the Globetrotters proved they were as good as any top-rated basketball team when they defeated a white professional club, the Minneapolis Lakers, in 1948.

The Globetrotters was able to attract some of best players until 1950. That was the year the Boston Celtics recruited Chuck Cooper. From that point on, teams like the Globetrotters had a hard time recruiting and retaining quality players. In order to make money and compete with the NBA teams financially, the Globetrotters incorporated comic routines, trick plays, fancy dribbling, and ball handling. They've been performing for crowds across the United States and overseas for almost eighty years. Some people say that they are more for entertainment than for competition, but the team stands behind their word that the games are real and competitive. That doesn't matter to me. All I know is that I love their games, and one day I'm going to take my grandchildren to their games too.

Charles "Chuck" Cooper
(1926–1984)
Professional Basketball Player

(CHUCK shares how he became the first African American to be drafted by an NBA team.)

CHUCK
(Enters dribbling a basketball, stops and fakes a shot.)

And Cooper makes the game-winning basket!

(Turns to the audience.)

I'm sorry. I wasn't trying to be rude, but sometimes I get caught up in my basketball fantasies. I guess every player dreams of being the game hero by making the winning shot at the buzzer. I don't know if that dream will come true, but one of my dreams has become a reality. Last year on April 25, 1950, I was drafted by the Boston Celtics. I became the first black man to be drafted by the NBA.

(Dribbles the ball off the stage.)

Nathaniel "Sweetwater" Clifton
(1922–1990)
Professional Basketball Player

(SPEAKER highlights Nathaniel Clifton's achievements in basketball.)

SPEAKER

Nathaniel Clifton was one of the first African Americans to sign a contract and play in the NBA. He signed with the New York Knicks in the summer of 1950, a few months after Chuck Cooper. He played his first game on November 3, 1950. In 1957 he played on the NBA All-Star team. He was over thirty-four years old. This was a career milestone, because it made him the oldest first-time All-Star in the history of the NBA.

Earl "Big Cat" Lloyd
(1928–)
Professional Basketball Player

(SPEAKER discusses Earl "Big Cat" Lloyd's success in basketball.)

SPEAKER

Earl Lloyd was drafted by the Washington Capitals on October 31, 1950. He became the first African American to play a game in the NBA. His debut was one day earlier than Chuck Cooper and four days prior to Nate Clifton's opening game. He was also the first African American to win an NBA championship. It was 1955 with the Syracuse Nationals.

John McLendon Jr.
(1915–1999)
Collegiate Basketball Coach

(JOHN recalls his success as a collegiate basketball coach.)

JOHN

My name is John McLendon Jr. A lot of people haven't heard of me, but I was one of the pioneers of college basketball during its early years of integration. I learned the game of basketball directly from its creator, James Naismith. As a college coach at the historically black college Tennessee A&I, later called Tennessee State University, our college was the first black school to be invited to a national tournament. We went to the National Association of Intercollegiate Athletes, or NAIA. Starting in 1957, we won the NAIA for three consecutive years.

I was also the head coach at Kentucky State College. In 1965 we made a European cage tour and won three of our four games. We ended our season at the top of the Midwestern Conference in 1966. Later in the 1960s, I transferred to a predominantly white college. I was the first African American to coach at a college with a majority white population. I coached collegiate basketball for thirty-four years and amassed over five hundred wins. I used sports to help promote peaceful integration and civil rights. I always say, "The best way to protest is to beat your adversary."

Wilton "Wilt" Chamberlain
(1936–1999)
Professional Basketball Player

(SPEAKER recounts Wilt Chamberlain's accomplishments in basketball.)

SPEAKER
There will always be debates about the greatest player of all time, but one legend that will always be at the top of the list is Wilt Chamberlain. His skills on the court are undeniable. His 7 foot 1 inch, three-hundred-pound frame was both strong and versatile. He holds NBA records in scoring, assists, and rebounds; in fact, the NBA had to rewrite the rules for offensive goaltending, inbounding, and free throwing because of his power. They even had to widen the lanes.

Chamberlain was born August 21, 1936, in Philadelphia, Pennsylvania. He began to make his mark in basketball early. At Overbrook High School in his hometown of Philadelphia, Chamberlain dominated high school basketball. By the time he graduated, he scored over 2,206 points and helped his team win two city championships. His college career was no less impressive. At the University of Kansas, he set scoring records and led the team to an NCAA championship final. Although the University of Kansas didn't win, Chamberlain was awarded Most Outstanding Player. At the end of his junior year, he decided not to finish his undergraduate career and spent one year playing for the Harlem Globetrotters.

By the time Chamberlain retired from the NBA in 1973, he was the only player to score 4,000 points in a season and accumulated over 31,419 points over his entire career. He won two championships, was a five time MVP, and a seven time All-NBA First Team player. Perhaps his most notable career milestone was his induction into the Naismith

Memorial Basketball Hall of Fame in 1978. He was also chosen by the NBA as one of the 50 Greatest Players in NBA History in 1996.

Bill Russell
(1934–)
Professional Basketball Player, Coach

Bill Russell

(SPEAKER recalls how Bill Russell became the first African American coach in the NBA.)

SPEAKER
Bill Russell was a five time MVP player for the Boston Celtics. In 1966 he became the team's head coach while playing for the team. He was the first African American head coach to win an NBA championship.

John Thompson
(1941–)
Collegiate Basketball Coach

(SPEAKER tells how John Thompson became the first African American head coach to win a Division I tournament.)

SPEAKER

In 1972 John Thompson accepted the head coaching position
at Georgetown University. His team won the NCAA Division I
championship in 1984. This victory made Thompson the first African
American head coach to win a Division I tournament.

Michael Jordan
(1963–)
Professional Basketball Player

(SPEAKER highlights Michael Jordan's prolific career in the NBA.)

SPEAKER

NBA . . . Nothing But Air. That's one way many people described the
unbelievable feats that 6 foot 6 inch Michael Jordan performed on
the courts. He would seemingly hang in the air, or elevate his body,
to amazing heights from the floor. So much so, that he earned the
nickname, Air Jordan.

Jordan wasn't born a superstar. In fact, in his sophomore year in high
school in North Carolina he was cut from the varsity squad. He grew
four inches over the summer and returned a star player. His additional
growth and determination drove him to become a high school
All-American.

His love for the Tar Heel state encouraged him to attend the University
of North Carolina. Jordan didn't start out as the team star. North
Carolina had two standout upper classmen who dominated the
spotlight. However, he became the center of attention later that year
in the NCAA finals. North Carolina was playing Georgetown for the
championship. With just eighteen seconds remaining on the clock, he
hit the game winning shot. His sixteen points and nine rebounds added
to their 63 to 62 victory.

His sophomore and junior years he was named College Player of the Year. During his junior year, he also received the Naismith and Wooden Awards. Jordan waived his senior year and made himself eligible for the NBA draft. He was picked in the third round by the Chicago Bulls.

Outside of his NBA awards, Jordan and his teammates won the Olympic gold medal in basketball in 1984 and 1992. His NBA career was marked with success almost from the first time he donned number twenty-three for the Bulls. Here's a summary of his court accomplishments:

- Rookie of the Year: 1985
- All-NBA First Team: 1987 to 1993 and from 1996 to 1998
- All-Defensive First Team: 1988 to 1993 and from 1996 to 1998
- Defensive Player of the Year: 1988
- League MVP: 1988 to 1991, 1992, 1996, and 1998
- All-Star MVP: 1988, 1996, 1998
- NBA Championship: 1991 to 1993 and 1996 to 1998
- Ten scoring titles, including tying Wilt Chamberlain's record of seven consecutive scoring titles

When Jordan retired at the end of the 2002–2003 season, he left the game with the highest scoring average: thirty points per game. In 1996 he was selected as one of the 50 Greatest Players in NBA History. Jordan was more than a player; he was a franchise and a legend. He will always be near the top of the list of the 50 Greatest Players in NBA History.

Team Owners

(Fictional character TINY CYNIA *describes her aspirations to be an NBA team owner.)*

TINY CYNIA

My real name is Cynia, but everybody calls me Tiny Cynia because I'm short. Nobody at school picks me to be on their basketball team but I don't care. I don't want to be a player; I want to buy a team just like Bertram Lee and Peter Bynoe did in 1989. They bought the Denver Nuggets for $65 million. They were the first African Americans to own an NBA team. When I own my team, some of these same friends of mine who wouldn't pick me to play with them will be working for me. I won't have to pass the ball, because I'll be passing the bucks.

Women Taking Basketball above the Rim

Characters:
DEIDRA, *female fictional character, high school basketball player*
YOLANDA, *female fictional character, high school basketball player*
ZAN, *female fictional character, high school basketball player*
Costumes:
Present-day basketball attire
Props:
Basketball, sports bag

(DEIDRA, YOLANDA, *and* ZAN *discuss their desires to join the WNBA.)*

DEIDRA

I hope we win tonight. If we do, we'll be district champions.

YOLANDA

A win will help my scholarship chances.

ZAN

It would be nice if we could go to the same college; if not, I'll beat you when I meet you.

DEIDRA

Keep dreaming.

YOLANDA

I'm going to keep dreaming. After college my dream is to play for the WNBA like Sheryl Swoopes. She was the first player to sign with the WNBA. That girl got game. She won Defensive Player of the Year three times, and she earned three Olympic gold medals with the U.S. women's basketball team in 1996, 2000, and 2004. She's the only woman to have a Nike shoe named after her, Air Swoopes!

ZAN

I'm going to be a star player like Lisa Leslie. Did you know that she scored 101 points in the first half of one of her high school games? She probably would've broken Cheryl Miller's record of 105 points if the other team hadn't forfeited the game. She won four Olympic gold medals as part of the U.S. women's basketball team. She also was one of the original players of the WNBA and the first woman to score 3,000 points as a pro. In 2002 she went above the rim and dunked the ball. She was the first woman in the WNBA to do that. Yep, she's my hero.

DEIDRA

They're both good. But me, I want the whole package like Cheryl Miller. Like Lisa Leslie, she scored over a hundred points in a high school game. She got a college basketball scholarship to the University of Southern California and later coached that team. She has four Olympic gold medals. She was offered several professional basketball contracts, even from the men's teams. No telling how many more records she would've set if she hadn't been forced to retire from the court when she injured her knee. But that didn't keep her from being active in the basketball world. She became a sports commentator on national TV, and she's still kicking it on the basketball scene as a sideline reporter for the NBA. Is that the total package or what?

ZAN

All three of them are fire. Now if we three could play just a fraction of the way they played in high school, we'll win the district championship tonight, and we'll be on our way to the state championship.

YOLANDA

I got hyped up just talking about them. Let's take it to the hoop like Miller, Leslie, and Swoopes!

BASEBALL

Baseball and the Birth of the Negro Leagues

(SPEAKER gives a brief history of African Americans and their role in baseball.)

SPEAKER

Baseball is the all-American game. Well it was at first, but racism and fear of competition entered the sport. African Americans had to create their own leagues to continue to showcase their talents and entertain their fans. During the 1880s, white teams established what was called "a gentlemen's agreement." The gentlemen's agreement was an unofficial pact in which team managers agreed not to recruit any black players and to phase out the existing ones. This agreement lasted for over fifty-five years. As African Americans were forced off the white teams, independent black clubs began to form. The Cuban Giants, established in 1885, was the first African American professional team. By pretending to be foreigners, they were able to play in the Southwest and Florida.

There were several Negro leagues, but the first leagues were loosely organized and didn't last long. After World War I, Negro leagues became better organized, and they spread across the country. Andrew "Rube" Foster was called the Father of Black Baseball. He established the National Association of Professional Baseball Club in 1920. Foster insisted that all the teams be controlled by African Americans, except for the Kansas City Monarchs. The club kept the same principles but was later renamed the Negro National League.

Baseball quickly became the main form of entertainment in the black community. The leagues enjoyed their best years from the 1920s until the Great Depression hit the country. But, even after becoming more structured, the teams faced numerous problems. The transportation was undependable. The accommodations were poor and sometimes unavailable in the South. The teams usually played in rented stadiums when the white teams were out of town. Even though they paid a rental fee, the black players weren't allowed to use the white-only dressing rooms. The salaries were low, so many of the teams had to barnstorm—which meant to travel from place to place and pick up games. In the off-season the black clubs played major league white teams in exhibition games and usually the Negro teams won.

The league began to fall apart when Rube Foster became too ill to manage things in 1926. It dissolved in 1931, a year after he died because of a lack of finances. In 1933 the league was reestablished. It continued to thrive until April 18, 1946, when Jackie Robinson signed to play major league baseball. He made his debut with the Brooklyn Dodgers in 1947. After Robinson established himself as an outstanding player, the major league began recruiting the best players from the Negro league. Soon the only players left were those who had either reached their prime or weren't popular enough to draw large crowds. The Negro National League disbanded in 1948.

The American Negro League was established in 1937. It was a combination of some of the best teams from the Western and Southern regions. After only ten years in existence, they too began to lose their top players to the major league. The loss of top players resulted in the loss of revenue. The American Negro League, which was the last of the major Negro league divisions, officially closed in 1952.

Although the Negro leagues were victims of progress, they offered a career for black athletes and entertainment for the black community. They also offered local heroes for African Americans. Equally important, they paved the way for Jackie Robinson and others. Many of the former Negro league players were standouts and broke numerous existing records before they entered the majors. In 1971 the Baseball Hall of Fame began inducting players from the Negro leagues, beginning with Satchel Paige.

John "Bud" Fowler
(1858–?)
Professional Baseball Player

(BUD describes how he became the first African American to play organized baseball.)

BUD

My name is John Fowler, but I'm better known by my nickname, Bud. I always loved baseball, and I could play every position on the field. In 1872 I joined a white team in New Castle, Pennsylvania. I was the first African American to play organized baseball. When I couldn't find a job with the white teams, I organized a black team called the All-American Black Tourists. We played in top hats and tuxedos.

Moses Fleetwood Walker
(1857–1924)
Professional Baseball Player

(MOSES describes how he became the first African American to play major league baseball.)

MOSES

My name is Moses Fleetwood Walker. In 1884 I joined the Toledo Mud Hens professional baseball team as a catcher. When the Mud Hens joined the American Association major league, I became the first Negro to play major league baseball.

Leroy Robert "Satchel" Paige
(1906–1982)
Professional Baseball Player

(SATCHEL recalls how he became the first player from the Negro leagues to be inducted into the National Baseball Hall of Fame.)

SATCHEL

I'm Satchel Paige. If you don't know me, you don't know baseball. I played for several teams in the Negro Leagues. I had a windup called the windmill.
(Demonstrates a windup.)
I was famous for my fastballs, but I had other pitches too. A lot of my pitches had nicknames. One of them was called the bee ball, because it "be where I wanted it to be." It made a whizzing sound as it crossed home plate. Some other names were midnight creeper, trouble ball, jump ball, bat dodger, and four-day rider. I even had one called the hesitation pitch. It was banned, because nobody could hit it.
(Laughs)
I played in the Negro leagues for over twenty years.

In 1948 I was drafted by the Cleveland Indians. I was forty-two years old. That made me the oldest rookie in the history of professional baseball. I was also the first black man to pitch in a world series. In 1971 I was inducted into the National Baseball Hall of Fame. I was also the first player from the Negro Leagues to be selected. Now that you've met Satchel Paige, remember my name when you go to the game.

Jackie Robinson
(1919–1972)
Professional Baseball Player

Jackie Robinson

(JACKIE recalls when he was drafted to the Brooklyn Dodgers.)

JACKIE

I'm Jackie Robinson. In 1887 Chicago White Sox manager, Cap Anson, refused to let his players take the field until the two black players on the opposing team left the ball diamond. His action led other clubs to follow suit. Owners stopped signing black players and dropped the remaining players shortly after. In 1947, sixty years later, I signed with the Brooklyn Dodgers. I became the first black man in modern times to play major league baseball.

Willie Mays
(1931–)
Professional Baseball Player

Willie Mays

(SPEAKER *recalls Willie Mays's success as a baseball player.*)

SPEAKER

Willie Mays was a star major league baseball player. He was nicknamed the Say Hey Kid, because "say hey" was usually how he greeted people. Mays learned to play baseball in Alabama where he was born and raised. Baseball has always been in his blood. His father and grandfather were ball players.

Mays was a center fielder and had a unique way of catching the ball. He would hold the glove close to his stomach and tuck the ball in. This came to be called the basket catch. When Mays was sixteen, he joined the Birmingham Barons, a team in the Negro Leagues. His father wanted to make sure he finished high school, so he was only allowed to play home games.

In 1950 the New York Giants bought his contract from the Barons, and Mays was sent to their minor league team for one season. He fought in the Korean War between 1951 and 1952. When he returned to the Giants in 1954, their team won the World Series. Some people say

Willie Mays was the best all-around player in the majors. He could hit, catch, run, and throw. In 1973 he retired. Willie Mays was voted the most valuable player twice, amassed a record of 660 home runs, 3,283 total hits, and a .302 batting average. In 1979 he was elected into the National Baseball Hall of Fame.

Hank "the Hammer" Aaron
(1934–)
Professional Baseball Player

(SPEAKER describes how Hank Aaron dominated professional baseball.)

SPEAKER

Hank Aaron, also known as the Hammer, was born and raised in Mobile, Alabama. He learned to play baseball there in a cleared pecan field. He began his career as a pro with the Indianapolis Clowns in 1952. The team paid Aaron $200 a month. In 1954 the Milwaukee Braves, who later relocated their team to Atlanta, purchased his contract for $10,000. Aaron played an all-around game, but he was better known as a home run hitter.

The 1970s were his best years as a hitter. In 1970 he made his three thousandth career hit. Aaron was the first player to combine three thousand hits with five hundred home runs. He also set a major league record by reaching his twelfth season with thirty or more home runs. Willie Mays, also an African American player, was one of the two players who had more homers than Aaron. The other player was white home run king, Babe Ruth. When Aaron broke Mays's record by hitting his 649th homer, the fans and media loved it; but when it seemed certain that he would break Babe Ruth's record, many people's attitudes changed.

As Aaron closed in on Ruth's 714 home run record, he started getting hate mail and threats on his life from racists across the country. The threats became so bad that the FBI had to get involved. He refused to let anything stop him from reaching his goal of being the new home run king. Aaron told media-regarding baseball fans, "I don't want them to forget Babe Ruth. I just want them to remember me." On the team's season home opener in Atlanta, on April 8, 1974, he finally did it! Hank Aaron hit his 715th homer and broke Ruth's record. He retired in 1976 with a total of 755 home runs. Aaron was elected into the National Baseball Hall of Fame in 1982. He told the public, "I had to break that record. I had to do it for Jackie [Robinson], and for my people, and myself, and for everybody who called me n——."

FOOTBALL

Collegiate Football

*(*SPEAKER 1, SPEAKER 2, SPEAKER 3, SPEAKER 4, *and* SPEAKER 5 *consecutively come to center stage and give a brief history of African Americans in collegiate football.)*

SPEAKER 1
The game of football as we basically know it today was instituted by Walter Camp in 1879. As always, black people desired to be a part of mainstream American culture. When those opportunities weren't readily opened, they created their own. The game of football was no exception, especially among historically black colleges.
*(*SPEAKER 1 *moves to stage right.)*

SPEAKER 2
Colleges in the North included African American players on their rosters, but even then it was on a limited basis. Usually when the teams from the North played white colleges in the South, they would

leave their black players at home or bench them on the sidelines. This was an unwritten agreement among the teams. Collegiate bowl games remained segregated by only inviting Southern teams to play each other. With the exception of one game in 1948, there were no integrated teams or games in the South until the 1950s.

(SPEAKER 2 *moves to stage right.*)

SPEAKER 3

In response to this exclusion, historically black colleges formed teams and conferences. In 1912 the Colored Intercollegiate Athletic Association was formed. The name was later changed to the Central Intercollegiate Athletic Association. In 1920 two black conferences were established: the Southern Intercollegiate Athletic Conference, or SIAC; and the Southwestern Athletic Conference, or SWAC. In 1970 the Mid-Eastern Athletic Conference was founded.

(SPEAKER 3 *moves to stage right.*)

SPEAKER 4

The first intercollegiate African American football game was played in 1892 between Biddle University—now Johnson C. Smith—and Livingston College, which were both in North Carolina. The Prairie View Bowl contest was the first African American college bowl game. It was played January 1, 1929, in Houston, Texas between Prairie View College and Atlanta University.

(SPEAKER 4 *moves to stage right.*)

SPEAKER 5

After the 1950s, as white Southern universities began to recruit African American players, it became harder and harder for black colleges to attract top players. Today these African American teams and conferences still compete with all-out heart and spirit, and students and alumni live for bragging rights among these rivalries.

(*Speakers exit stage.*)

Professional Football

*(*SPEAKER 1, SPEAKER 2, SPEAKER 3, *and* SPEAKER 4
*consecutively come to center stage and give a brief history of African
Americans in professional football.)*

SPEAKER 1

The general accepted date for the start of professional football is
November 12, 1892. African Americans were able to join during the
game's initial stages and through 1933. From 1934 until World War
II, black players were banned from the professional game. One of
the leaders in the movement was team owner George Marshall, who
refused to sign any African Americans to his team—the Washington
Redskins. The Redskins was also the last professional team to integrate
and had to be forced to do so in 1962.
*(*SPEAKER 1 *moves to stage right.)*

SPEAKER 2

In 1947 the NFL broke color barriers in professional football for the
first time since 1933. On March 21 the Los Angeles Rams signed
Kenny Washington, and on May 7 they signed Woody Strode. The
Cleveland Browns signed Bill Willis on August 6 and Marion Motely
on August 9. Other teams gradually followed; however, the teams had
a "two man" unwritten rule. The owners would only have an even
number of African American players on their teams at a time. That was
to prevent a white player from having to share a room with a black
player during road trips.
*(*SPEAKER 2 *moves to stage right.)*

SPEAKER 3

The AFL was the alternative professional football league to the NFL
from 1960 to 1970. It was much more aggressive in recruiting black
players. They had more African American scouts and focused on small

colleges that the NFL ignored. This gave players from historically black colleges a better opportunity to make the pros. When drafted, most black players' contracts were less than the contracts offered to white players. C. A. Wells from the Kansas City Chiefs was the first African American full-time scout in professional football. *(SPEAKER 3 moves to stage right.)*

SPEAKER 4

When African American players were drafted to professional teams, most found that they would no longer play their former positions. Many were changed to wide receivers or other speed positions like defensive ends. Quarterbacks, no matter how great their collegiate record, weren't assigned that position. It was generally felt that they weren't intelligent enough to play a complicated position and lead a team. In 1953 that perception began to change when Willie Thrower was drafted by the Chicago Bears and became the first black quarterback in the NFL.

(Speakers exit stage.)

Charles W. Follis
(1879–1910)
Professional Football Player

(CHARLES shares his success in professional football.)

CHARLES

My name is Charles Follis. I played for the Blues of Shelby County, Ohio, in 1904. I was the first black professional football player.

Frederick Douglas "Fritz" Pollard
(1894–1986)
Professional Football Player, Coach

(FRITZ highlights his groundbreaking success in collegiate and professional football.)

FRITZ

I'm Fritz Pollard. In 1916 I was the first black man to play in the Rose Bowl. In 1919 I joined the Akron Indians as a player. A few years later, I also became the team's coach. This made me the first black coach in professional football.

Paul "Tank" Younger
(1928–2001)
Professional Football Player

(TANK highlights his achievements in collegiate and professional football.)

TANK

I'm Paul "Tank" Younger. I was nicknamed Tank, because I ran over everything in front of me. I played football at Grambling State University, in Grambling, Louisiana. I was the first black person to play professional football from an all-black college. I signed with the Los Angeles Rams in 1949.

Ernest "Ernie" Davis
(1939–1962)
Collegiate Football Player

Ernie Davis

(SPEAKER *describes how Ernie Davis became the first African American Heisman Trophy winner.*)

SPEAKER

Ernie Davis was the first African American to win the coveted Heisman Trophy. He won the Heisman in 1961 during his senior year at Syracuse University. He was drafted by the Cleveland Browns. Unfortunately, Davis never played a game of professional football. He was diagnosed with leukemia and died before he began his professional career.

Emlen "the Gremlin" Tunnell
(1925–1975)
Professional Football Coach

(EMLEN *shares his success in professional football.*)

EMLEN

My name is Emlen Tunnell, but many people know me by my nickname—the Gremlin. I signed with the New York Giants as a free agent in 1948. I was an assistant coach for the team from 1965 to 1973. This made me the first African American coach after the league's twelve-year ban on black players, which ended in 1946.

Alonzo Smith "Jake" Gaither
(1905–1994)
Collegiate Football Coach

(JAKE shares his success as a collegiate football coach.)

JAKE

I'm Jake Gaither of the Florida A&M University Rattlers. I'm also called the Papa Rattler. In 1969 I became the first African American collegiate coach to win more than two hundred football games.

Eddie Robinson
(1919–2007)
Collegiate Football Coach

(EDDIE shares his success as a collegiate football coach.)

EDDIE

I'm Eddie Robinson. I was the head football coach at Grambling University in Grambling, Louisiana. I was the first collegiate coach of any race to win 368 games. As of 1988 I sent sixty-nine players to the pros. That was also more than any other collegiate coach as of that date.

Arthur "Art" Shell
(1946–)
Professional Football Coach

(SPEAKER shares Art Shell's success in professional football.)

SPEAKER

In 1989 Art Shell became the head coach of the Los Angeles Raiders. This made him the first African American head coach in professional football since Fritz Pollard in 1933.

Dennis Green
(1949–)
Professional Football Coach

(SPEAKER describes Dennis Green's success in professional football.)

SPEAKER

Dennis Green was the head coach with the Minnesota Vikings from 1992 to 2001. In 1994 Green and his quarterback Warren Moon made national football history by becoming the first NFL team to have an African American head coach and an African American starting quarterback.

Lovie Smith
(1958–)
Professional Football Coach

(SPEAKER shares Lovie Smith's success as a professional football coach.)

SPEAKER

Lovie Smith, for the Chicago Bears, became the first African American head coach to lead a team to the Super Bowl when his team won the NFC championship in 2006. Hours later Tony Dungy, for the Indianapolis Colts, became the second African American head coach to lead a team to the Super Bowl when he won the AFC championship. The coaches made NFL history. Not only was it the first time the Super

Bowl had an African American head coach, it was the first time two black head coaches competed.

Tony Dungy
(1955–)
Professional Football Coach

(SPEAKER highlights Tony Dungy's success as a professional football coach.)

SPEAKER
Tony Dungy was the head football coach for the Indianapolis Colts. In 2006 his team won Super Bowl XLI in Miami, Florida. That historic game made him the first African American head coach to win a Super Bowl.

Mike Tomlin
(1972–)
Professional Football Coach

(SPEAKER describes Mike Tomlin's success as a professional football coach.)

SPEAKER
On February 1, 2009, Mike Tomlin—head coach for the Pittsburg Steelers—led his team to victory in Super Bowl XLIII. Tomlin was the second African American head coach to win a Super Bowl. He was also the youngest head coach of any race to accomplish this feat.

Quarterbacks

(SPEAKER 1, SPEAKER 2, SPEAKER 3, and SPEAKER 4 come to center stage consecutively and highlight African American quarterbacks in the NFL.)

SPEAKER 1

From 1934 to 1946, the National Football League had an informal racial ban on recruiting black players. When they did lift the ban, team owners would only recruit an even number of players. They did this so that white players would not have to share a room with black players on road trips.
(SPEAKER 1 moves to stage right.)

SPEAKER 2

Black quarterbacks were overlooked, or their positions were changed once they were drafted to professional football teams. Most team owners didn't believe that African American athletes were smart enough to play the quarterback position. It wasn't until the Chicago Bears drafted Willie Thrower in 1953 that the NFL had a black quarterback.
(SPEAKER 2 moves to stage right.)

SPEAKER 3

In 1988 Doug Williams of the Washington Redskins became the first African American quarterback to win a Super Bowl. He led his team to defeat the Denver Broncos in Super Bowl XXII. He was also voted the game's most valuable player. He completed eighteen of twenty-nine passes for a record 340 yards and 4 touchdowns.
(SPEAKER 3 moves to stage right.)

SPEAKER 4

Once they were given a chance, black quarterbacks destroyed the myth that they were not intelligent enough to play the position of team leader. Here are the names of some of the NFL's African American starting quarterbacks from the past through 2010:

- Charlie Batch
- Tony Banks
- Marlin Briscoe
- Aaron Brooks
- Jason Campbell
- Daunte Culpepper
- Randall Cunningham
- Vince Evans

- David Garrard
- Joe Gilliam
- James Harris
- Major Harris
- Tarvaris Jackson
- Shaun King
- Bryan Leftwich
- Donovan McNabb

- Steve McNair
- Warren Moon
- Akili Smith
- Kordell Stewart
- Willie Thrower
- Michael Vick
- Andre Ware
- Doug Williams

(Speakers exit stage.)

TENNIS

Althea Gibson
(1927–2003)
Professional Tennis Player

Althea Gibson

(ALTHEA *recalls how she was the first African American woman to play in major international tennis tournaments.*)

ALTHEA

My name is Althea Gibson. I played tennis during a time when players used wood-frame racquets and when the sport was considered a game for wealthy whites. Opportunities to learn even the basic skills were limited. There weren't many tennis courts in black neighborhoods, and the private country clubs were off-limits to people of my race. African Americans weren't invited to major international tournaments and were barred from national tournaments in the United States.

Despite all this, I loved the game. I improved my skills, because I wanted to be ready when the opportunity came. Even though I won numerous tournaments sponsored by the all-black American Tennis Association, or the ATA, I was still ignored by the white tennis world. In 1950 things changed when an article written in the *American Lawn Tennis* magazine criticized the tennis community for dismissing me. Three months later, I received an invitation to compete in a national tournament. My opportunity had finally come.

I continued to compete. My career highlights were in the 1950s. My first grand slam singles was the French Open in 1956. Between 1956 and 1958, I earned five singles grand slam titles. I won at the French Open, Wimbledon, and the U.S. Open. I won six double titles in grand slams in France and Australia. In 1957 I was named Female Athlete of the Year. I was the first African American to achieve these honors in the world of tennis. But I had people who had faith in me and helped me reach success. Always remember, "No matter what you accomplish, somebody helps you."

Arthur Robert Ashe
(1943–1993)
Professional Tennis Player

Arthur Ashe

(ARTHUR describes his success as a professional tennis player.)

ARTHUR

I'm Arthur Ashe. I was born and raised in Richmond, Virginia, during a period when segregation kept black people from receiving an equal education and fair employment. I knew I was a good tennis player, but trying to reach my potential wasn't easy. Jim Crow laws kept me from playing on most of the public tennis courts, and black players weren't allowed to compete in the white tournaments. But I refused to allow these obstacles to hinder me. I had faith in myself. I knew I was a good player and could be a champion if I got the opportunity. My goal was to be the number one men's singles player in the world. So instead of focusing on how segregation restricted me, I focused on preparing myself by improving my skills.

I believed that an important key to success was to be prepared. My preparation paid off as I was awarded a tennis scholarship to UCLA in 1963. This was also the year I became the first African American male to play on the Davis Cup team. I remained a team member for fifteen years and set a record of twenty-seven victories. In 1968 I won the U.S. Open. In 1969 I joined the professional circuit. In 1970 I won the Australian Open and the French Open. In 1971 I won the French Open again. In 1975 I won the Wimbledon Open, and I was ranked the number one male singles tennis player in the world. My dream finally came true.

It wasn't easy being the only black man on the professional tour. Many times I wanted to argue with the umpire about a bad call or throw a temper tantrum like some of the white players, but I had to remain cool. I knew the world was watching me. I was representing my country and my race. I didn't want my actions to prevent other black players from having the opportunity to become a part of the professional association. I also didn't want to leave a negative legacy. I firmly believe that "if one's reputation is a possession, then of all possessions reputation means the most."

Venus Williams and Serena Williams
(1980–) (1981–)
Professional Tennis Players

Characters:
TIFFANY, *female fictional character, recreational tennis player and* LAINI'*s older sister*
LAINI, *female fictional character, recreational tennis player*
Costumes:
Present-day tennis attire
Props:
Two tennis racquets, two sports bags, can of tennis balls, magazine

(TIFFANY *and* LAINI *discuss Venus and Serena's success as professional tennis players.*)

TIFFANY
You played a good game, little sis.

LAINI
Thanks, you weren't too bad yourself. If we keep winning like this, we may become another Venus and Serena Williams.

TIFFANY
Anything is possible, but it will be a long time before our game is anywhere near theirs.

LAINI
I know, but they had to start somewhere too. We have to believe in ourselves the way they do.

TIFFANY
Who do you think is the better player, Venus or Serena?

LAINI
That's a hard question to answer. They both have power serves and strong ground strokes; they can play the net and seem to run everything down that comes across it. Each of them has been ranked the number one tennis player in the world. When they're at the top of their game, they seem invincible.

TIFFANY
(Takes a tennis magazine from her bag.)
According to this tennis magazine, as of August 2008 when Serena won the U.S. Open Women's Singles title, she earned nine grand slam singles victories. She also has seven grand slam doubles titles with her sister Venus. She has earned over $21,774,000 since she turned pro in 1995.

LAINI

Let me see that magazine.

TIFFANY

(Passes the magazine to LAINI.*)*

LAINI

Venus hasn't done too badly for herself either. Since she turned pro in 1994, she has a total of seven grand slam singles titles, and she won two Olympic gold medals for women's doubles with Serena: one in 2000 and another in 2008. And she's not poor either. As of August 2008 Venus earned $20,445,911.

TIFFANY

It would be nice if we could be rich like them, but more importantly, I hope we will always be best friends the way they are.

LAINI

There's no reason why we can't be like them. They're good role models for all sisters to follow.

(End scene.)

Recognizing Other Professional Tennis Players

*(*SPEAKER 1, SPEAKER 2, SPEAKER 3, SPEAKER 4, *and* SPEAKER 5 *share the accomplishments of other black professional tennis players.)*

SPEAKER 1

Venus and Serena Williams have helped popularize the tennis game in the African American community. But there are, and have been, other successful male and female black tennis players since Althea Gibson,

Arthur Ashe, and the rise of the Williams sisters. These other players achieved high rankings on the pro tour and became multimillionaires.
(SPEAKER 1 moves to stage right.)

SPEAKER 2
Malivai Washington was born in 1969. He became a professional tennis player in 1989. He was ranked as high as number eleven in the tennis world. His career earnings were over $3 million.
(SPEAKER 2 moves to stage right.)

SPEAKER 3
Zina Garrison, born in 1963, was ranked number four in women's tennis. In 1988 she won an Olympic gold medal for the doubles competition. She was a Wimbledon runner-up in 1990 and a finalist in 1991. She also won three mixed doubles grand slam tournaments. During her career, she won over $4.5 million.
(SPEAKER 3 moves to stage right.)

SPEAKER 4
Chandra Rubin, born in 1976, became a professional player in 1991 when she was fifteen. Although she never won a grand slam, she had a good career and won several titles in the WTA. Rubin earned over $3.2 million as a professional player.
(SPEAKER 4 moves to stage right.)

SPEAKER 5
James Blake was born in 1979. He started playing tennis when he was only five years old. He began his professional career in 1999. Blake hasn't won a grand slam yet, but he's always a serious threat as he has beaten some of the top players. He's been ranked as high as number eleven in men's singles. As of 2008 his career earnings were nearly $6 million.

(Speakers exit stage.)

BOXING

Jack Johnson
(1878–1946)
Professional Boxer

Jack Johnson

(JACK describes the trials he endured as a result of his boxing success.)

JACK

Feast your eyes on Jack Johnson, the first black heavyweight champion of the world. I had to get the title the hard way. I learned to box when I was young. A lot of us boys would have what we called royals. We would put up money and fight for it. The last man standing would win it all. It was violent, because there weren't any rules. I took that same brutal style with me into the ring.

In 1903 I beat the black heavyweight champion in a twenty-three-round decision. We had long bouts back then. I tried hard to get a fight with Jim Jefferies, the white champion, but was turned down because the boxing world was still segregated. In 1908 Tommy Burns, a Canadian,

became champion. I had to follow him all the way to Australia to get the fight. I beat him for the title. He couldn't do anything.
(Laughs)
I beat him so bad that in the fourteenth round I knocked him clear out of the ring. The police had to stop the fight.

I defended my title five times against white contenders. After a while, nobody wanted to fight me. White fans didn't like my fighting style. I would make a mockery out of the match. I would taunt my opponents. I would even applaud them when they hit me. The white crowds would shout racial slurs, boo, and hiss at me. Many of my victories caused racial riots and lynchings. Even President Teddy Roosevelt, who was a boxing fan, turned against the sport. In some cities Christian groups tried to keep films of my fights from being shown. I wasn't just another boxer; I was a threat. I was a symbol of black masculinity and a threat to what they thought was their racial superiority. I dated white women and black women of all social classes, dressed fancy, and drove luxury cars.

I was labeled public enemy number one. They had to find a way to stop me. Boxers tried to beat me in the ring, but I was too good. I used strategy, technique, size, and violence. Men were scared to fight me. This led to pleas to white contenders to challenge me. They sent out a call for the Great White Hope. A writer for the *New York Herald* spoke on behalf of white Americans when he wrote a first-page column begging Jim Jefferies to wipe that smile off my face. They finally convinced him to come out of retirement and fight me.

In 1910 I fought Jefferies in Reno, Nevada. Everybody was so sure that he would defeat me that they scheduled the fight on the Fourth of July. White pride and white supremacy was riding on his win. They planned a double celebration. I whipped that poor man so bad I almost felt sorry for him.
(Laughs)

My victory caused racial riots all across the country. Two hundred and fifty-one people were injured, and nineteen others were killed. Some states even passed laws forbidding interracial boxing.
(Grows silent and takes a sip of water.)

White America couldn't defeat me as a boxer. They couldn't beat me socially, because I wouldn't let them tell me how to live. I did whatever I wanted to do and with whoever I wanted to do it. They kept coming up with ways to break me down. Finally, they used the legal system. In 1913 I was traveling with my white wife when I was arrested and convicted under the Mann Act. It was also called the White-Slave Traffic Act. This law made it illegal for men to take women across state lines for immoral purposes. Even though she was my legal wife, the courts defined interracial marriages as immoral. I was forced to leave the country to keep from going to prison. I continued to fight overseas, but I saw a lot of hard times and wanted to return to my country. That was a costly decision. I had to spend ten months in Leavenworth prison.

But I survived it. I survived it all, and I still lived my life the way I chose. I refused to let anybody dictate how I had to live as a man! Who would have thought a black fifth grade dropout from a poor Texas family would cause all that racial, political, religious, social, and legal controversy?

Joe Louis
(1914–1981)
Professional Boxer

Joe Louis

(JOE describes how he became the first black heavyweight to be inducted into the Boxing Hall of Fame.)

JOE

My name is Joe Louis. I was nicknamed the Brown Bomber. I was born to a sharecropping couple in Chambers County, Alabama. My parents had eight children. When I was young, we moved to Detroit, Michigan. I've always been a natural fighter, but I didn't like to bully people—and I didn't like to be bullied. I remember four boys picking on me when I was eight years old. I knocked all four of them out!

In 1934 I became a professional fighter while living in Detroit, Michigan. During that time, boxing was the only major professional sport where blacks could compete against whites. I won the heavyweight championship in 1937. Without planning it, I became a role model and icon to my race. Every time I won a fight, black people all over America would have big parties and celebrate.

I wasn't the first black heavyweight champion, but I was the first to achieve some career highlights. On September 24, 1935, I became the first to draw a million-dollar gate. In 1936 I became the first to win *Ring* magazine's Fighter of the Year Award. I was also the first black heavyweight elected to the Boxing Hall of Fame. Not bad for the son of poor sharecroppers.

Muhammad Ali
(1942–)
Professional Boxer

Muhammad Ali

(SPEAKER describes Muhammad Ali's successful career in boxing.)

SPEAKER

Muhammad Ali was born Cassius Clay in Louisville, Kentucky. When he joined the Nation of Islam, Clay changed his name to Muhammad Ali. But in the boxing world, he nicknamed himself the Greatest. In 1960 Ali won an Olympic gold medal. As a professional fighter, he successfully defended his title nineteen times.

In 1967 Muhammad Ali was ordered to join the U.S. Army but he refused. Because of his religious beliefs, he didn't support the Vietnam War. The government really got mad when Ali told them, "No Vietcong ever called me n———." He was sentenced to five years in prison and stripped of his title. Ali had never been defeated in the ring and was determined not to be defeated outside the ring. He fought all the way to the U.S Supreme Court. He won his case in 1971 and later regained his title. Muhammad Ali retired in 1979 with fifty-six wins and five losses. If anybody asks you who he is, tell them he's the greatest!

Champions of the Ring

Characters:
NARRATOR 1, *male or female, voice over*
NARRATOR 2, *male or female, voice over*
JOE LOUIS, *male, professional boxer, nonspeaking role*
MUHAMMAD ALI, *male, professional boxer, nonspeaking role*
Costumes:
Boxing attire of the early 1970s
Props:
At director's discretion

*(*NARRATOR 1 *and* NARRATOR 2 *recall Joe Louis and Muhammad Ali's boxing success.)*

NARRATOR 1
Boxing has always been a sport that offered the lower economic class, especially African Americans, opportunities for a route out of poverty. Many enslaved men have boxed since colonial times. Usually they were trained by their masters to fight other slaves. Some even gained their freedom by boxing. If their owners won a lot of money from wagers on their matches, a few would sometimes be granted their freedom. By the owner's gratitude, fighters were sometimes allowed to bet on themselves. They would save their winnings to purchase their freedom.

NARRATOR 2
African Americans have dominated the boxing world for many years. There has only been one white heavyweight champion since 1937.

Let's look at two outstanding champions. Meet Joe Louis, nicknamed the Brown Bomber.

JOE

(JOE steps forward; light shines on him while he shadowboxes.)

NARRATOR 2

When Louis turned professional, boxing was the only major sport where African Americans could compete with whites. He held his title for twelve years. That's longer than any boxer in history. He successfully defended his title twenty-five times. He was elected to the Boxing Hall of Fame in 1954.

NARRATOR 1

Float like a butterfly sting like a bee; no one did it better than Muhammad Ali.

ALI

(ALI steps forward; light shines on him while he shadowboxes.)

NARRATOR 1

This is the type of poetry Ali would use to describe his boxing skills and taunt his opponents. He proclaimed himself the greatest.

ALI

(ALI raises both hands over his head.)

NARRATOR 1

Ali had his first professional fight October 29, 1960. In 1964 he defeated Sonny Liston to become the heavyweight champion of the world. Some of his championship fights had colorful titles, such as the Fight of the Century, Rumble in the Jungle, and Thrilla in Manilla.

In 1978 he became the first boxer to win the heavyweight title three times."

(End scene.)

GOLF

Dr. William Powell and Renee Powell
(1916–2009) (1946–)
Golf Course Owner; Professional Golfer

(SPEAKER tells how Renee and Dr. William Powell made advances in professional golf.)

SPEAKER
The family that plays together stays together. Renee Powell received her first golf lesson from her father, William Powell, when she was only three years old. In 1967 Renee became the second African American to play on the LPGA tour. She followed behind former tennis champion Althea Gibson.

Dr. William Powell always had a love for the game of golf; however, finding a place to play wasn't easy for African Americans, even in Ohio where he lived. Dr. Powell decided to do something about it rather than just complain about it. He began designing a golf course. In 1946 he became the first African American to design, construct, own, and operate a course. He built it in Canton, Ohio, and named it Clearview Golf Course.

The Powells' accomplishments have also been recognized in society. Clearview is now listed on the National Register of Historic Places. Renee and Dr. Powell have received numerous awards and honors from the golf world, including the 1992 Jack Nicklaus Gold Family of the Year Award. In 2007 the Powells were inducted into the Ohio Golf Hall of Fame. In 2009 William Powell was the recipient of the PGA Distinguished Service Award.

Joseph Rice and the U.S. Supreme Court

(SPEAKER *describes how Joseph Rice fought for equal rights for African American golfers.*)

SPEAKER
Joseph Rice was a Florida resident. He enjoyed playing golf and believed he should have the right to play anytime he wanted. However, the city of Miami Springs didn't feel the same way. The town had one public golf course, and African Americans were only allowed to play one day a week. In October 1950, with his NAACP lawyer Frank Williams, he appealed a ruling by the Florida Supreme Court that agreed with Miami Springs. Joseph Rice took his case to the U.S. Supreme Court. The Court ruled in his favor, and Miami Springs was ordered to reconsider their decision. Rice's case was a victory for other African Americans also, as this influenced other black golfers to demand equal access to public facilities.

Charles "Charlie" Sifford
(1922–)
Professional Golfer

(SPEAKER *recalls Charlie Sifford's success as a professional golfer.*)

SPEAKER
On November 10, 1957, Charlie Sifford won the Long Beach Open. This victory made him the first African American to win a major professional golf tournament.

Lee Elder
(1934–)
Professional Golfer

*(*SPEAKER *recalls Lee Elder's success in professional golf.)*

SPEAKER
In 1975 Lee Elder became the first African American to play in the Masters Tournament in Augusta, Georgia. Elder was also the first to qualify for the Ryder Cup team and to earn a million dollars in a single season.

Calvin Peete
(1943–)
Professional Golfer

*(*SPEAKER *shares how Calvin Peete overcame an injury and became a successful golfer.)*

SPEAKER
Calvin Peete was the most successful African American on the PGA tour until 1996; he had twelve wins. He grew up poor and had a broken arm that was never properly set, because his family couldn't afford better medical treatment. Peete didn't learn to play the game of golf until he was in his twenties because of this injury. He was still poor as an adult and worked as a migrant laborer near Rochester, New York. It was at Genesee Valley Park in Rochester that Peete learned to play the game. He was ranked in the top ten of the Official World Golf Rankings for several weeks after he turned pro in 1986. He never allowed poverty or injury to stop him from excelling in the sport he enjoyed.

HORSE RACING

Monkey Simon
(ca. 1806–?)
Professional Jockey

(MONKEY SIMON recounts his successful career as a jockey.)

MONKEY SIMON

People call me Monkey Simon. But I don't monkey around when it comes to horse racing. I'm considered the best jockey of my day. I get paid $100 a race. I'm also the first known Negro jockey that anybody's heard of.

Oliver Lewis
(1856–1924)
Professional Jockey

(OLIVER recalls his success in the Kentucky Derby.)

OLIVER

I'm Oliver Lewis. In 1875 I became the first black jockey to win the Kentucky Derby.

Isaac Murphy
(ca. 1861–1896)
Professional Jockey

Isaac Murphy

(ISSAC recalls his success in the Kentucky Derby.)

ISSAC

I'm Isaac Murphy. I was the first jockey of any race ever to win three
Kentucky Derbies.

OTHER SPORTS AND INFLUENTIAL ATHLETES

Marshall W. "Major" Taylor
(1878–1948)
Professional Cyclist

(MAJOR highlights his success as a cyclist.)

MAJOR

I'm a bicycle racer. My name is Marshall Taylor. I got the nickname
Major when I was young, because I used to perform bicycle stunts
in a military uniform to earn money. I was banned from a lot of
races, because I was black; but when I got the opportunity, I outrode

everybody. I raced in the United States, New Zealand, Australia, and Europe. I won my first professional race at Madison Square Garden in 1898. I was the second Negro world champion and dubbed the Fastest Bicycle Rider in the World.

Willy T. Ribbs
(1956–)
Professional Race Car Driver

(SPEAKER shares Willy Ribbs's success as a race car driver.)

SPEAKER
In 1991 Willy T. Ribbs became the first African American race car driver to qualify for the Indianapolis 500.

Ron Simmons
(1958–)
Professional Wrestler

(SPEAKER describes Ron Simmons's success in wrestling.)

SPEAKER
In 1992 Ron Simmons captured the World Championship Wrestling title making him the first African American heavyweight champion in the history of the sport.

ENTERTAINMENT

THE BIG SCREEN

African Americans in the Motion-Picture Industry

(SPEAKER 1, SPEAKER 2, and SPEAKER 3 consecutively come to center stage and give a brief history of African Americans in film.)

SPEAKER 1
Acting roles were available for African Americans as early as 1905. Typically the women were typecast as faithful, bossy maids and the men as slow-talking, dim-witted servants. The scripts were filled with broken grammar, mispronounced words, and exaggerated facial expressions. In many films, instead of using black actors, whites would paint their faces black and portray similar derogatory images. In addition, many of the films' titles that portrayed African Americans were inflammatory, for example, *The Dancing Nig, The Wooing and Wedding of a Coon,* and *For Massa's Sake.*
(SPEAKER 1 moves to stage right.)

SPEAKER 2
Tired of these negative screen images, African Americans started producing movies. These films were called race movies. Race movies were created by black independent filmmakers, for black audiences. The movies included such genres as westerns and comedies, and such roles as detectives and heroes. Between 1915 and 1923 there were

about six hundred theaters on the race circuit. The movies were shown in the northern inner-city theaters. In the South they were shown in segregated movie houses and occasionally at schools, African American churches, and social gatherings.

(SPEAKER 2 moves to stage right.)

SPEAKER 3

In the late 1920s movies changed from silent films to talking, or sound films. These talking films opened the door for many African American entertainers and gave them a respectable place in mainstream Hollywood. Agents started looking in the New York black nightclubs and the black theaters for performers. Producers not only wanted actors who sounded nice, they wanted actors who looked nice too. From the silent films of yesterday to the high-technology films of today, African American actors have evolved from negative stereotypes to superstars and Oscar winners.

(Speakers exit stage.)

George Johnson and Noble Johnson
(ca. 1876–?) (1881–1978)
Screenwriters, Directors, Producers

Characters:

GEORGE, *male, movie producer, studio owner, and* NOBLE'*s older brother*

NOBLE, *male, movie producer and studio owner*

Costumes:

Casual attire of the early 1900s

Props:

Two chairs

(GEORGE and NOBLE *describe the struggles they faced as African American film producers.)*

GEORGE

Noble, do you ever wonder how we made it as long as we did in the motion-picture industry?

NOBLE

I think about it a lot, George. It wasn't easy to pursue our goal of becoming black producers in a world controlled by white Hollywood studios.

GEORGE

And 1918 was a tough year to do it, but we founded the Lincoln Motion Picture Company, and it was the first to be owned by blacks in the United States. We put a lot of energy into our enterprise. We needed to show the black actor in movies other than comedies. By 1920 we had completed five films, three dramatic subjects, two pictorials, and that five-reel feature *A Man's Duty.* You remember? We had to really work hard.

NOBLE

Yes, I do. Our biggest problem was that our market for selling movies was limited. The majority of white audiences weren't interested in all-black films, and we didn't have any theatres where we could present them. Our promotion depended on our road men. They traveled around the country with reels of film and showed them in churches, social halls, and schools. Against these odds, it was hard to survive in a business that depended on being able to reach the masses. But we were movie entrepreneurs. We stood firm on our belief that black people should invest in the business aspect of film so that our race could have powerful roles both in front of and behind the camera.

(End scene.)

Oscar Micheaux
(1884–1951)
Independent Filmmaker

(OSCAR describes his struggles as an African American filmmaker.)

OSCAR

I'm Oscar Micheaux. I was one of the early black filmmakers. Between 1918 and 1948, I wrote, directed, and produced thirty to forty films. I wanted my films to portray the importance of race in black life. I sometimes took a typical Hollywood plot and redirected it with a black slant, like my gangster films. Other times I would exclusively use race as the focus.

I knew the importance of publicity and promotion. I would tour the country promoting my films. When I toured the Southern towns, I would contact the theater managers and owners and try to persuade them to show my films to black people at special matinees or as a late special for interested white audiences.

Many of my films were controversial, even within my race. Black critics said my pictures focused on the upper-middle-class professional Negro. I was also accused of making all my leading stars very light complexioned with straight hair and white features. Despite these criticisms, my goal was to give my audiences something "to further the race, not hinder it." I wanted to present movies that showcased Negroes as intelligent, not as buffoons, as they were portrayed in white scripts.

Paul Robeson
(1898–1976)
Actor, Singer

Paul Robeson

(PAUL explains the struggles he faced as an African American actor in the United States.)

PAUL

I'm Paul Robeson. I was blessed to be multitalented. I grew up in New Jersey, where I attended Rutgers College. I played college football, baseball, basketball, and ran track. I also excelled in academics. I was elected to the national honors society, Phi Beta Kappa. I played professional football on weekends while studying law at Columbia Law School. When I graduated two years later, I decided to become an actor, rather than an attorney. I won rave reviews for several hit plays, but I was most remembered for my leading role in *Othello*. I continued to showcase my talents and became a singer. I made over three hundred records.

In my personal life, I was active in the fight against racial discrimination. I joined a picket line in front of the White House to protest lynching. Whenever I was asked to perform, I would only do so if the audience was allowed to be integrated. Because I was so outspoken, the government called me to testify before Congress where they questioned me about being a communist. I refused to answer. The State Department retaliated by revoking my passport. They made it impossible for me to work abroad. I was labeled a communist, so hardly anyone would hire me in the United States. In 1947 my income dropped from $104,000 to $2,000 per year. The state department made me a political prisoner in my own country. In 1958 the U.S. Supreme Court made a ruling in another case that was similar to mine. The outcome of that case forced the government to return my passport. By that time my prime years as an entertainer had passed, and I had to retire because of poor health. I lost my career, respect, and rights as a citizen, but I don't have any regrets. The Constitution gave me the freedom of speech. I voiced my opinions and was penalized for it. The government took my rights, but they couldn't take my manhood.

Hattie McDaniel
(1895–1952)
Actress

Hattie McDaniel

(HATTIE *reflects on her trials and successes as an actress in Hollywood.)*

HATTIE
(Looks into a mirror.)
Mirror, mirror on the wall, am I the fairest of them all?

(Turns to audience.)

I know I'm not the fairest of them all; but when you work in the entertainment industry, looks and image are important. Trust me; I know what I'm talking about. I'm Hattie McDaniel, and I've been entertaining for years. When I was young, I used to travel around the country with my father. We would perform minstrel shows in his big tent. I also did vaudeville back then. I was the first black woman to sing a solo on the radio. It wasn't long before I moved to Hollywood and became an actress.

Unfortunately, there wasn't much variety in roles for black actors when I started my career. If you were a popular bandleader or a successful dancer, there were occasional roles where you could show your stuff. Aside from that, the other roles were based on Hollywood's image of us. Image.

(Shakes her head.)

Hollywood didn't give us many choices. Roles for the black male usually consisted of the slow-witted, slow-talking, head-scratching, wide-eyed, shuffling character that was afraid of his own shadow. It wasn't much better for the black females either. Our parts were limited to the role of the overweight, headscarf wearing, sassy, bossy—but faithful—maid or mammy. Hollywood made sure our lines were full of mispronunciations and broken verbs. We didn't like it, but we took what was offered and made the most of it. I even had a clause in my contract forbidding me to lose weight.

This image put black actors in a conflict between Hollywood and the black community. Hollywood did all it could to maintain stereotypical roles. Our community was fighting to change the way we were portrayed on the screen. When the NAACP became organized, we were criticized for accepting those parts. These criticisms hurt me personally, because I've always been proud of my race; and I've always had pride in myself. I told the black community, from what I considered a realistic point of view, that I would rather play a maid for $700 a week than to be one for $7 a week. Well, that shut some of them up and angered some others. I also decided that the best way to make the most of my success was to help others. I gave numerous scholarships to black students and I volunteered to entertain our black troops during World War II. But you didn't hear much about that.

The best way I knew to deal with criticism and racism was to throw myself into my work. And that's what I did. When I heard about the movie *Gone with the Wind*, I read the book three times. I fit the image. I was big and dark enough for the part. I dressed the way I knew Hollywood thought a mammy should look when I auditioned. After I tried out, I got the role on the spot. They didn't even look at anyone else. I played Mammy to the best of my ability.

Regardless of our important roles in *Gone with the Wind*, none of the black actors were allowed to attend the premiere in Atlanta. My portrait was even removed from the promotional programs that were distributed in the South. Despite it all, my hard work paid off. In 1939 I won an Oscar for best supporting actress and became the first black person to win an Academy Award.

I took what life gave me and made the most of it. No I wasn't the fairest of them all, but I believed in myself. Remember, beauty will only last for a while, but talent will last forever.

Lena Horne
(1917–2010)
Actress

Characters:
BILL, *male fictional character, World War II veteran*
V. J., *male fictional character, World War II veteran*

Costumes:
Casual attire of the early 2000s
Props:
Dining table, two chairs, photographs

(BILL *and* V.J. *reflect on Lena Horne's successful career as an actress and entertainer.*)

BILL
(Passes picture to V. J.*)*
I know you remember who she is.

V. J.
You know I know who she is. She's the woman I was supposed to marry. That's Lena Horne.

BILL
Lena Horne didn't want you; she only had eyes for me. That's why she autographed this picture. Look at what it says, "To Bill from Lena." You know what that means, don't you?

V. J.
Yeah, it means Lena Horne knows how to write. She sent pictures to thousands of GIs. She was the black soldier's official pinup girl. You were just another lovesick admirer.

BILL
What's that the young people say, "You're just hating." Lena Horne loved all us black GIs. Remember when she came to our camp in Europe to perform?

V. J.

Stop asking me if I remember things about Lena. I was there that night too. I remember real well, because she pitched a fit when she saw that our military officers made us black soldiers sit behind the Nazi war criminals. She refused to perform. She stood up for black soldiers anytime she entertained American troops. She made clear that she didn't just come to lift our morale; she wanted us to know that she cared about our treatment too.

BILL

Her protests got back to Hollywood, and her career suffered as a result. But she stood firm and never apologized for her actions. It's not every day that you find a woman who's beautiful and that courageous too.

V. J.

I hated that she was victimized for speaking the truth. She certainly paid her dues as an entertainer. When she was only sixteen years old, she was a chorus girl at the Cotton Club in Harlem. Later, she took lessons and became a singer. Her career as a successful actress didn't begin until the early 1940s. Unfortunately during those years, just about the only roles open to black women were as maids or mammies. She refused to accept those parts. Lena also demanded that MGM Studios stop cutting out her scenes when her pictures played in the South. Lena's roles changed the way Hollywood portrayed the black female.

BILL

Count Basie saw her career as a milestone. He told people that before Lena, Americans had never been given the opportunity to see the black woman as a woman. Although she hated the title, she was called the first black sex symbol.

V. J.

She may have hated to be called a sex symbol, but she was all that and more. She will always be remembered as one beautiful, classy lady.

(End scene.)

Dorothy Dandridge
(1922–1965)
Actress

Dorothy Dandridge

*(*DOROTHY *recounts her success and trials as an African American actress in Hollywood.)*

DOROTHY

My name is Dorothy Dandridge. I was the first black woman to be nominated for an Oscar for best actress in a leading role. The nomination was for my role as Carmen in the 1954 film *Carmen Jones,* which featured an all-black cast. I didn't win, but my talent was recognized by the Academy and the American public. Even though I was a proven actress, it was three years before I made another film. Racism was an ever-present factor in determining roles. I know there are uncounted talented black actors in America. One day we will get the recognition we deserve.

Shelton "Spike" Lee
(1957–)
Director, Actor, Producer

Characters:
JIMMY, *male fictional character,* SPUD*'s uncle*
SPUD, *male fictional character, undergraduate film major*
Costumes:
Present-day casual attire
Props:
Sofa, television, popcorn, sodas

(JIMMY and SPUD *discuss Spike Lee's success as a director and producer.)*

JIMMY
Man, I'll be glad when you graduate in a few months. I'm tired of renting all these movies. I know you'll hook your uncle up.

SPUD
Yeah, I'll hook you up as long as you promise not to bootleg my movies on the street like you do everybody else's.

JIMMY
I wouldn't do that to you; you're family. You know me.

SPUD
That's right; I know you. But that probably won't be for a while anyway. It's hard for an unknown to break into Hollywood.

JIMMY

Well, how do you get from the unknown to the well-known? It sounds like trying to get a credit card for the first time. Nobody wants to give you credit, because you don't already have credit.

SPUD

I made a few short films in school, which my professors said were pretty good. They encouraged me to go to graduate school. I might get lucky with a motion-picture company, but I'm not going to sit around waiting on that. There are nearly a hundred black filmmakers, and a lot of them are actors too. I plan to be an independent film producer like Spike Lee. He's my film producer and director hero. He's known for being controversial and he earned that reputation as early as college. After he graduated from Morehouse College, he enrolled in graduate school at New York University's Institute of Film and Television in 1979. He almost got expelled, because he made a film called *The Answer*. It was about a young black screenwriter who was asked to remake D. W. Griffith's film *The Birth of a Nation*. In *The Answer* he exposed and attacked the racist stereotypes in Griffith's film, which had been hailed a masterpiece.

Also, he's not afraid to make us look at the attitudes and issues within our race. He deals with things like skin complexion and hair texture hang-ups, like in *School Daze*. He made us examine our attitudes about gender roles in *She's Gotta Have It*. He focused on northern race relations in *Do the Right Thing* and racial romance in *Jungle Fever*. Spike does his own thing. Nobody's in control but him, and he tells it like it is.

JIMMY

I love Spike Lee movies. They're some of my best sellers. He and Denzel should've gotten an Oscar for *Malcolm X*. I sold out of copies I don't know how many times.

SPUD

See Uncle, that's what I'm talking about. You know that's not right. You're taking money from people who earned it. When people use their talents and money to produce something, you shouldn't be out there hustling their investments.

JIMMY

You're looking at it all wrong. I wasn't selling the movies for a profit. I sold them for educational purposes. You know how many young people didn't know anything about Malcolm? I provided a community service for folks who couldn't afford the movie.

I have to give Spike credit, he is smart. He's made over ten films and the cameras are still rolling, thank goodness. He's made some documentaries too, like *Four Little Girls* and *When the Levees Broke: A Requiem in Four Acts*. Those two films made me angry and they made me cry too, but don't tell nobody about the crying part. But his *Kings of Comedy* had me rolling on the floor. It was one of my best sellers too. Yep, I'm a big fan of Spike Lee. He really helps supplement my income. I'll be glad when you make your first film so we can make some money. What's your first film going to be about?

SPUD

It's going to be about a hardworking film director whose uncle bootlegs films.

(End scene.)

Academy Award Winners

(NARRATOR and twelve speakers consecutively come to center stage and cite African Americans' accomplishments in film.)

NARRATOR
Today, to see African American actors on the screen is commonplace. They have excelled in the trade and have won numerous Oscar nominations and Academy Awards. The following speakers will share the names of some of these talented individuals and their Oscar winning performances.
(*NARRATOR exits stage.*)

SPEAKER 1
Hattie McDaniel was the first African American to win best actress in a supporting role. She won for the movie *Gone with the Wind* in 1939.
(*SPEAKER 1 moves to stage right.*)

SPEAKER 2
In 1948 James Baskett received an Oscar statuette for his characterization of Uncle Remus in Walt Disney's 1946 movie *Song of the South*.
(*SPEAKER 2 moves to stage right.*)

SPEAKER 3
In 1963 Sidney Poitier became the first African American actor to receive an Oscar for best actor in a leading role. Poitier starred in *Lilies of the Field*. In 2002 at the Academy Awards ceremony, he was presented with the honorary Lifetime Achievement Award.
(*SPEAKER 3 moves to stage right.*)

SPEAKER 4
In 1982 Louis Gossett Jr. received an Oscar for best actor in a supporting role for the film *An Officer and a Gentleman*.
(*SPEAKER 4 moves to stage right.*)

SPEAKER 5

In 1989 Denzel Washington received an Oscar for best actor in a supporting role for the movie *Glory.* In 2001 he received an Oscar for best actor in a leading role for the film *Training Day.*
*(*SPEAKER 5 *moves to stage right.)*

SPEAKER 6

Whoopi Goldberg received an Oscar for best actress in a supporting role for the film *Ghost* in 1990.
*(*SPEAKER 6 *moves to stage right.)*

SPEAKER 7

In 1996 Cuba Gooding Jr. was awarded an Oscar for best actor in a supporting role for the movie *Jerry Maguire.*
*(*SPEAKER 7 *moves to stage right.)*

SPEAKER 8

In 2001 Halle Berry became the first African American actress to receive an Oscar for best actress in a leading role. She starred in the film *Monster's Ball.*
*(*SPEAKER 8 *moves to stage right.)*

SPEAKER 9

Jamie Foxx received an Oscar in 2004 for best actor in a leading role for the movie *Ray.*
*(*SPEAKER 9 *moves to stage right.)*

SPEAKER 10

In 2004 Morgan Freeman's long career reached a milestone when he received an Oscar for best actor in a supporting role for the film *Million Dollar Baby.*
*(*SPEAKER 10 *moves to stage right.)*

SPEAKER 11

Forest Whitaker received an Oscar for best actor in a leading role in 2006 for the movie *The Last King of Scotland.*
(SPEAKER 11 moves to stage right.)

SPEAKER 12

In 2006 Jennifer Hudson received an Oscar for best actress in a supporting role for the movie *Dreamgirls.*
(SPEAKER 12 moves to stage right.)

SPEAKER 13

In 2009 Mo'Nique won an Oscar for best supporting actress for her role as Mary Lee Johnson for the movie Precious.
(SPEAKER 13 moves to stage right.)

SPEAKER 14

In 2009 Roger Ross Williams won the Academy Award for Documentary Short Subject for his film Music by Prudence.
(SPEAKER 14 moves to stage right.)

SPEAKER 15

In 2009 Geoffrey Fletcher became the first black winner of the Academy Award for Writing an Adapted Screenplay for the film Precious.

(Speakers exit stage.)

TELEVISION

Nat King Cole
(1919–1965)
Television Show Host, Singer

(NAT reflects on his success as a talk show host.)

NAT

My entertainment name is Nat King Cole, but I was born Nathaniel Adams Coles in Montgomery, Alabama. My family moved to the South Side of Chicago in the 1920s. My father was a preacher. By the time I was twelve, I was playing the organ and singing in his Baptist church. That didn't last too long, because shortly afterward I started playing in my brother's jazz band. I officially broke into the jazz world when I was sixteen. I had a successful career as a jazz artist by 1950. Later that year, I recorded the hit song "Mona Lisa." It sold over 3 million copies and popularized me as a pop balladeer.

I want to be remembered as a singer, but I also want the public to remember me as a television pioneer. I was the first black person to have a television show and host it. In 1956 *The Nat King Cole Show* made its debut. The show only lasted sixty-four weeks, because NBC couldn't get a solid sponsor. But it was a racial breakthrough in the television industry. I was the first of my race to host a show, but I was sure I wouldn't be the last.

Bill Cosby
(1937–)
Television Show Host, Writer, Actor

(SPEAKER highlights Bill Cosby's success in television.)

SPEAKER

Bill Cosby broke into television with the hit series *I Spy* in 1965. He costarred with actor Robert Culp in this action show. Cosby's role portrayed an image of African Americans that television viewers weren't accustomed to seeing. His character called for intelligence and heroism. The four-year hit catapulted Cosby into an overnight television star. He won three Emmy Awards for his role. His character, Alexander Scott, was typical of Cosby's future roles in that it didn't focus on race, stereotypes, or negative images of black life.

Cosby starred in two other television programs, *The Bill Cosby Show* and *The New Bill Cosby Show*. Neither show sustained long-term airing. Cosby, however, continued to move forward with new ideas. In 1972 he created the *Fat Albert Show*. The show ran from 1972 to 1979. Cosby was the animated show's host and writer. Fat Albert and his buddies created a fad for T-shirts and other items. The familiar, "Hey! Hey! Hey!" was heard daily by fans everywhere. Bill Cosby had another animated show in 2000. It starred the cartoon character Little Bill.

His biggest success was in 1984 with the megahit series *The Cosby Show*. The show starred Bill Cosby and Phylicia Rashad as his wife. It became one of the most successful situation comedies in television history. When *The Cosby Show* went syndicated, he received a reported $600 million.

Cosby and his wife Camille have generously shared their wealth. They've donated to numerous organizations and colleges, including a $20 million donation to Spelman College. It was the largest donation ever given to a historically black college.

Oprah Winfrey
(1954–)
Talk Show Host, Actress

Characters:

ANGELA, *female fictional character, undergraduate media communications major*

ROZLYN, *female fictional character, undergraduate early childhood development major*

Costumes:

Present-day casual attire

Props:

Two desks, two chairs

(ANGELA and ROZLYN discuss their future aspirations and Oprah Winfrey's success.)

ROZLYN

I can't wait until I graduate. I might teach for a few years, but I want to open a daycare center. What do you want to do?

ANGELA

I want to host a talk show. I love interviewing people.

ROZLYN

Nah, not for me. That's too competitive. You have to work too hard for too long or know somebody. You know what they say, "It's not what you know, but who you know." If you don't know the right people, you may never get any further than working as an office assistant. I'm sticking to little kids, because I know people will always have babies.

ANGELA

That's good if that's what you want. I think I can be self-made like Oprah Winfrey. She said, "It doesn't matter who you are, where you come from. The ability to triumph begins with you." I believe that. She motivates me by her accomplishments.

ROZLYN

I can't argue with you about that. In 1993 she was on Forbes Fortune 500 list. It's reported that she has a net worth of $1.5 billion. She was the first African American to become a billionaire. I'd have to take care of every child in America for the rest of my life to make that much money. How did she get started anyway?

ANGELA

Oprah Winfrey began her broadcasting career working at a radio station in Nashville, Tennessee, while she was still a high school student. At age nineteen she was an anchorwoman at a Nashville television station. This made her the youngest African American woman to anchor the news. In 1977 she moved to Baltimore, Maryland, to join an ABC affiliate station. She coanchored the *Six O'clock News*. She later cohosted a Baltimore local talk show called *People Are Talking*.

Oprah moved to Chicago in January 1984 to cohost a morning TV talk show called *AM Chicago*. She had only been at the station a month and her show surpassed all her competition. Within a year the program was expanded to an hour and named after her. In June 1984 *The Oprah Winfrey Show* won three Daytime Emmy Awards. The next year she won a second Daytime Emmy Award for Outstanding Talk/Service Program. In 1988 she became the youngest person ever to receive the International Radio and Television Society's Broadcaster of the Year Award. In 1986 her show was nationally syndicated and became the highest rated talk show in the history of television. It remained at the number one position for twenty-two consecutive years. It is broadcast in 139 countries and has over 44 million viewers. Things just snowballed for her.

ROZLYN

It was as though she had the Midas touch.

ANGELA

She isn't successful because she's lucky; she's smart and hardworking. She created Harpo Productions Inc., expanded her talents by becoming an actress, and produced movies, plays, and television projects. She has her own magazine and founded a book club in 1997. Her recommended book lists almost guarantee a best seller. Oprah's a partner in Oxygen Media Inc., and she's already starting a new venture. In 2008 Oprah and Discovery Communications began plans to create OWN: The Oprah Winfrey Network. It's scheduled to debut in 2009.

ROZLYN

I know she's generous. She built a school for girls in South Africa. She gave them an opportunity they never could've imagined. She has her Angel Network that gives $100,000 to people who make sacrifices in their lives to help others. What would you do if you had that much money?

ANGELA

I'm sure I would be a philanthropist like Oprah. But knowing me, I would also shop 'til I drop.
(Both laugh.)

(End scene.)

THE STAGE

Bill "Bojangles" Robinson
(1878–1949)
Dancer

(BOJANGLES recalls his accomplishments as a tap dancer and actor.)

BOJANGLES

Have you ever heard of a pickaninny? It was a term that white people
in show business used to describe little black kids that performed in
musical stage productions. These children were also called picks,
because they were "picked" for their cute appearance and talents. They
could sing, dance, or act comically. They would be in the background
during the grand finale of a white female star's solo act. I started my
career as a pick and made fifty cents a night. I'm a tap dancer. My
name is Bill Robinson, but most people know me by my nickname,
Bojangles.

I started dancing for a living at an early age. Both my parents died, and
I was orphaned by the time I was seven. When I was older, I teamed
with another black dancer named George Cooper. We entertained
on the vaudeville circuit when it was just beginning to accept black
entertainers. We were allowed to perform without black face, which
we liked, because black face was a common mockery of our race.
Sometimes I would appear as a solo act. I billed myself as the Black
Cloud of Joy. I developed my own style. I wore a top hat, full dress,
and carried a cane. I exited the stage with my signature dance, the
Camel Walk. But my favorite routine was the Old Man, where I
pretended to be an elderly man when I danced. I also performed in
fourteen films, including one with child star Shirley Temple.

I was proud of my professional accomplishments, but the recognition from my people gave me equal pride. The Negro Actors Guild made me their honorary president. My race showed me additional love by calling me the Honorary Mayor of Harlem. I earned a lot of money during my career, but I gave most of it away. I didn't worry about it. To me, everything was copasetic. That's a word I created to mean better than alright, it's really wonderful.

Josephine Baker
(1906–1975)
Dancer, Singer

(JOSEPHINE *describes the adversity she faced as an African American* *dancer.*)

JOSEPHINE

I'm Josephine Baker. I was born Freda Josephine McDonald in Saint Louis, Missouri. I married my first husband when I was fifteen. I kept his name, Baker, for my stage name. I admit fifteen was young for a girl to marry, but I did a lot of things when I was young. I quit school when I was eight and ran away from home when I was thirteen. Shortly after that, I started dancing professionally in vaudeville and on Broadway as a chorus girl. When I was nineteen, I went to Paris, France, to perform in a Negro revue. It was sponsored by a wealthy white female who wanted to show Parisians what she called real Negro entertainment. The revue had mixed results, but my comic antics and jazz dancing were noticed by the Folies Bergere. I was asked to star in their new production. My performances from that point on were highly successful and controversial. The Bergere was known for elaborate scenery and costumes. It was also known for its nudity. It presented its female performers nude from the waist up. I was invited to the socially elite events and was treated like a first-class citizen in France. I wasn't confronted with the racism I experienced in the United States. I decided to make France my permanent home. In 1937 I became a French citizen.

During World War II, I supported the Allies by gathering intelligence for the French Resistance. I also performed for the troops in Africa and the Middle East. I returned to the United States quite a few times after moving to Paris; however, I remained disillusioned about the racial conditions. On one of my visits in 1951, I went to the famous Stork Club in New York. I was refused service. No one came to my defense. I was angry! It seemed black people were still experiencing racism in the North as well as the South. Even though I no longer lived there, I remained concerned about race relations. During the 1960s, I came to the United States several times for benefit performances to raise funds for the civil rights movement. I returned again in 1963 to participate in the March on Washington.

I believed people everywhere should accept each other as human beings regardless of color. That's one reason I love children, they accept everyone. I adopted twelve children of all nationalities. I called them the Rainbow Tribe. I came out of retirement to raise money to support them. I had a successful performance at Carnegie Hall in New York and in Paris. Even though I was sixty-nine, the show was a success. I never let age prevent me from performing when I was young, and I wasn't going to let it stop me when I was older. I loved the stage. I always felt that the day I could no longer go on stage would be the day I'd die.

Katherine Dunham
(1910–2006)
Dancer, Choreographer, Activist

(KATHERINE chronicles her career as a dancer and an activist.)

KATHERINE

I'm Katherine Dunham. I'm a choreographer, dancer, anthropologist, and author. I became intrigued with dance at an early age. When I was fifteen, I organized a fund-raising cabaret. I even started a dance school for black children before I finished high school. Not only was I interested in the beauty of dance, but I was also interested in the cultures in which they were rooted. In 1936 while working on my doctorate in cultural anthropology, I received a fellowship that allowed me to study dance as it related to black cultures in Haiti, Martinique, Jamaica, and Trinidad. I became a part of their ethnic practices in order to gain a better understanding of Afro-Caribbean history and how it influenced dance.

I formed the Katherine Dunham Dance Company when I returned to the United States. It consisted of dancers, singers, musicians, and actors. It was the first African American modern dance company in the country. I incorporated the dances I learned in the Caribbean and used them in my dance troupe. I continued to study other dances from numerous cultures. I used dance as a language to teach people about themselves and others around the world.

In 1939 my husband and I moved to New York. I formed a dance troupe there. We were so successful that the entire company was involved in the Broadway production *Cabin in the Sky*. In 1941 the troupe stayed in Los Angeles, and I made my first movie. In 1943 we returned to New York, where we had 156 successful performances; then we went on tour throughout the country.

I enjoyed my success as a performer; however, I didn't believe we should ignore the hardships of others. I was a political activist in the United States and abroad. This caused conflict in many areas where we performed. When my troupe entertained in the South during the 1940s, I refused to perform unless African Americans were allowed to attend the performances too. I turned down a generous Hollywood contract, because I was told I would have to replace some of my darker performers. We also had problems finding decent lodging while touring different parts of the South because of Jim Crow laws. My political stands caused the State Department—which subsidized many troupes—to refuse to support us, even when we entertained U.S. servicemen.

In 1992 I was at the ripe old age of eighty-two. I went on a hunger strike to protest the United States' discriminatory foreign policy against Haitian refugees who were attempting to enter our country by boat. My strike was highly publicized. *Time* magazine did a coverage piece of my protest. The magazine reported, "She went on a forty-seven-day hunger strike to protest the U.S.'s forced repatriation of Haitian refugees." President Aristide of Haiti called me the spiritual mother of Haiti and awarded me a medal of Haiti's highest honor. All artists want to be recognized and famous, but that wasn't my priority. As I told the reporter for *Time* magazine, "My job is to create a useful legacy."

Alvin Ailey
(1931–1989)
Dancer, Choreographer, Director

(ALVIN chronicles his successful career as a dancer and choreographer.)

ALVIN

I'm Alvin Ailey. When I was in junior high school on a field trip, I saw a ballet. That inspired me to take dance lessons. I studied initially under Katherine Dunham. In 1949 I studied under another great choreographer, Lester Horton, in Los Angeles. Horton had a racially mixed troupe that included Native American and Japanese influences. I made my performance debut in 1953. Horton died that same year, and I took over the troupe. I made my Broadway debut in 1954 in a Truman Capote play. When the play closed, I studied ballet, acting, and modern dance.

For the next ten years, I performed on and off Broadway in a variety of capacities and choreographed for several productions. My first financial and critical success came in 1958 for my choreography for *Blues Suite*. In 1965 I changed my priorities to choreographing shows and managing my company, Alvin Ailey American Dance Theater. My dance company performed for nearly 21 million people in forty-eight states and six continents. We have received numerous awards and have been recognized as cultural ambassadors.

Arthur Mitchell
(1934–)
Dancer, Choreographer

(SPEAKER describes Arthur Mitchell's success as a ballet dancer.)

SPEAKER
When Arthur Mitchell heard the statement that black people couldn't perform ballet, he was determined to break that myth. Other critics said African Americans didn't have the body for ballet. Mitchell knew that he was a talented ballet dancer, and he was determined to prove that statement false. Mitchell entered the challenging and segregated world of ballet. He joined the New York City Ballet in 1955 and performed with them for fifteen years. Mitchell was the first African American in a major ballet company. In the 1960s he established the National Ballet Company of Brazil and traveled there to work with the troupe. The assassination of Martin Luther King Jr. in 1968 had a deep impact on him. He was on his way to Brazil when he heard the news. He decided then and there that he wanted to do something for disadvantaged African Americans.

Early in his dancing career Arthur Mitchell wanted to prove that if given the same opportunity as white children that black children could be great dancers also. He proved that in just a few years. In 1969 he set up a dance studio in a basement in Harlem. It was open to any neighborhood child who wanted to learn. Mitchell wanted to give black children a route out of the ghetto through the arts. Within two months, his studio had over four hundred students. This was the start of the Dance Theater of Harlem. The performers' movements combined Afro-ethnic, ballet, and jazz dance. The troupe debuted in 1971.

The Dance Theater of Harlem continues to excite audiences worldwide. They have received numerous awards. If anyone still believes the stereotype that African Americans can't perform ballet, come to one of their performances. You'll not only be enlightened, you'll be enthused! The myth has been broken.

Garth Fagan
(1940–)
Dancer, Choreographer

(SPEAKER *defines Garth Fagan's success as a dancer and choreographer.*)

SPEAKER
Garth Fagan was born in Kingston, Jamaica, in 1940. A gymnastics class initially drew his attention to dance. While in high school, he studied with Ivy Baxter at the Jamaica Dance Company. He later moved to the United States to earn a Bachelor of Arts degree at Wayne State University in Detroit, Michigan. In 1970 he moved to Rochester, New York. In 1973 he established his dance company, which was originally named the Bucket BUT . . . Dance Theatre. He choreographed for several distinguished dance companies.

He has been a premiere performer, and his dance troupe has been equally successful. As of 2007 he had twenty-five stage productions to his credit. In 1998 he received the Drama Desk Award for outstanding choreography for *The Lion King*.

MUSIC

Innovative Music Styles

African Americans and Music

(SPEAKER *gives a brief history of African Americans and music.)*

SPEAKER
(Listening to music through headphones.)
My bad. I didn't see you out there. I'm telling you, I just block everything else out when I get into my music. I love music, my family loves music, and all my friends love music too. I believe the whole world loves music. But for us African Americans, I think music has a special place in our culture. I say that because we can trace our rhythms and some of our instruments all the way back to the mother country. Some of our singing styles, like call-and-response, came across the Atlantic Ocean with us on the slave ships. The work songs that slaves sang, spirituals, gospel, blues, R&B, ragtime, jazz, and rap—all have their origins in Africa.

Music makes us feel good; it makes us cry. It makes your grandma sing at the kitchen stove while she's cooking a pot of soul food. It makes your mama and daddy remember when they were teens, and it makes you remember your first date. Music makes you party on Saturday night and shout in church on Sunday morning. Don't get mad! I'm not talking about everybody, but some of you know I'm telling the truth.

Well I better shut my mouth. I don't want to step on anybody's toes, especially if they're wearing their dancing shoes.

Work Songs

(SPEAKER highlights the roll of call-and-response in African American work songs.)

SPEAKER
Work songs incorporated a style of singing called call-and-response. Call-and-response is a method of singing in which one singer belts out a phrase and a group of singers responds to that phrase. Africans used call-and-response to pace labor, and they carried the tradition to the colonies as slaves. Along with pacing labor, they also used call-and-response to communicate about their daily lives. Frequently the songs would entail codes to talk about their masters and overseers.

Later, this singing style was used on prison chain gangs. Prisoners often sang about their unfair sentencing or the meanness of the sheriff's guards. They referred to the warden or sheriff as the boss man. Singing in code gave the prisoners an opportunity to express their feelings in a manner that the guards couldn't understand.

Spirituals

(SPEAKER shares how African American slaves used spirituals to pass messages.)

SPEAKER
Slaves developed spirituals on the plantation. Spirituals are a blend of Christian hymns, West African rhythms, and vocal music. The slaves employed call-and-response, a singing style rooted in tribal African villages, into their spirituals. Often they incorporated their masters'

Christian hymns in order to mask antislavery lyrics. The songs often expressed sorrow and the desire to be free. Slaves also used certain lyrics to pass escape plans. For example, "the promised land" meant the joy of freedom. "Down by the riverside" came from the New Testament and symbolized overcoming hardship and oppression through faith. "This little light of mine" represented faith that the future would be better. "Get on board, little children" meant taking a ride on the Underground Railroad. "Wade in the water" told runaways to wade in the rivers and streams so the dogs couldn't pick up their scent. "Swing low from the sky" referred to a way to escape from slavery in America and be transported back to Africa.

Did any of these songs sound familiar? How many times have you heard them? I bet too many times for you to count. Did you know their meanings? I bet you didn't. The next time you hear one, think about what it meant to the slaves.

Ragtime

*(*SPEAKER *shares ragtime's history.)*

SPEAKER
Ragtime was the first music style of African American origin that was significantly popular in both the black and white populations. It was a lively style of music, and at the time of its birth it was associated with popular dances. Ragtime reached its peak between the 1890s and the late 1910s. Early ragtime was composed of stereotypical dialect, negative themes of black men and women, and was sometimes called *coon songs*. Scott Joplin popularized piano ragtime and is called the King of Ragtime Composers.

Blues

(SPEAKER explains the origin of blues music.)

SPEAKER

Blues is another style of music that African Americans created. The blues, as it's often called, got its start in the Mississippi Delta in the 1890s. Its style is rooted in Negro spirituals. Blues got its name from what are called blue notes, which are the third and seventh notes of a major scale. They are flatted, which means played lower than the intended pitch.

Blues gave black people a way to express their lives' experiences. Similar to spirituals, the blues had coded messages. The lyrics would sometimes express the harshness of life or the unfairness of certain sheriffs, judges, and prison bosses. For example, the lyrics from "Chain Gang Blues" state, "It was early in the morning when I had my trial, ninety-nine days on the county road and the judge didn't even smile."

As blues singers migrated north and west because of poverty or racism, their music migrated with them. They performed in traveling minstrel shows and carnivals. In the North, blues singers and entertainers played in urban clubs and dance halls. "Crazy Blues," written by Mamie Smith in 1920, was the first blues song recorded by a white studio. It sold over seventy-five thousand copies the first month it was released. It proved that the blues had commercial appeal.

Jazz

(SPEAKER *explains the origin of jazz.*)

SPEAKER
Jazz is a style of African American music that is rooted in the blues.
Jazz began to surface in New Orleans around the 1890s when the bands
in the city played for Mardi Gras celebrations and funeral processions.
The smaller bands played in bars in New Orleans's notorious Storyville
district. When the U.S. Navy placed most of Storyville off limits to
its sailors, a lot of the jazz musicians who played there lost their jobs.
Many of them moved to Chicago, including the two jazz legends
Louis Armstrong and Joe "King" Oliver. Many musical legends were
jazz musicians and singers, including Nat King Cole, Sarah Vaughan,
Ella Fitzgerald, and Lionel Hampton. These, and many other talented
artists, helped take jazz from the city of New Orleans to countries all
over the world.

Gospel

(SPEAKER *gives a brief history of gospel music.*)

SPEAKER
Gospel music evolved in the 1930s from blues and Christian spirituals.
Originally, the melodies incorporated shouts, moans, hand clapping,
and dancing. Gospel music was later popularized outside the church
by solo recording artists, groups, and choirs. Mahalia Jackson, Shirley
Caesar, the Five Blind Boys of Mississippi, the Mighty Clouds of Joy,
and the Mississippi Mass Choir were a few of gospel's prominent
artists.

Rhythm and Blues

(SPEAKER gives a brief history of rhythm and blues.)

SPEAKER
Rhythm and blues, or simply called R&B, emerged around the late 1930s. It was created and performed by black musicians, and targeted black audiences. It combined blues, jazz, and gospel music. In its early stages, R&B was only played on African American radio stations; in addition, because it hadn't yet become popular in mainstream America, most of the R&B singers had to travel around the country and play in local clubs. Some of the pioneers of R&B music were Louis Jordan, Fats Domino, Little Richard, Frankie Lymon and the Teenagers, Sam Cooke, Bo Diddley, and Big Joe Turner.

Rap

(SPEAKER 1, SPEAKER 2, SPEAKER 3, and SPEAKER 4 consecutively come to center stage and give a brief history of rap music.)

SPEAKER 1
The roots of rap can be traced back to the poet-storytellers, or griots, of West Africa. As the griots spoke, their words were set to a musical background. The term "rap" is credited to the 1960s black nationalist H. Rap Brown, who incorporated hip rhyme into his political speeches. In the late 1960s, groups like the Last Poets set Brown's rapping style to music in their performances.
(SPEAKER 1 moves to stage right.)

SPEAKER 2
Also in the late 1960s and 1970s, there were two other kinds of rap: soul rap and funk rap. Soul rap was a monologue about love. It was

275

popularized by Isaac Hayes in his hit song "By the Time I Get to Phoenix." Funk rap was about partying. George Clinton and his group Parliament introduced party funk. Unlike the political rap of the Last Poets, soul rap and funk rap were not rhymed. Contemporary rap began in the city streets of New York. The release of *Rapper's Delight* by the Sugar Hill Gang in October 1979 marked the beginning of rap as a popular music form.
(SPEAKER 2 moves to stage right.)

SPEAKER 3

As new artists got involved, rap music became more diverse by including female and white rappers. In the 1990s many of the lyrics changed from a fun party-style to a more hard-core form that exposed the violent side of inner-city life. These forms were referred to as gangsta rap.
(SPEAKER 3 moves to stage right.)

SPEAKER 4

At first many people felt rap music was a fad that would soon fade away; however, over thirty years later it still remains an important branch of American music that appeals to and influences the lives of both the young and old.

(Speakers exit stage.)

MUSICIANS AND VOCALISTS

Thomas Green "Blind Tom" Wiggins
(1849–1904)
Musician

Blind Tom Wiggins

(SPEAKER recounts the tragic story of musical genius Blind Tom Wiggins.)

SPEAKER

I hope you have a fresh tissue handy, because the story I'm about to tell you is true; but many of you may find it somewhat sad. The year was 1849. A baby boy named Thomas was born in Columbus, Georgia. He was born to enslaved parents, Charity and Mingo Wiggins, which by law made him a slave. To add to his misfortunes, he was also born blind. It's reported that Tom had some degree of mental illness. His verbal skills and ability to walk were significantly delayed. When he was two, he and his family were sold to the general James Neil Bethune.

Tom could barely speak or walk, but he possessed a great ability to imitate sounds. When he was only four, he shocked everyone by playing note for note one of the musical pieces he heard Bethune's daughter play during her piano lesson earlier that day. The family had left Tom asleep in the hall. When they heard the music, they came running down the stairs and saw Tom sitting at the piano in ecstasy; he was breaking out at the end of each successive fugue in shouts of laughter, while kicking his heels and clapping his hands.

Today's medical professionals would probably identify Tom as a person with extraordinary skills but extremely limited socially and cognitively. When he was five, he composed his first original composition. His first works were "The Rainstorm" and "Sewing Song." They were impressions of everyday sounds. General Bethune recognized Tom's talents and provided him with music lessons. Three years later, eight-year-old Tom made his musical debut in Columbus, Georgia. The following year General Bethune hired Tom out to a farmer from Savannah, Georgia, named Perry Oliver for $15,000. Oliver was known for his talent as a show-business promoter. He gave Tom the name Blind Tom and targeted the middle class as his market audience.

Tom was known for his writhing when he played. Most people found this fascinating. Oliver decided to highlight this as part of the act. In short, Tom's performances were presented as a kind of freak show. Tom would also frequently introduce himself in the third person and clap for himself in exhilaration. All these natural antics proved to be crowd-pleasers. Oliver pushed Tom's skills to the maximum of physical endurance. He advertised that Tom could repeat long and complex compositions after only hearing them one time. Tom showcased his ability to turn his back to the piano and play the same song with his hands reversed. He could sit next to a musician who was playing a tune he'd never heard then spontaneously pick out a bass accompaniment that blended perfectly. His concerts were long and included taking requests from the audience from the hundreds of compositions he knew.

He played for President Buchanan at the White House in 1860. Similar to his other performances, it was long and included audience requests. He was asked to replay two selections. One was thirteen pages long, the other was twenty pages. He played them without any difficulty.

Tom's natural ability to recall provided another talent from which Perry Oliver could capitalize. These demanding performances took their toll on Tom. His shows would last for hours. He was booked for as many as four shows per day and multiple-city schedules. His later career tours took him throughout the United States, England, South America, France, Scotland, and Canada. Ironically he got a temporary relief during the Civil War. In January 1861 he was performing in New York when Georgia seceded from the Union. Oliver canceled all of Tom's performances and returned to the South. He quickly booked Tom to give concerts to raise money for the Confederacy. In July of that same year, Tom had been listening to people around him read the newspaper's accounts of the war. Based on what he heard, he sat down at his piano and wrote "The Battle of Manassas." It was comprised of a melody of popular tunes and was a tremendous success.

When the Civil War ended in 1865, General Bethune persuaded Tom's parents to sign a contract making him Tom's manager until he turned twenty-one. The agreement was that he would give the parents $500 a year, plus food and shelter. Tom would receive $20 per month, food, clothing, shelter, and a piano. Meanwhile, Tabbs Grossa—former slave and promoter—sued Bethune. He alleged that Bethune accepted a down payment of $20,000 in gold in exchange for custody of Tom. When the case went to court, doctors interviewed sixteen-year-old Tom. They concluded that Tom was too emotionally violent to be put in a new environment and in the custody of strangers. When Tom turned twenty-one, General Bethune had Tom declared insane and appointed himself his legal guardian.

The Bethune family made a fortune off Tom. Historians believed they acquired at least $750,000. Many speculated that Tom was the highest paid pianist of the nineteenth century. It's estimated that he earned over $100,000 per year, which would be equal to $1.5 million by today's standards. Of course Tom was never paid any part of the money. It was reported however, that he was well cared for, and the Bethunes treated him like a member of the family.

General Bethune's son John became Tom's protector and guardian when he was on tours. He had been Tom's playmate since childhood. It seems Tom's favorite times were between concert seasons on the Bethunes' farm in Virginia. It was told that when it was time to start touring again, John would have someone summon Tom. At that point Tom would yell, "Tell him to go to hell, Tom ain't coming."

John Bethune died suddenly in 1884. General Bethune resumed the role as Tom's guardian, but John's wife, Eliza, didn't want to lose custody of Tom and control of his career. She initiated a long custody battle. The case ended up in a federal court in Virginia. The court ordered General Bethune to surrender custody of Tom to Eliza and Tom's mother, who Eliza shrewdly brought with her from Georgia to add weight to her case. Some say Tom was heartbroken by the decision, but he left meekly without complaint. General Bethune swore he would continue his fight to get Tom back.

Eliza relocated to New Jersey and kept Tom with her. He then performed under the name Thomas Greene until he retired in 1904. His retirement may have been in part because he suffered a stroke and was paralyzed on his right side. Less than two months after his stroke, he sat down to his piano for the last time. He rose and said, "I'm done, missus, all gone," and died. Sadly, Tom died poor, exhausted, exploited, and maybe unloved.

Scott Joplin
(1868–1917)
Ragtime Composer

(SCOTT recounts his contributions to ragtime music.)

SCOTT

My name is Scott Joplin. I'm a musician and composer of ragtime music. I began studying the piano when I was a child. People noticed almost immediately that I had an unusual style. During my first years as a musician, I concentrated on classical music and toured the Midwest when I was a teenager.

I focused most of my time on writing my own music. My most famous rag was the "Maple Leaf Rag." In 1911 I wrote and choreographed *Treemonisha*, a ragtime folk opera. Some of my music was adapted for the 1973 movie *The Sting*. It was an Academy Award-winning movie score. I have been called the King of Ragtime Composers.

Thomas Dorsey
(1899–1993)
Gospel Singer

(THOMAS describes his career as a blues and gospel artist.)

THOMAS

My name is Thomas Dorsey. I'm known as the Father of Gospel Music. My father was a country preacher, and I grew up in the church. When I was nine, my father moved to Atlanta. It was there that I was exposed to secular music, including the blues. I became a piano player by the time I was twelve. When I was seventeen, I left Atlanta and moved to Chicago to study music. I began to write gospel and blues music.

In 1920 I wrote my first blues song called "If You Don't Believe I'm Leaving, You Can Count the Days I'm Gone." Two years later, I wrote my first gospel song called "If I Don't Get There." Even though I loved gospel as much as I loved the blues, I chose to write blues music, because it allowed me to make more money. I became known as Georgia Tom and started my blues career. I recorded over twelve songs. Some of them were pretty suggestive and left little to the imagination. One of my songs sold a million copies.

In 1932 when I was out of town on the blues circuit, my wife and baby died. Their deaths changed my life. From that point on, I wrote nothing but gospel. I wrote and recorded over the following sixty years. Many of my songs are still played today, for example, "Precious Lord, Take My Hand," "Peace in the Valley," and "Standing Here Wondering Which Way to Go." I worked with and trained many gospel singers who became very famous. Some of them were Mahalia Jackson, James Cleveland, and Rosetta Tharpe. Many black recording stars started out singing in the church the same as me, but unlike some, I returned to my gospel roots and never looked back.

Marian Anderson
(1902–1993)
Opera Singer

Marian Anderson

(MARIAN *gives a brief history of her career as an opera singer and a U.S. delegate.*)

MARIAN

I'm Marian Anderson. I was a contralto opera singer. That's the lowest voice for a female singer. I've even been dubbed the world's greatest contralto. I was born and raised in South Philadelphia. When I was six, I sang in my church's junior choir; I was the youngest member. When I was thirteen, I was leading songs and singing solos. I started taking private voice lessons from a voice teacher when I was in high school. She was kind enough to train me for free, because my parents were too poor to afford the lessons. Later, I started earning money by singing in recitals in Philadelphia. I was fortunate enough to have many supporters who donated money to help pay for my musical education.

When I was nineteen, I auditioned to study with a well-known, excellent voice teacher in New York. In 1925 I won a contest that included a guest appearance with the New York Philharmonic Orchestra. The next year I won a scholarship from the National Association of Negro Musicians. The scholarship gave me the opportunity to study in England. I gave a number of recitals while living there. In 1933 I won another scholarship to study in Germany. From 1933 to 1936 I performed in three continents and five countries and gave seventy-five concerts in sixty cities.

I received high praises and red-carpet treatment everywhere I went, except in the United States. In 1939 my manager tried to book me for a concert at Constitution Hall, in Washington, D.C. The Daughters of the American Revolution owned the hall. Their organization refused to allow me to perform there because I was black. I was insulted and hurt. Most Americans were outraged. When First Lady Eleanor Roosevelt learned what had transpired, she resigned from the Daughters of the American Revolution and arranged for me to sing at the Lincoln

Memorial on Easter Sunday. A crowd of over seventy-five thousand attended the concert.

In 1955 I became the first black person to give a performance at the Metropolitan Opera House in New York City. In 1958 President Eisenhower appointed me as a member of the American delegation to the United Nations. In 1961 I was asked to sing "The Star-Spangled Banner" at President Kennedy's inauguration. In addition to these honors, President Johnson presented me with the Medal of Freedom.

In 1965 I gave my farewell concert at Carnegie Hall. I knew early in my career that the operatic world wasn't a welcoming place for black opera singers. Who knows how many talented singers were discouraged by this. I tried to be a symbol of inspiration to others. As I once said, "Not everyone can be turned aside from meanness and hatred . . . I have a great belief in the future of my people and my country."

Mahalia Jackson
(1911–1972)
Gospel Singer

Mahalia Jackson

(*MAHALIA recounts her career as a gospel singer.*)

MAHALIA

My name is Mahalia Jackson. I grew up in a very religious environment. My father was a preacher, and religion had a lot of influence on my life. I started singing in my father's church in New Orleans when I was five years old.

I started recording my music in the 1930s. My style of gospel blended religious music, blues, and jazz. I sold millions of records during my career and made several films. I performed on television, radio, and at Carnegie Hall. I even sang at President Kennedy's inauguration.

I turned down bookings in Las Vegas and New York clubs. I refused thousands of offers to record pop music and blues. I made a promise to God that I would only sing to glorify him, and that's what I did.

Mary Violet Leontyne Price
(1927–)
Opera Singer

Leontyne Price

(SPEAKER recounts Leontyne Price's success as an opera singer.)

SPEAKER

Leontyne Price began singing as a little girl in her hometown of Laurel, Mississippi. She also learned to play the piano when she was young. Following high school, she was awarded a scholarship at the prestigious Julliard School of Music in New York. In 1952 she won the starring role of Bess in the Broadway production of *Porgy and Bess.* In 1955 she became the first African American to sing opera on television. In 1966 the Metropolitan Opera opened at Lincoln Center in New York, and she starred in the opening evening production. She continued her career until 1985. Price gave her farewell performance at Lincoln Center. She sang her signature song from her role in Verdi's *Aida.*

James Cleveland
(1932–1991)
Gospel Singer, Minister, Musician

(JAMES recounts his career as a gospel artist.)

JAMES
I'm James Cleveland. I'm a Baptist minister, pianist, and arranger. I'm also the founder and director of the James Cleveland Choir. I wrote over four hundred gospel songs including, "Peace, Be Still" and "Everything Will Be Alright." I sold millions of records and received three Grammy Awards. I was the first gospel singer to have a star on Hollywood's Walk of Fame.

Riley "B. B." King
(1925–)
Blues Singer

(SPEAKER gives a brief history of B. B. King's blues singing career.)

SPEAKER
Riley King is more popularly known as B. B., or Blues Boy, King. He also has an equally famous guitar named Lucille. Some people call him the King of the Blues. B. B. King was born in Mississippi in 1925. His

early life was sad and hard. His mother died when he was only nine. King was left on his own and had to survive the best way he could. He did farm work and odd jobs for $15 a month. King only went to school every now and then. When he was around fourteen years old, he was reunited with his father. It was then that he learned to play the guitar.

King had hits on the R&B charts in the 1950s, but his music didn't reach mainstream America until the 1960s. Since then he's sold millions of records and performed before sold-out crowds around the world. A lot of new blues artists have come along since early pioneers like B. B. King. I'm sure it makes him and those other artists feel good to know that the blues is still appreciated.

The Jackson 5

(SPEAKER gives a brief history of the Jackson 5.)

SPEAKER
The Jackson 5 began their musical career in their hometown, Gary, Indiana. They competed in local talent shows and eventually became an opening act for Gladys Knight and the Pips in 1958. Jackie, Tito, Jermaine, Marlon, and Michael were the total entertainment package. They were singers, dancers, musicians, and choreographers.

In 1968 Bobby Taylor, an entertainer with Motown Records, sent a tape of the Jackson 5 to Motown's founder, Berry Gordy. He launched the group's career in 1969. Beginning in January 1970, the Jackson 5 boasted four number-one hits within a nine month period. The hits were "I Want You Back," "ABC," "The Love You Save," and "I'll Be There." The group recorded for Motown from 1969 to 1975. In 1976 they decided to sign with Epic Records; however, Jermaine chose to remain with Motown to begin a solo career. He was replaced by younger brother Randy, and they were renamed the Jacksons. In

1978 they recorded their biggest album, *Destiny*, with Epic Records. Although Michael remained a member of the Jacksons, he had begun recording solo albums. The Jacksons recorded two more albums with Epic: *Triumph* in 1980 and *Victory* in 1984. They began the *Victory* tour in 1984, which was Michael's last tour as a member of the Jacksons. Afterward, Michael went on to pursue his already successful solo career.

The Jackson 5 has been honored with awards both within and outside the music industry. In 1970, 1971, and 1972 they received the NAACP Image Award for Best Singing Group of the Year. In 1971 they won a Grammy Award for their song "ABC." Also in 1971 the city of Gary, Indiana, awarded them the keys to the city. In 1975 they were inducted into the Black Caucus as honorary members. Out of their many awards, possibly one of the greatest honors they received was their 1997 induction into the Rock and Roll Hall of Fame.

Michael Jackson
(1958–2009)
Pop Singer

*(*SPEAKER *details the prolific career of Michael Jackson.)*

SPEAKER
Michael Jackson was born in Gary, Indiana, into a musical family. This child star started performing at age five with his four older brothers. They later became known as the Jackson 5. When the siblings began their debut career for Motown in 1969, Michael was only eleven years old, but he immediately captivated audiences. It seems as though he was born to entertain.

Michael's impact on the entertainment industry and his history-making accomplishments are almost too numerous to document. He is among the few artists to leave a successful group and have a long history of individual success.

When Michael decided to launch his solo career, he became a legend and earned the title the King of Pop. Five of his solo albums—*Off the Wall, Thriller, Bad, Dangerous, and HIStory*—are ranked among the all-time top sellers. *Thriller* sold more than 70 million units worldwide; that is more than any album in music history. Singles from the *Thriller* album also sold more than 100 million copies, a feat that no other album has been able to accomplish to date.

It is estimated that Michael sold over 750 million records worldwide during his years as a performer. He has over five hundred awards and accomplishments, including thirteen Grammys, over fifty RIAA gold and platinum record certifications, and multiple NAACP Image Awards. He earned twenty Billboard Awards and twenty American Music Awards. He received the Soul Train Music Award four times and eight Rolling Stone Awards. Michael is one of the few artists to be inducted into the Rock and Roll Hall of Fame twice. Michael Jackson is the King of Pop.

Academy Award Winners for Music

(NARRATOR and ten speakers consecutively come to center stage and share African American Academy Award winners for music.)

NARRATOR
Black singers and musicians have had a presence in Hollywood since the early days of talking films. In the earliest films, African Americans typically had parts where they performed as a group. They sang Negro spirituals or work songs. Their songs often expressed sorrow after a tragedy and were set in a Southern atmosphere.

Later, Hollywood agents scouted northern nightclubs and theaters looking for talent. African Americans could now showcase their genius by performing some of their original music. These were usually bit parts in a nightclub setting. The roles provided them an opportunity to dress in fancy gowns, tuxedos, and suits. It showed the mainstream another side of their culture. The roles were more dignified than those in earlier films.

Times have changed, and African Americans have come a long way. They've moved up from bit musical parts to writing musical scores for feature films. The following speakers will highlight some of these musical geniuses and their Academy Award winning music. *(NARRATOR exits stage.)*

SPEAKER 1
In 1971 Isaac Hayes became the first African American to win an Academy Award for Best Music, Original Song. He won for the song "Theme from Shaft" from the movie *Shaft*.
(SPEAKER 1 moves to stage right.)

SPEAKER 2
In 1983 Irene Cara won an Academy Award for Best Music, Original Song for "Flashdance . . . What a Feeling" from the movie *Flashdance*.
(SPEAKER 2 moves to stage right.)

SPEAKER 3
Prince won an Academy Award for Best Music, Original Song Score for the film *Purple Rain* in 1984.
(SPEAKER 3 moves to stage right.)

SPEAKER 4
Stevie Wonder won an Academy Award for Best Music, Original Song for "I Just Called to Say I Love You" from the film *Woman in Red* in 1984.

(SPEAKER 4 *moves to stage right.*)

SPEAKER 5
Lionel Richie won an Academy Award for Best Music, Original Song for "Say You, Say Me" from the film *White Nights* in 1985.
(SPEAKER 5 *moves to stage right.*)

SPEAKER 6
Herbie Hancock won an Academy Award for Best Music, Original Score for the film *'Round Midnight* in 1986.
(SPEAKER 6 *moves to stage right.*)

SPEAKER 7
Willie D. Burton won an Academy Award for Best Sound for the film *Bird*, along with Les Fresholtz, Rick Alexander, and Vern Poore in 1988. Burton also won an individual Academy Award for Best Achievement in Sound Mixing for *Dreamgirls* in 2006.
(SPEAKER 7 *moves to stage right.*)

SPEAKER 8
Russell Williams II was the first African American to win two Academy Awards in the music category. He won Best Sound for the movie *Glory,* which he shared with Donald O. Mitchell, Gregg Rudloff, and Elliot Tyson in 1989. Williams won Best Sound again for the film *Dances with Wolves* along with Bill W. Benson, Jeffrey Perkins, and Gregory H. Watkins in 1990.
(SPEAKER 8 *moves to stage right.*)

SPEAKER 9
Quincy Jones was recognized for his musical contributions when the Academy honored him with the Jean Hersholt Humanitarian Award in 1995.
(SPEAKER 9 *moves to stage right.*)

SPEAKER 10
Jordan Houston, Cedric Coleman, and Paul Beauregard, also known as Three 6 Mafia, won an Academy Award for Best Music, Original Song for "It's Hard Out Here for a Pimp" from the movie *Hustle and Flow* in 2005.

(Speakers exit stage.)

A Viable Medium

Race Records

*(*SPEAKER *gives a brief history of race records.)*

SPEAKER
Race records were recorded on wax records that looked like this.
(Holds up a large wax phonograph record.)
Race records were divisions of record companies that sold music written and performed by African Americans. The music was also specifically marketed to the black community. Initially, race music was only recorded in Northern studios. Later, it was recorded in the segregated South in what were called field studios. These studios were typically hotel rooms, schools, and rental halls and the music was recorded on portable equipment. The microphones had to be kept on ice to avoid cracking, because they were sensitive to heat.

From 1927 to 1930 race records reached their peak. Blues and gospel were the biggest sellers and were produced at a rate of about ten per week. Unfortunately, the Great Depression forced the race record industry out of business. This ended the recording careers of many black musicians. However, during the brief time that race records existed, many unknown singers were able to break into the industry because of these companies. After the Depression, only a few were able to continue to record.

Black Swan Records

(SPEAKER *gives a brief history of Black Swan Records.*)

SPEAKER
In 1921 African American Henry Pace founded Black Swan Records. It was the first black-owned record company and produced race records. Pace advertised his label as "the only genuine colored records, others are only passing for colored." The label's artists included blues singers and balladeers, which were marketed to both poor and well-to-do African Americans. Black Swan Records' success, however, was short-lived. By 1924 the company had to close, because it couldn't compete with white-owned record labels, which had a growing interest in black performers.

Motown Records

(SPEAKER *gives a brief history of Berry Gordy's Motown Records.*)

SPEAKER
Berry Gordy was the founder of Motown Music. He was born and raised in Detroit, Michigan. He had a talent for music but didn't pursue it at first. Gordy had a brief career as a prizefighter. Next he got a job at a car factory. While there he operated a record store in his spare time and started writing songs. He entered a lot of contests but never won. In 1957 a dazzling singer named Jackie Wilson recorded a song Gordy wrote with his sister and a friend called "Sweet Petite." It was a success and launched Gordy and Wilson's careers. Soon other singers started recording Gordy's songs. It didn't take long for him to realize that every time one of his records was sold, he was only getting a small

percentage of the sale. The publishing company that owned Gordy's songs was getting the majority of the profit. He felt that this wasn't right, since he was the one who created the music.

In 1959 Gordy borrowed $700 from his family, rented an apartment, and set up a recording studio. That was the birth of Motown Records. He focused on new talents rather than the more well-known artists. Through these young performers, Gordy created the Motown sound, which became a stylistic legend in the music industry. By the 1970s the company amassed sales of over $10 million per year.

In 1972 Gordy moved the Motown headquarters to Los Angeles, California. He also began producing movies and television shows. In 1988 Gordy sold the company to MCA Records for $61 million. Motown became one of the most successful African American enterprises in the United States.

Def Jam

(SPEAKER *discusses the origin and importance of Def Jam to hip hop music and culture.)*

SPEAKER
Rick Rubin and Russell Simmons met in 1984 at a club in New York City. By 1984 both Russell Simmons and Rick Rubin had begun to make names for themselves in the hip hop community. Rubin had started Def Jam in his NYU dorm room and had produced T. La Rock and Jazzy J's song "It's Yours." Simmons was at the center of the budding hip hop industry. His company Rush Management had become the largest management company in hip hop. It managed multiple artists including Kurtis Blow, who had two RIAA gold singles: "Christmas Rappin'" and "The Breaks." Simmons was also working as a producer for his younger brother's group, Run-D.M.C., which had

celebrated rap's first RIAA gold album. *King of Rock,* their second album, had reached platinum status.

Rick Rubin and Russell Simmons combined their talents to coproduce Run-D.M.C.'s third album, *Raising Hell.* Simmons, Rubin, and Run-D.M.C. appreciated the rebellious attitude that both rap and rock had in common. Rubin used his connections to convince Aerosmith to collaborate with Run-D.M.C. for "Walk this Way." By the end of 1984, Simmons and Rubin had become partners for Def Jam; and in 1985 they signed a deal with CBS to be Def Jam's distributor.

As smaller rap recording labels were forced to close, Def Jam Recordings became the conduit for hip hop music and culture and the largest rap recording label in existence. It was home to the groups whose popularity forced mainstream America to play their music and recognize hip hop culture. Def Jam boasted artists like L.L. Cool J, Slick Rick, the Beastie Boys, Public Enemy, and Jay-Z. Def Jam was also linked with Simmons's company Rush Management, which represented many artists, including RUN D.M.C., Jazzy Jeff and the Fresh Prince, and Whodini.

By the early 1990s, Rubin and Simmons began to move in different directions creatively. Rubin began to migrate back to his rock roots and Simmons to his R&B roots. Eventually, Rubin moved to the West Coast where he started Def Jam America and focused on producing rock and roll artists. In 1999 Simmons sold Def Jam to PolyGram Records, and became the label's chairman. Today Def Jam is a part of Island Def Jam, which houses several labels. However, Def Jam Recordings remains a leader in the music industry and the home of many music stars and legends like Rihanna, Kanye West, Nas, the Roots, Ne-Yo, Chrisette Michele, L.L. Cool J., and Patti LaBelle. Def Jam has been on the cutting edge since its founding in 1984 and continues be a leader in the music industry over twenty-five years later.

ARTISTS AND PHOTOGRAPHERS

Edmonia Lewis
(1845–1890)
Sculptor

(EDMONIA explains what prompted her to become a sculptor.)

EDMONIA

My name is Edmonia Lewis and I'm a sculptor. Some people say I make stones talk. I don't know about all that, but I do enjoy my work. After college I moved to Boston to develop my talents further. Later, I moved to Rome, Italy, where I set up a studio.

I loved to sculpt people who helped bring slavery to an end. This perspective seen in my art was probably influenced by my struggle to help emancipate slaves. I was involved in the Underground Railroad and helped organize one of the earliest Negro regiments to fight in the Civil War. One of my most famous works is *Forever Free*. It portrays a black man with one of his fists clenched while the other hand is protecting his wife. I completed this sculpture in 1867 to represent emancipation.

Edward M. Bannister
(1828–1901)
Painter

(EDWARD shares the circumstances that motivated him to become a painter.)

EDWARD

My name is Edward Bannister. I was born in 1828 in Nova Scotia but later moved to Boston, Massachusetts. I was orphaned when I was young and supported myself by working a variety of menial jobs. I always loved to draw. I began sketching when I was ten years old. I took art lessons at the Arts Academy in Boston and the Lowell Institute. I was able to study with a renowned sculptor at Lowell but found it difficult to interact with the white students, because they ostracized me.

One day I read an article in an 1867 edition of the *New York Herald*. I couldn't believe my eyes. The article stated, "The Negro seems to have an appreciation of art while being manifestly unable to produce it." It was an insult! I knew that I—as a member of the Negro race—was more than capable of producing art, and was sure there were many other talented black artists.

In 1870 I relocated to Providence, Rhode Island. In 1876 my talents as a painter gained me an entry into the Centennial Exhibition that was held in Philadelphia. My painting *Under the Oaks* won the gold medal. The judges wanted to reconsider their decision when they learned I was a Negro, but the white competitors forced the judges to let their decision stand. Later that year, *Under the Oaks* sold for $1,500.

My following continued to grow after the Centennial Exhibition, and I secured a comfortable income. I specialized in landscape themes. My work can be seen at several universities and galleries throughout the United States. I proved that the Negro could produce art.

Henry Ossawa Tanner
(1859–1937)
Painter, Photographer

(HENRY highlights his achievements during his career as a painter.)

HENRY

I'm Henry O. Tanner. Some people regard me as the Dean of African American Art. When I was thirteen, I watched an artist take paint from tubes and his palette and form an image on his easel. I was intrigued. It inspired me to become a painter. I didn't realize at the time how difficult my life would be as an artist, especially a black artist. I studied until I became comfortable enough to send some of my paintings to New York publishers. I was disappointed, because most of them were returned. I finally sold my first painting for $40 then another one for $80.

As a young adult I expanded my horizons by traveling. I earned a modest living by selling my art and photography. I sold one of my photographs for $15, which I thought was a good price until I found out later that it was resold for $250. In 1879 I enrolled at the Pennsylvania Academy of Fine Arts. The faculty was open-minded, but I experienced a large degree of prejudice from my art peers. I decided to leave the academy and move to France. I studied at an academy in Paris and received a lot of encouragement from one of the leading French painters. I developed a unique style that highlighted the use of color, light, and symbolic mystical figures. Some of my works, such as the *Banjo Lesson* and the *Thankful Poor*, featured Negro subjects; but most of my works focused on biblical themes. Some of my most famous religious paintings are *Daniel and the Lion's Den,* the *Destruction of Sodom and Gommorah,* and the *Raising of Lazarus.* Later in my career, I sold paintings and worked as an art instructor at Clark University in Atlanta. I was very passionate about art and the plight of my people. I hope that my work helped black painters become recognized in the international art world.

James Van Der Zee
(1886–1983)
Photographer

(JAMES describes the focus of his photography during the Harlem Renaissance.)

JAMES

I'm James Van Der Zee. I documented the lives of black people during the Harlem Renaissance. In 1917 I opened a portrait studio on 135th Street in New York City. I earned a good living by taking original portraits and retouching them. I saw photography as an art. I used elaborate backdrops and soft-focus techniques to capture my subjects. My pictures presented a side of black life that was different from the negative stereotypes shown in white media advertisements and comic strips. I showed the black race for what it really was. I wanted others to appreciate the beauty and culture of this period in Harlem.

Richmond Barthe
(1901–1987)
Sculptor

(RICHMOND describes the focus of his works during his career as a sculptor.)

RICHMOND
My name is Richmond Barthe. I'm a sculptor. I wanted to attend college in my hometown in Mississippi, but I had to go to school in the North because of segregation laws. I attended the Art Institute of Chicago. I studied dance and incorporated a sense of movement and flow into my art. I created busts of numerable black Americans, but my preference was to focus on the sensitive nature of the racial problems that were going on at the time. One of my favorites was *Mother and Son*. It was a sculpture of a mother holding the body of her son, who had been lynched.

I also sculpted figures of black foreign heroes. My portrait of Haitian hero Toussaint L'Ouverture appears on the Haitian coin. My statues of Jean-Jacques Dessalines are displayed in Haiti also. I hoped my art would express the joys and sorrows of black people everywhere.

Gordon Parks
(1912–2006)
Photographer, Movie Director, Writer

(GORDON describes his life and career as a photographer.)

GORDON
I'm Gordon Parks. Some people say I'm a jack-of-all-trades. I guess that's because I've done so many things during my career. I'll tell you about some of my accomplishments, if you promise not to think I'm bragging. I don't boast when talking about myself. Rather, I like to use my life as an example of what can be achieved despite poverty, hardships, and discrimination.

I learned to turn the anger and hatred from my youth into something constructive. I was the youngest of fifteen children. My mother died when I was a teenager. I did various jobs to support myself. In 1938, when I was about twenty-five, I purchased a camera for $7.50 and became a freelance photo journalist. Three years later, I received a prestigious award for photography. In 1942 I became the first African American to work for the Farm Security Agency, or FSA. The agency was established to document poverty in the United States. I took pictures of impoverished people living in our nation's capital.

In 1943 the Office of War Information included the FSA in its agency. I was assigned to cover the 332nd Fighter Group of the Tuskegee Airmen. This all-black squadron was a bomber escort unit during World War II. Following that assignment, I became a fashion photographer for *Vogue* magazine. I was the first African American photographer to work for *Vogue*. In 1948 I became the first African American to work for *Life* magazine. I was assigned a photo documentary of gang life in Harlem. My other work in the United States included photographing poverty in Harlem, crime in Chicago, Dr. Martin Luther King Jr., the civil rights movement, Muhammad Ali, and the Black Panther Party.

In 1961 my documentaries depicting poverty took me on assignment to Brazil, where I photographed the slums of Rio de Janeiro. I featured twelve-year-old Falvio da Silva, who was dying of asthma. My pictures of Falvio and his family's poverty were so shocking that the story attracted international attention. The concern for this family resulted in them receiving medical treatment, gifts, and a new home.

My career also included music. I wrote a piano concerto while living in Paris, France, and the music for a ballet about Dr. King. I was also an author and wrote twelve books. My first book, *The Learning Tree,* was published in 1963. It was later made into a movie, which I directed. This made me the first African American to direct a full-length film. I directed several other films, including *Shaft* and *Shaft's Big Score.*

When I've been asked about my view on life, I've said this to people,
"I've liked being a stranger to failure since I was a young man
and I still feel that way. I'm still occupied with survival, still very
single-minded about keeping my life moving, but not for fame or
fortune."

Jacob Lawrence
(1917–2000)
Painter

(JACOB highlights his contributions to the field of art.)

JACOB

I love being an artist. Do you like to paint? I'm Jacob Lawrence.
Some people say I'm the most popular African American artist of
the twentieth century. I think what makes me unique as a black artist
is that most of my art teachers were black, and I grew up in black
neighborhoods. I have a strong interest in black history, and many of
my pictures and panels reflect the history and everyday lives of African
Americans. I painted one of my best-known works in the early 1940s.
It was called the *Migration of the Negro.* In this series I portrayed black
Americans migrating from the rural South to the industrial cities of the
North in search of a better life. I became the first African American
artist to have works displayed by a major gallery, which was the
Downtown Gallery in New York City.

When was the last time you visited an art gallery? If you've never been
to one, you're missing something special. If you haven't been lately,
hurry back. I would consider it a special honor if you saw some of my
paintings.

Annie Lee
(1935–)
Painter

(SPEAKER highlights Annie Lee's success as an artist.)

SPEAKER

Annie Lee's art is known for its humor, faceless characters, and depictions of African American life. Annie Lee grew up on the Southside of Chicago, where she lived with her mother and older brother. Lee's artistic skills were apparent at an early age. Her mother saved her childhood drawings and motivated her to continue. However, her mother was also a practical person. She did not see art as a practical career. Lee must have shared those sentiments, because when she was seventeen, she turned down a full scholarship to study art at Northwestern University. Instead she enrolled in a clerical school with the goal of starting a career in government. She also wanted to be a wife and mother.

Lee had two short-term marriages. Her first husband died when he was in his early twenties, and her second marriage ended in divorce. She found herself a young single parent with two small children. She loved to paint, but finances wouldn't allow her to make painting her priority; however, she made time to pursue it as a hobby. Lee also juggled her schedule to take college courses at night. She earned both a bachelor's and master's degree.

When a long-time friend of Lee saw her artwork, he was so impressed that he bought some of her art for his gallery. The gallery's visitors loved what they saw. Being a good friend and a good businessman, he offered her a private exhibition. The exhibit was so successful that every piece of her art sold.

Lee also began doing in-home art shows after a woman she met on a train saw her portfolio. The lady convinced her employer to present some of Annie Lee's work for his company's art show parties. Once Lee's work was exposed to the public, her art became an instant sensation. The requests were so huge that she deliberately left the faces blank as a time saver.

Annie Lee wanted the security of a nine-to-five job, but she still dreamed of becoming a professional painter. Unfortunately in December 1996, her twenty-eight-year-old son was killed in an automobile accident. It was at this point that she made the decision to make art her life's work. She found that painting was a form of therapy, because it kept her mind focused. This helped her through her period of grief.

Lee's business evolved from a mail-order enterprise to a gallery of her own. It was called Annie Lee and Friends. It wasn't long before the gallery proved too small. Annie Lee and Friends is now located in an 8,000 square foot gallery and business complex for the sale and shipping of her artwork.

Annie Lee's art has expanded also. Her work features over twenty-five categories, including paintings and reproductions, calendars, figurines, clocks, and dolls. Her products can be purchased on the internet and in over two thousand galleries, malls, and private stores across the country.

EDUCATION

The Spirit of African American Education

James Meredith accompanied by U.S. Marshalls while walking to class

(SPEAKER challenges African American students to honor their ancestors' struggles to receive an education.)

SPEAKER
(Wearing a graduation robe; turns to audience.)
I am the spirit of African American education. I represent generations of black people who sacrificed and struggled to achieve the dream of a quality education. I came to challenge you today. I challenge you to have perfect attendance. I challenge you to make the honor roll. I challenge you to never get suspended. I challenge you to respect all your teachers, school personnel, and your classmates, because they deserve to learn.
(Pause)
I see some of you out there laughing and rolling your eyes. Do you think I'm asking too much? Do you think I'm asking the impossible? If that's what you're thinking, listen to me while I give you a little history on the education of African Americans in the United States.

Prior to the end of the Civil War in 1865, it was illegal for black people to learn to read and write in the South. Even in the North, some of the schools were segregated or wouldn't provide a school for black children. Some Northern schools were destroyed, and their teachers were threatened for trying to teach black pupils.

During the Reconstruction period, which followed the Civil War, hundreds of churches and private philanthropists in the North sent teachers to the South, built schools, and established colleges for African Americans. It was the first opportunity for thousands of former enslaved children to receive an education.

After Reconstruction, the federal government pulled the army troops from the South. Life for black people became more harsh and dangerous. Many children remained illiterate or had little education, because they had to drop out at an early age to help support their families.

Black schools in the South were inferior, overcrowded, and had limited resources. Some towns wouldn't even provide a high school for black students. Often black children had to walk several miles, because they didn't have school buses. Yet Southern states justified this by claiming schools were equal even though they were segregated. Schools remained in this unfair condition until 1954, when the U.S. Supreme Court ruled that separate schools were illegal in the *Brown v. Board of Education* case.

Even though schools were ordered to desegregate, many towns dragged their feet as long as possible to avoid integration. Prince Edward County, Virginia for example, closed all its schools for five years to avoid integration. In 1964 the Supreme Court ordered their schools to reopen.

Suppose you had to walk to school every day when a school bus with white children passed right by you? What if you had to stick together like the Little Rock Nine, who the president had to send federal troops to protect when they integrated Central High School in Little Rock, Arkansas, in 1957?

Imagine being six-year-old Ruby Bridges, the only African American child in her school in 1960. She had to have federal troops escort her to school every day, because the other children's parents threatened her with bodily harm. Could you man up like James Meredith, an Air Force veteran who served his country, yet had to face danger every day after he enrolled in the University of Mississippi in 1962? Could you survive the campus riots like he did and endure the violence that got so bad that two people were killed? Would you be able to tolerate these extreme acts of hatred just because you were black and wanted an education?

And all I ask is for you to accept the easy challenges of today. Can you do it? Will you do it? You not only owe it to yourself, you owe it to those who endured the unimaginable, so you could be entitled to the same high standard of education afforded to everyone else.

The Fisk Jubilee Singers

Characters:
MELINDA, *female fictional character, undergraduate student and a member of the college choir*
TALIA, *female fictional character, undergraduate student and a member of the college choir*
Costumes:
Present-day casual attire
Props:
A Fisk Jubilee Singers brochure

(MELINDA *and* TALIA *discuss the Fisk Jubilee Singers' mission to save their college.)*

MELINDA

Hi Talia, what are you doing here so early?

TALIA

You know me; I'd rather be early than late. What are you doing here early? You're a last-minute person.

MELINDA

I wanted to meet with Mrs. McArthur. She's supposed to tell us about the Fisk Jubilee Singers. She's planning to invite them to the school to put on a concert. I've been reading their history. Do you know they saved their college, Fisk School in Nashville, Tennessee, when they were only students? Look at this brochure. It has a history of their group.
(Hands her the brochure.)

TALIA

They weren't just students; they were also singers like us. It says the original nine performers were organized in 1866 by George White, who was a Freedman Bureau official. The school was in debt and needed money to remain in existence. Eight of the nine students were former slaves, so they sang spirituals that they learned on the plantations. In 1871 the troupe began traveling.
(Hands the brochure back to MELINDA.*)*

MELINDA

Oh, listen to this. It says that at first white audiences didn't know how to receive them. They were used to blackface entertainment and some of them, especially in the North, hadn't been exposed to spirituals. Apparently the Jubilee Singers were the first musical group to make spirituals popular among white people. It even says that at times the group got discouraged. But that's how they got their name. Mr. White decided to name them Jubilee after a passage in the Bible.

TALIA

They continued traveling, and before long they were well received everywhere they performed. They raised $25,000, which was enough to pay off the school's existing debts and purchase land for the new school.

MELINDA

The Fisk Jubilee singers still perform all over the world. Tell me Talia, do you think we could save our college if the university needed us to raise money?

TALIA

I think so. We just have to step out on faith like they did. They set the standard for motivating young people by showing that age didn't matter. They proved that when given a challenge, you're never too young to be a hero.

(End Scene.)

Booker T. Washington
(1856–1915)
Educator

(BOOKER explains his role in founding the Tuskegee Institute.)

BOOKER

I was nine years old when the Civil War ended. My family moved to West Virginia after the war. We considered ourselves blessed because although we were poor, we were free. As a child, I had to work to help support my family. My name is Booker T. Washington, and like you, I wanted a good education. I knew my family needed my help, so every morning I would begin my workday at 4:00 a.m. then go to school. At night I would study. When I was fourteen, I traveled by foot from West Virginia to Hampton Institute in Virginia to enroll into college.

The school's founder, General Armstrong, made a strong impression on me. He believed manual labor promoted honesty, discipline, and intelligence. I later became a teacher and taught Indian children at the Hampton Normal School. In 1881 the state of Alabama decided to establish a training school for Negroes. White leaders wanted to hire an older white man to head the school, but the principal at Hampton Institute persuaded them to hire me. I carried Armstrong's concepts of manual labor with me to Alabama. I was twenty-five years old when I was commissioned as principal of the Tuskegee Institute. I was given only $2,000 to establish the school. The money was to be used for teachers' salaries. No money was allocated for books, supplies, land, or buildings. I started by locating a place to hold classes. I raised money to buy land for the school. I persuaded white businessmen to donate funds to support us. I found a building, but it was so raggedy that a student had to hold an umbrella over my head whenever it rained.

I recruited some of the best Negro teachers in the country, including George Washington Carver. The teachers and freshman students built the first buildings and provided their own food. By 1888 Tuskegee Institute owned 540 acres of land and had enrolled four hundred students. I established my school's priority on vocational skills rather than traditional intellectual pursuits. I realized that most former slaves only knew the trades they had learned during slavery. I knew those trades would keep them dependent on white landowners and in poverty.

My philosophy was that in order to be totally free black people had to own property. Owning property would give them power and put them in their rightful place in society. It would also earn them voting rights. I admit my philosophy was controversial to some of the other Negro leaders, but I always did what I thought was best for the survival of my people in the South and my school.

Mary McLeod Bethune
(1875–1955)
Educator, Political Advisor

Mary McLeod Bethune

(MARY shares her passion for educating African Americans.)

MARY

My name is Mary McLeod Bethune. I have been an advisor to five U.S. presidents and held high offices in several national organizations. I fought to help improve the lives of Negroes through self-help programs. These things influenced my first love, which was teaching. I was born in Mayesville, South Carolina. I was the fifteenth of the seventeen children born to my parents. They were former slaves and became farmers. My family was very poor. I had to work during most of my childhood. I picked cotton and took in laundry to aid my family. I didn't use poverty as an excuse for not succeeding in life. I was determined to get an education. I walked five miles to and from school each day for six years. At night I would teach my sisters and brothers what I had learned that day. When I attended college, one of my mentors taught us to believe in ourselves. She insisted that we believe we were intelligent, moral, and upright human beings.

In 1896 I attended a conference for black educators at Tuskegee Institute. I was impressed by the way Booker T. Washington raised money by petitioning donations from wealthy benefactors. His success influenced me to use this same technique when I moved to Daytona, Florida. With faith in a higher power and $1.50, I established the Daytona Normal and Industrial School for Negro Girls. Tuition was $0.50 a week. I sold sweet potato pies and received donations to keep my school going. I only had five girls when I opened, but within two years 250 students had enrolled. My normal school later became Bethune Cookman College. I stand before you with my head held high, because my historically black college is still educating students today.

I want all black people, especially children and women, to have self-respect, dignity, and increased opportunities in life. I never want my race to become disillusioned. I leave these words of encouragement to them: "The Negro's growth will be great in the years to come. Yesterday, our ancestors endured the degradation of slavery, yet they retained their dignity. Today, we direct our economic and political strength toward winning a more abundant and secure life. Tomorrow, a new Negro, unhindered by race taboos and shackles, will benefit from more than 330 years of ceaseless striving and struggle. Theirs will be a better world. This I believe with all my heart. I leave you love . . . I leave you hope . . . I leave you a thirst for education . . . I leave you a responsibility to our young people."

Linda Brown
(1943–)
Elementary Student Integrationist

(SPEAKER explains Linda Brown's role in desegregation.)

SPEAKER

Schools in the South were segregated in every town
But America changed, thanks to Linda Brown
Everyone knew there were too many flaws
In the separate but equal Jim Crow Laws
Black families had long realized
Their schools weren't as nice and lacked supplies
White parents refused to change the situation
They supported separate schools in education
Black citizens in Topeka, Kansas began to insist
That they had taken enough of this
A change is what Linda's parents wanted to see
Her father got in touch with the NAACP
Thurgood Marshall was sent to give legal support
He fought Linda's case all the way to the U.S. Supreme Court
The landmark decision came on May 17, 1954
The Court ruled schools couldn't be segregated anymore

The Little Rock Nine

The Little Rock Nine

(Nine speakers consecutively come to center stage and recount Central High's integration.)

SPEAKER 1

The U.S. Supreme Court ruled against segregation in public schools in 1954, but some towns in the South refused to obey the Court's order.

(SPEAKER 1 *moves to stage right.*)

SPEAKER 2
School officials in Little Rock, Arkansas, finally planned to
desegregate the local high school in 1957.
(SPEAKER 2 *moves to stage right.*)

SPEAKER 3
Seventy-five African American students registered to attend Central
High, which was the all-white high school. However, the school board
cut the number down to twenty-five, but only nine enrolled. They
became known as the Little Rock Nine.
(SPEAKER 3 *moves to stage right.*)

SPEAKER 4
Governor Faubus didn't believe in integration. He said, "blood will
run in the streets" if the school integrated. He also announced that
he couldn't guarantee the black students' safety, which seemed to
encourage violence.
(SPEAKER 4 *moves to stage right.*)

SPEAKER 5
He sent 250 National Guard soldiers to keep the black students from
entering the school. The NAACP had to get the federal district court to
order that the integration of Central High continue.
(SPEAKER 5 *moves to stage right.*)

SPEAKER 6
It was a horrible time. A mob of over a thousand angry white people
gathered around the school grounds; some even broke into the school
trying to get to the black students. They were often spat on, tripped,
and called the "n" word.
(SPEAKER 6 *moves to stage right.*)

SPEAKER 7

Things got so bad that President Eisenhower had to send 350
paratroopers from the 101st Airborne Division of the U.S. Army
to protect the black students. Everybody in the African American
community was glad to see the federal troops, especially the Little
Rock Nine.
(SPEAKER 7 moves to stage right.)

SPEAKER 8

People around the world who saw the students going to school every
day hailed them as being brave. Yes, they were brave and determined.
Would you be brave enough to go to school every day in that kind of
situation?
(SPEAKER 8 moves to stage right.)

SPEAKER 9

The Little Rock Nine proved that there is more than one way to fight
your enemy. They risked their lives to pave the way for other African
American students to be able to receive an equal education. I hope you
appreciate their sacrifice.
(SPEAKER 9 moves to stage right.)

SPEAKER 1

The names of the brave Little Rock Nine are: Minniejean Brown

SPEAKER 2

Gloria Ray

SPEAKER 3

Elizabeth Eckford

SPEAKER 4

Terrence Roberts

SPEAKER 5
Jefferson Thomas

SPEAKER 6
Ernest Green

SPEAKER 7
Thelma Mothershed

SPEAKER 8
Carlotta Walls

SPEAKER 9
Melba Pattillo

(Speakers exit stage.)

Ruby Bridges
(1954–)
Elementary Student Integrationist

(SPEAKER describes the role of six-year-old Ruby Bridges in school desegregation.)

SPEAKER
When Ruby Bridges attended school in New Orleans
She was discriminated against and treated mean
She was the only black child in her school all year long
But six-year-old Ruby remained valiant and strong

Federal marshals protected her so that angry mobs couldn't reach her
Only one person in her school would agree to teach her
She went to school each day with her head held high
And ignored the bad names and threats as she passed by
Just like her name Bridges, she helped bridge the gap in education
This courageous little girl helped end school segregation

RELIGION AND THE BLACK CHURCH

Denominations and Religions

Church and Religion

(SPEAKER 1, SPEAKER 2, SPEAKER 3, SPEAKER 4, *and* SPEAKER 5 *consecutively come to center stage and explain the evolution of African Americans and religion in America.)*

SPEAKER 1
Religion and the church have always been a dominant and influential factor in the lives of African Americans. From the early days of slavery when Christianity was forced on the kidnapped Africans, to their gradual acceptance of European religion, faith in God was their only source of endurance.
(SPEAKER 1 *moves to stage right.)*

SPEAKER 2
Religion in the antebellum South primarily consisted of slaves listening to sermons delivered by their masters' ministers. If a black preacher was allowed to speak, he was only able to do so if a white person was present to monitor the sermon. The slaves remedied this by escaping at night into the woods to hold services in what they called hush harbors. In 1773 David George, a slave, became the pastor of the first known black church in America

(SPEAKER 2 *moves to stage right.*)

SPEAKER 3

By the end of the Civil War, many African Americans began to seek independence from white congregations. They had grown tired of limited memberships and forced segregation within the churches. Others wanted to worship in a style that was less formal and have a pastor who better understood their needs. By 1900 independent all-black churches and denominations began to appear throughout the United States. These sects primarily existed in the Methodist, Baptist, and Pentecostal denominations. Also, African Americans began to create new religions of their own. By the mid-1900s, religions like the Nation of Islam provided both a social and spiritual voice for the race. (SPEAKER 3 *moves to stage right.*)

SPEAKER 4

Regardless of religious affiliation, traces in history reflect the importance of the church in African American culture. Prior to the end of the Civil War, many Northern black churches served as Underground Railroad stations. During the Great Migration, when thousands of African Americans left the South, the black church helped many adjust to the urban North. They also provided food and other charities to the impoverished new arrivals. After the Civil War, African American Christian churches—either solely or in conjunction with white affiliates—quickly began to establish schools and colleges for black students in the former Confederate states. (SPEAKER 4 *moves to stage right.*)

SPEAKER 5

Today most churches and religions are growing with the needs of black congregations and communities. Churches have progressed from meeting in hush harbors to meeting in mega churches that have three thousand or more members. Providing day care centers, health awareness programs, investing in real estate, and establishing nursing homes for the elderly are just a few of the new roles that the black sects have undertaken. The black church continues to be an essential institution in African American society.

(Speakers exit stage.)

Congregationalists

*(*SPEAKER *describes the role of Congregationalists.)*

SPEAKER
Dixwell Church was founded in New Haven, Connecticut, in 1820. It was the first all-black Congregationalist church. Congregationalists highly valued education. After the Civil War, they founded or supported five hundred black schools and colleges. Five of those colleges are still in existence.

Colored Methodist Protestant Church

*(*SPEAKER *gives a brief history of the Colored Methodist Protestant Church's founding.)*

SPEAKER
The Colored Methodist Protestant Church was formed in Elkin, Maryland, in 1840. They separated from the white Methodist Episcopal Church. The Colored Methodist Protestant Church was structured on the same core beliefs as the Methodist Protestant Church.

United American Free Will Baptist Church

(SPEAKER gives a brief history of the United American Free Will Baptist Church.)

SPEAKER
In 1867 African Americans established Shady Grove Free Will Baptist Church in North Carolina when they formed a separate congregation from the white governing body. It was the first all-black church within the United American Free Will Baptist Church denomination. It was also the first independent United American Free Will Baptist church in America.

In 1901 the first general conference of the United Free Will Baptists was formed. In 1968 there was a split in the conference. As a result, the United American Baptist Conference Inc. was created. It is the smaller of the two organizations. The United American Free Will Baptist Conference Inc. is headquartered in Lakeland, Florida, and Dr. Henry J. Rodman serves as general bishop.

Christian Methodist Episcopal Church

(SPEAKER gives a brief history of the CME Church's founding.)

SPEAKER
There were a number of African Americans in the South who wanted to remain in the Methodist denomination after the Civil War. But they wanted independence from white Methodist control and didn't want to join the already established African Methodist Episcopal or African Methodist Episcopal Zion churches.

On December 16, 1870, forty-one African American men met in Jackson, Tennessee, to petition the Methodist Episcopal South for the right to establish a colored branch of the denomination. On December 20, the delegation adopted the Methodist South's Book of Discipline. On December 21, William Miles from Kentucky and Richard Vanderhorst from Georgia were elected as bishops. This was the beginning of the Colored Methodist Episcopal Church. In 1954 the church changed its name to the Christian Methodist Episcopal Church, or the CME Church. The CME Church is the third largest of the African American Methodist denominations.

The Reformed Methodist Union Episcopal Church

(SPEAKER *recounts the Reformed Methodist Union Episcopal Church's founding.*)

SPEAKER
The Reformed Methodist Union Episcopal Church consecrated their first bishop in 1885. They withdrew from the African Methodist Church. They consist of a small body of churches, and as of 1923 they have been mainly located in South Carolina and Georgia.

United Holy Church of America Inc.

(SPEAKER *gives a brief history of the United Holy Church of America Inc.*)

SPEAKER
The United Holy Church of America Inc. is a predominantly African American Pentecostal Holiness Christian denomination. It was established as an outgrowth of a revival near Raleigh, North Carolina, in 1886. Originally, it was called the Holy Church of North Carolina. In 1916 the name was changed and it became known as the United Holy Church of America. It is the oldest black Pentecostal Church in the United States.

Black Jews

(SPEAKER describes the origin and doctrine of the Black Jews.)

SPEAKER
There are several groups of black Jews in the United States. The earliest group seems to have been the Church of God and Saints in Christ, which was founded in 1896 in Lawrence, Kansas, by William Crowdy. Today it is also probably the largest of the groups, having over two hundred churches. Another group, the Church of God, was founded in Philadelphia by Prophet F. S. Cherry. Between 1919 and 1920, a Nigerian-born man called Rabbi Matthew founded the Commandment Keepers in Harlem, New York. Some black Jews assert that they are descendants from the Falasha Jews of Ethiopia. The commonality of their doctrine is a little more than a dislike for Christianity and a love for the Old Testament. Only a few orthodox rabbis recognize black Jews.

Primitive Baptists

(SPEAKER explains the founding and principles of the Primitive Baptists.)

SPEAKER
African Americans, many of whom spent most of their lives as slaves, began to separate themselves from the white Primitive Baptists shortly after the end of the Civil War in 1865. The black denomination continued to grow in membership, and the Reverend C. F. Sams of Key West, Florida, initiated the plans for a national movement. On July 17, 1907, the National Meeting of Colored Primitive Baptists of America had its first meeting. The meeting was held in Huntsville, Alabama, and hosted by Saint Bartley Primitive Baptist Church. The attending members voted unanimously for a temporary organization, and on July

19, 1907, the organization became permanent. The black Primitive Baptist churches continue to thrive today.

Fire Baptized Holiness Church of God of the Americas

(SPEAKER *establishes the founding and beliefs of the Fire Baptized Holiness Church of God of the Americas.)*

SPEAKER
The Fire Baptized Holiness Church of God of the Americas is of the Pentecostal denomination. It was established in 1908 as the Colored Fire Baptized Holiness Church when the black members broke away from the integrated Fire Baptized Church, which was established in 1898. The church changed its name in 1926 to the Fire Baptized Holiness Church of God of the Americas.

The logos on their flag—the cross, dove, and fire—express much of their beliefs. The cross is called "the Cross of Triumph," which signifies Christ's victory over sin and death and the provision of salvation. The dove signifies innocence, purity, and the Holy Spirit. The flame represents the means by which God often appeared to man biblically and emphasizes God's cleansing power and relationship to mankind.

The Oneness Pentecostal Movement

(SPEAKER *defines the Oneness Pentecostal doctrine.)*

SPEAKER
The Oneness Pentecostal movement began in 1913 in Los Angeles, California. The Oneness Pentecostals don't believe that the Father, the Son, and the Holy Spirit—or the Trinity—are three separate beings. They teach that there is one God who reveals himself in three different

forms: God the Father, God the Son—who is Jesus—and God the Holy Spirit. Therefore, Jesus is fully God. Oneness Pentecostals only baptize in the name of Jesus.

Apostolic Overcoming Holy Church of God

(SPEAKER *explains the Apostolic Overcoming Holy Church of God's doctrine.*)

SPEAKER
The Apostolic Overcoming Holy Church of God was incorporated in Alabama in 1919. It is a Pentecostal church and was originally established as the Ethiopian Overcoming Holy Church. Their doctrine stresses holiness, sanctification, and the power of divine healing.

The Church of Our Lord Jesus Christ of the Apostolic Faith

(SPEAKER *defines the doctrine of the Church of Our Lord Jesus Christ of the Apostolic Faith.*)

SPEAKER
The Church of Our Lord Jesus Christ of the Apostolic Faith is a Oneness Pentecostal church. It is also known as the Church of Our Lord Jesus Christ. It was founded in 1919 by Robert C. Lawson, who claimed to have received salvation by the Holy Spirit in 1913.

The United House of Prayer for All People

(SPEAKER *gives the origin of the United House of Prayer for All People.*)

SPEAKER

The United House of Prayer for All People is also known as the United House of Prayer for All People of the Church on the Rock of the Apostolic Faith. It is of the Pentecostal Holiness denomination. It was founded in Massachusetts in 1919 by Charles Manuel Grace, who was born in Brava in the Cape Verde Islands. Bishop Grace, also known as Sweet Daddy Grace, built the church himself. It is particularly known for its shout bands. The church music for these bands is mostly brass and predominantly trombone based. The music is inspired by jazz, blues, Dixieland gospel, and old-time spirituals.

African Orthodox Church

(SPEAKER briefly recounts the African Orthodox Church's origin.)

SPEAKER

The African Orthodox Church was founded by Archbishop George McGuire, who was a former minister in the Protestant Episcopal Church. He was also a chaplain for Marcus Garvey's Universal Negro Improvement Association, but Garvey opposed his efforts to establish a new denomination. However, in 1921 McGuire founded the African Orthodox Church anyway. Their doctrine adheres to an orthodox confession of faith. The Orthodox Church is an independent body of worshippers.

Mt. Sinai Holy Church of America Inc.

(SPEAKER gives a brief history of the founding of Mt. Sinai Holy Church of America Inc.)

SPEAKER

Mt. Sinai Holy Church of America was established in the Pentecostal tradition and is Episcopalian in governance. It consists of approximately 130 congregations in four states and four countries with over eight thousand members. It is headquartered in Philadelphia, Pennsylvania. It is unique, because it is one of the few—if not the only—church organization established by a female. It was founded by Ida B. Robinson in 1924. Mother Robinson was converted as a teenager in Florida and later moved to Philadelphia with her husband. She began street evangelism in Philadelphia under the auspices of the United Holy Church of America. She was installed as a pastor of Mt. Olive Holy Temple, which is a small mission affiliated with the United Holy Church.

While fasting and praying for ten days in 1924, she stated that she received a revelation from God. She believed the Holy Spirit spoke to her and said, "Come out on Mount Sinai." She interpreted this as God calling to her. On May 20, 1924, she was granted a charter for her church under the name Mt. Sinai Holy Church of America. On April 20, 1946, she died in Winter Haven, Florida, while visiting her churches in that state.

Spiritual Israel Church and Its Army

(SPEAKER *highlights SICIA's founding and beliefs.*)

SPEAKER
The Spiritual Israel Church and Its Army, or SICIA, is a Christian spiritual church that emerged from the Church of God in David. It was founded in Alabama in the mid-1920s by Bishop Derks Field. When Bishop Field died, W. D. Dickson took over leadership and changed the name to its current title. The Spiritual Israel Church and Its Army believes that Adam, Noah, Moses, and Jesus were all black men. The members are called Israelites, not Israelis. The head of the church holds the title of King of Israel within the church. There are over twenty-five

SICIA temples in the United States. They are mostly located in urban areas.

The Nation of Islam

(SPEAKER briefly highlights the Nation of Islam's history and beliefs.)

SPEAKER
Wallace Fard Muhammad, who also used the name Wallace D. Fard, founded the religious group called the Lost-Found Nation of Islam. The Lost-Found Nation of Islam later became known as the Nation of Islam, or the Black Muslims. In 1930 Master Fard, as he is called within the Nation of Islam community, established his first mosque in Detroit, Michigan.

Fard's exact identity, date of birth, and date of death has aroused speculation and rumors; however, those in the Nation of Islam recognize his birth year as 1877. In 1934 he disappeared and was never heard from again. But during his three years as founder of the Nation of Islam, Master Fard was a major influence and leader in the religious lives of non-Christian African Americans.

Fard's ideology combined his theories with traditional Islam. He believed that black people were naturally divine and created by Allah from the dark substance of space. He also believed that Earth's original people were black, that Christianity was the religion of slave owners who forced their doctrine on enslaved people, and that Armageddon was impending. He established a temple, a newspaper, the University of Islam, the Muslim Girls Training Class, and the Fruit of Islam, which is a group of male security guards.

Members of the Nation of Islam assume Arabic names to replace their birth names, or what they consider their slave names. They are required to dress modestly and to abstain from alcohol, drugs, and tobacco. They also believe in and promote self-sufficiency, economic development, and learning more about the black race.

Elijah Poole, who later changed his name to Elijah Muhammad, became the new leader of the Nation of Islam after Fard disappeared in 1934. He was one of Fard's first followers. Muhammad preached, "Allah, came to us from the Holy City of Mecca, Arabia, in 1930." He believed that Master Fard is the Mahdi and the true and living God. In the Nation of Islam his birth date is celebrated as Savior's Day.

Peace Mission Movement

(SPEAKER describes the role of the Peace Mission Movement.)

SPEAKER
The Peace Mission Movement was one of the alternative black religions. It was started by George Baker, who changed his name to Father Divine. He eventually settled in Harlem where his mission prospered. He acquired property, which he called heavens. Father Divine provided housing and jobs for his followers. Hundreds of people flocked to him for spiritual guidance and physical and mental healing.

Antioch Association of Metaphysical Science

(SPEAKER establishes the founding of the first predominantly black Antioch Association of Metaphysical Science.)

SPEAKER
In 1932 the first predominantly African American Antioch Association of Metaphysical Science was founded in Detroit, Michigan, by H.

Lewis Johnson. The church was founded on the Christian Science background and believes in healing through mental power.

The Church of the Lord Jesus Christ

(SPEAKER defines the founding of the Church of the Lord Jesus Christ.)

SPEAKER
The Church of the Lord Jesus Christ was founded by Bishop Sherrod C. Johnson in 1933. It is of the Apostolic faith and has congregations throughout the United States and internationally.

Bible Way Church of Our Lord Jesus Christ World-Wide Inc.

(SPEAKER establishes the founding and principles of Bible Way Church of Our Lord Jesus Christ World-Wide Inc.)

SPEAKER
The Bible Way Church of Our Lord Jesus Christ World-Wide Inc. is a member of the African American Pentecostal denomination. It was founded in 1957 in Washington, D.C., by Smallwood Edmond Williams. Williams became the leader of Bible Way when a group of followers withdrew from the Church of Our Lord Jesus Christ of the Apostolic Faith, or COOLJC. After Bishop Williams's death in 1991 there was a split in the organization, which resulted in two organizations called Bible Way Church of Our Lord Jesus Christ World-Wide. One is headquartered in Brooklyn, New York, and the other is headquartered in Baltimore, Maryland. Both organizations' doctrines emphasize the following principles: (1) the inspiration of the Bible as the word of God, (2) the baptism of the Holy Spirit with

evidence of speaking in tongues, (3) salvation as the only possible way to Jesus Christ, (4) the second coming of Christ, (5) the final judgment of the dead, and (6) the establishment of a new earth and heaven.

Fundamental Baptist Fellowship Association

(SPEAKER gives a brief history of the FBFA.)

SPEAKER
The Fundamental Baptist Fellowship Association, or FBFA, is an association of independent fundamentalist African American Baptist churches. It was established in 1962 by Reverend Richard C. Mattox in Cleveland, Ohio. Each congregation is independent and autonomous. It provides fundamental black Baptist churches a means of fellowship in areas like foreign missions and evangelism.

United Church of Jesus Christ for All People

(SPEAKER explains the doctrine of the United Church of Jesus Christ for All People.)

SPEAKER
The United Church of Jesus Christ for All People was founded in 1958 by Frederick J. Eikerenkotter II, more popularly known as Reverend Ike. Reverend Ike was a very colorful nontraditional preacher. He has been both criticized and praised for his Prosperity Now religious philosophy. His self-image psychology, which is still practiced, intends "to motivate people into the kind of positive thinking and faith and interaction, which produces good health, healing, joy, love, success, prosperity, good fortune, and more money."

Apostolic Assemblies of Christ Inc.

*(*SPEAKER *defines the founding of the Apostolic Assemblies of Christ Inc.)*

SPEAKER
The Apostolic Assemblies of Christ Inc. was organized in 1970 by George Marshall Boone, a former bishop in the Pentecostal church. It is of the Oneness Pentecostal faith. Its doctrine holds that repentance, water baptism in the name of Jesus Christ by immersion, and Holy Spirit baptism with the evidence of speaking in tongues are necessary to enter the kingdom of God.

Imani Temple African-American Catholic Congregation

*(*SPEAKER *recounts the founding of Imani Temple African-American Catholic Congregation.)*

SPEAKER
The Imani Temple African-American Catholic Congregation was founded in Washington, D.C., by a former Catholic priest named George Stallings. He broke away from the traditional Catholic Church in 1989. Stallings was very vocal about his views regarding the church and African Americans. He didn't feel that the Catholic Church was addressing the needs of its black members. He stated, "We could no longer afford to worship white gods in black homes." He broke away from the Roman Catholic Church by performing a mass based on an experimental rite that was being used in Zaire, Africa. He declared that there weren't enough black priests, black churches, or black members. He alleged that the few churches that existed were being closed or consolidated. His views created controversy within the church and created mixed feelings from African American Catholic bishops and

members. Yet he created a following, and in 1991 he assumed the title of Archbishop of Imani Temple.

Full Gospel Baptist Church Fellowship, International

(SPEAKER explains the principles of the Full Gospel Baptist Church Fellowship, International.)

SPEAKER
The Full Gospel Baptist Church Fellowship, International is a fellowship of churches and individuals representing various spiritual gifts. Led by Bishop Paul S. Morton, the movement of spiritual gifts began around 1992. In 1994 the first Full Gospel Baptist Church Fellowship Conference was held in New Orleans, Louisiana. The term "full gospel" means the belief in the entire Bible, whereas some denominations only believe in certain parts of the Bible. It has a traditional Baptist foundation but sees itself as a bridge between Baptist and Pentecostal doctrines. It endorses a variety of beliefs such as speaking in tongues, prophecy, and the baptism of the Holy Spirit. It also believes in the fivefold ministry, which is the apostles, prophets, pastors, teachers, and evangelists. In addition, there is an acceptance of women in the ministry on all levels.

RELIGIOUS LEADERS

David George
(1742–?)
Baptist Minister

(DAVID explains how he became the pastor of the first black church in the country.)

DAVID

I'm Reverend David George. Master Gaplin owned me, but I learned that my real master was the Lord Jesus. Master Gaplin wasn't too bad as far as masters go. I say that because in 1773 he gave us an old empty barn on his plantation in Silver Bluff, South Carolina, and let us use it for a church. We named it Silver Bluff Baptist Church. Reverend Wait Palmer helped us established it, and we became the first black church in this country. I had the honor of being the pastor. Reverend George Liele, who was the first Negro to be ordained in Georgia, and Reverend Palmer baptized me and trained me to become the pastor of the church. We only had eight members at first, but eventually we grew to thirty members. We existed until the start of the Revolutionary War.

Richard Allen and Absalom Jones
(1760–1831) (1746–1818)
Methodist Bishop; Episcopal Priest

Characters:

RICHARD, *male, bishop in the Methodist Church*

ABSALOM, *male, priest in the Episcopal Church*

Costumes:

Typical attire for a priest and bishop of the early 1800s

Props:

Two chairs

(RICHARD *and* ABSALOM *describe how they founded all-black congregations within the Methodist and Episcopal denominations.)*

RICHARD

Praise the Lord, Reverend Jones. It's good to see you again. How are things going at your church, St. Thomas?

ABSALOM

We're blessed and still growing. It's good to see Mother Bethel Church is thriving. Doesn't it feel good to have a place where you can worship like you want to and don't have to worry about nobody telling you to stop and get up?

RICHARD

(Nods in agreement.)

I clearly remember the day we walked out of St. George's Methodist Episcopal Church on Fourth Street in Philadelphia in 1787. That Sunday morning when we got to the church, the sexton met us as we entered and told us to go in the gallery and find out where we were going to sit. We assumed we were going to have the same seats we always had. By the time we got to our seats, the service had already begun, and the singing was just about over. Then the elder said, "Let us pray." We had barely gotten down on our knees when I heard some mumbling and saw one of the trustees grabbing you.

ABSALOM

Yeah, he was pulling me up off my knees and saying, "You must get up . . . you must not kneel here." I replied, "Wait until prayer is over." He said, "No, you must get up now, or I will call for aid and force you away." I told him again, "Wait until prayer is over, and I will get up and trouble you no more." That wasn't good enough for him. He called for another trustee to come over and assist him. Next thing I knew, he went to Brother William White and started pulling on him too. By that time, we colored parishioners got up and walked out together and haven't been back since.

RICHARD

That's right. After all that trouble and embarrassment they caused us, the white congregation got mad when we left. They threatened to disown us if we continued to worship in the place where we were meeting. Some white members truly missed us, but they also missed our money.

ABSALOM

Well, it's sad but true. The walkout had been coming for a long time. St. George's was becoming more and more un-Christian and more and more prejudiced. That's why we raised money and built our own house of worship.

RICHARD

Our friendship has lasted many years. We have so much in common. We were both slaves but managed to purchase our freedom. We also shared a mutual concern for the social and spiritual welfare of black people. I remember that being one of our reasons for forming the Free African Society religious group. I'm glad we were able to remain friends after we established separate churches.

ABSALOM

Me too. I guess the main difference was that the majority of us wanted to remain Episcopalian rather than Methodist. That's why we started a black congregation and established St. Thomas Episcopal Church within the white-led national Episcopal Church in 1787. Because I was elected to lead that flock, I became the first black priest in the United States.

RICHARD

You sure did. My followers and I established Mother Bethel Methodist Church, because we wanted to be totally independent of white rule. St. George's still wanted to control us. They tried and tried until 1816. That's when the Pennsylvania Supreme Court ruled we were independent. Within a few months of the court's decision, black ministers from across the mid-Atlantic region met to form the African

Methodist Episcopal Church. The AME Church elected me their first bishop.

ABSALOM

We never let our different church denominations prevent us from saving souls and working for the best interest of our people.

(End scene.)

James Varick
(1750–1827)
Methodist Bishop

(JAMES explains how he helped found the African Methodist Episcopal Zion Church.)

JAMES

My name is James Varick. I'm a bishop in the African Methodist Episcopal Zion Church. I joined the congregation of John Street Methodist Church in New York City. The church was built in 1750, and I joined around 1766. John Street was integrated, but that was only in name. The black members of the congregation had to sit in the back of the church during services, and we were tiring of the unwelcome attitude of the white members toward us.

Around 1780 we started asserting our independence and held separate classes and prayer meetings. We didn't have any problems with the Methodist doctrine; our concern was the racism that was practiced within the church. We created our own doctrine, but it only differed slightly from the original Methodist text. We had services on Sunday afternoons and midweek evenings. Although some of us were ministers, someone else had to give sermons and communion, because the church wouldn't ordain black ministers.

In 1796 I led the fight to obtain more independence. In 1799 we made the decision to establish a separate church. We remodeled a house for a place to hold our meetings. In October 1800 we dedicated the African Methodist Episcopal Zion Church, which became our mother church. I was one of the leaders who led the pursuit to obtain an independent charter and necessary legal documents. We wanted to make sure our investments were protected from the white Methodist organization. In 1801 our church was officially incorporated under New York law.

Eighteen twenty was a stellar year for us. In July we met and pushed for the ordination of black ministers. In August, Zion began erecting a new permanent building. Also in that month, we had perhaps our most significant meeting. We made two major decisions: one, we decided against uniting with the black Methodists led by Bishop Allen; two, we elected not to return to the John Street Methodist Church. We were determined to become totally independent. September 13, 1820, Abraham Thompson and I were chosen by the congregation to become elders. Finally in 1821, the white Methodist elders agreed to ordain Thompson, Leven Smith, and me. On July 22, 1822, I became the first bishop of the African Methodist Episcopal Zion denomination.

John Gloucester Sr.
(ca. 1776–1822)
Presbyterian Minister

(JOHN *describes his founding of the first all-black Presbyterian Church.*)

JOHN

I'm Reverend John Gloucester Sr. In 1807 I organized the First African Church in Philadelphia, Pennsylvania. It was the first all-black Presbyterian Church in the United States.

Thomas Paul
(1773–1831)
Baptist Minister

*(*THOMAS *explains how he started one of the largest African American Baptist churches in the United States.)*

THOMAS

My name is Reverend Thomas Paul. I'm a Baptist minister, and I led a movement to inspire black people to form separate denominations from their white counterparts. Traditionally, black people worshipped with whites in the white churches. However, former slaves began to migrate north and worship with whites after the Revolutionary War. Integrated worship quickly became uncomfortable for both races. Blacks especially were growing tired of their inferior status in the white Baptist churches.

I was ordained in 1805. I established a congregation of free Negroes in Boston. Word of my preaching spread among free blacks, and I never refused a request to preach. By 1808 word spread to white congregations in New York. I delivered a series of sermons there too. After my sermons in New York, it was generally agreed on among the whites and Negroes that separate congregations could exist. The First Baptist Church subsequently issued letters of honorable dismissal to sixteen of its Negro members. Under my leadership, we organized a Baptist congregation and became known as the Abyssinian Baptist Church of New York City. I continued my life's work of organizing churches in America and Haiti.

Peter Spencer
(1782–1843)
Methodist Minister

(PETER recounts how he founded the African Union Church.)

PETER

My name is Reverend Peter Spencer. I was a minister and the primary founder of the African Union Church. I'm known as the Father of the Black Independent Church Movement in Delaware; however, in the Wilmington community, where I was very active, I was often called Father Spencer. I tried to live my life in such a way as to be an example to my people. I felt education and religion shared equal importance. I taught numerous black people how to read and write. I studied law, so I was also able to help with legal issues as well.

I was concerned about the spiritual worship and lack of spiritual brotherhood that black people experienced in white churches. We were treated unfairly by the white Methodist congregations. In 1813 we rejected their domineering control and founded our own church, the African Union Church. Keeping to my philosophy that religion and education were twins, I established thirty-one churches and several schools. I believe I fulfilled my purpose in life by helping others.

Mary Elizabeth Clovis Lange
(ca. 1784–1882)
Catholic Nun

(MARY describes how she opened the first black Catholic church in the United States.)

MARY

My name is Mother Mary Elizabeth Clovis Lange. In 1828 I established the Oblate Sisters of Providence in Baltimore, Maryland. It was the first black Roman Catholic religious order of nuns in the United States. We never had enough funds, and we were confronted with persecution from whites in the community; but we were a vital source within the black community. We provided a school for black children, and in 1836 we erected a chapel. No other black Catholic church existed in our country prior to our chapel.

Elijah Abel
(?–1884)
Mormon Elder

(ELIJAH explains how he became the first black Mormon elder.)

ELIJAH

My name is Elijah Abel. In 1836 I became the first Negro seventy in the Mormon Church. After the early years of our church, the Mormons established a ban which prevented us from becoming elders. I was the last Negro to advance to that status during my lifetime.

Jehu Jones
(1786–1852)
Lutheran Minister

(JEHU explains how he came to found the first all-black Lutheran church.)

JEHU

My name is Jehu Jones. In the 1820s I joined St. John's Lutheran Church in Charleston, South Carolina. In 1832 I was ordained in the Lutheran Church's New York synagogue. After I was ordained, I went back to the city of Charleston. However, when I returned I was jailed briefly. I was charged with violating a law that was passed by the state of South Carolina, which made the immigration of free blacks illegal.

I later moved to Philadelphia, Pennsylvania. In June 1833 I was appointed as a missionary to work among the colored people in that city. I worked hard among my brethren and was able to build a congregation. On February 16, 1834, I began the process of establishing my own church in that city. We petitioned other Lutheran churches for donations. Four months later, we were able to purchase two lots on Quince Street.

By the time our building was dedicated in 1836, we had paid almost 40 percent of the expenses. Unfortunately, we were unable to raise enough money to pay off the balance of approximately $1,300. In 1839 our building went up for sale at a sheriff's auction. It was a heartbreaking experience for us, but we persevered. I continued to serve my St. Paul congregation until 1851. My members and I stayed active in the community, especially in the area of civil rights. We joined an association of African American churches called the Moral Reform and Improvement Society. The organization's goal was to make improvements in the social conditions of its residents.

Rebecca Cox Jackson
(1795–1871)
Shaker Minister

*(*REBECCA *explains how she established the first largely black Shaker family.)*

REBECCA

I'm Rebecca Cox Jackson. I'm an elderess in the Shaker religion, or the United Society of Believers in Christ's Second Coming. The Shaker religion is a Christian denomination that believes in communal living and observing celibacy. I was blessed with gifts from God at a young age. As a child I wanted dearly to learn to read and write, because I wanted to read the Bible. When my brother didn't teach me as he promised, I prayed to God to give me that knowledge. One day as I was finishing a dress I was sewing, I heard the voice of the Lord tell me that he could teach me to read. I laid down my dress, picked up my Bible, and rushed upstairs. I prayed to God Almighty and asked that he would teach me to read his word, if it was his will. I looked in the Bible and began to read. I called this "my unspeakable gift of Almighty God." I did not take this gift for granted. I became the first woman elderess in the Shaker religion. I also established the first black Shaker congregation in 1859, which was in Philadelphia, Pennsylvania.

Edward H. Chippey
(1825–1900)
Methodist Minister

(EDWARD explains how he cofounded the African Union First Colored Methodist Protestant Church.)

EDWARD

I'm Reverend Edward Chippey. I was pastor of the First Colored Methodist Protestant Church in Delaware. In 1866 Reverend Spencer and I decided to merge. We founded a new church called the African Union First Colored Methodist Protestant Church. Our membership flourished rapidly following the Civil War. In 1886 we purchased another site for members residing in the Hockessin community. This church was named Chippey Chapel in my honor. It was rebuilt in 1896 and officially incorporated as Chippey African Union Methodist Protestant Church in 1896.

The Healy Family

(NARRATOR comes to center stage and gives a brief history of the Healy family; siblings PATRICK, JAMES, and ELIZA consecutively come to center stage and explain their roles in the Catholic Church.)

NARRATOR
The Healy siblings were the most prominent black Catholics in the nineteenth century. They were born in Georgia to a white Irish Catholic plantation owner and a black mother, who had nine children with him. It was illegal for their parents to marry, but their father cared for them and their mother. He sent his children north to receive an education. It is not clear whether many people knew that their mother was African American, but the Healy children were black pioneers in the Catholic Church.
(NARRATOR exits stage.)

PATRICK
I'm Patrick Healy. I was the first black Jesuit priest in the United States. I was also president of Georgetown University for eight years.
(PATRICK moves to stage right.)

JAMES
I'm James Healy. I was the first black Catholic bishop in the United States. I was the presiding bishop of Portland, Maine.
(JAMES moves to stage right.)

ELIZA
My name is Eliza Healy. I became headmistress of a Catholic school in Vermont after taking my vows as a nun.

(PATRICK, JAMES, and ELIZA exit stage.)

Charles Mason
(1866–1961)
Church of God in Christ Minister

(CHARLES recalls his role in the founding and growth of the Church of God in Christ.)

CHARLES

My name is Charles Mason. Initially, I was a Baptist minister. In 1895 I met another Baptist minister named Charles Jones. Both of us were influenced by the Holiness movement. Because of this, we were expelled from our respective churches. Shortly after we were expelled in 1895, we began a series of successful revivals in Tennessee and Mississippi. The result was the birth of the Church of God in Christ, or COGIC church. COGIC became one of the leading black churches in America.

Charles Price Jones
(1865–1949)
Church of God in Christ Minister

(CHARLES describes how he cofounded the Church of God in Christ.)

CHARLES

I'm Charles Price Jones. I began my ministry as a Baptist preacher. In 1895 I met another Baptist preacher named Charles Mason. Both of us were growing dissatisfied with the traditional Baptist and Methodist churches. Mason, two other radical preachers, and I held a faith healing revival and presented the doctrine of sanctification in 1896 in Jackson, Mississippi. This doctrine was rejected by my church. In 1897 Mason and I were expelled from our respective churches for our belief in the Holiness movement. That same year we started a church by preaching in the homes of our supporters. This marked the beginning of a major new black denomination that we called the Church of God in Christ. Our services appealed to many people, partly because of Mason's preaching and the abundance of hymns that I wrote.

Mason and I continued our pastoral relationship until 1907. We split over his support of the creed of speaking in tongues as evidence of the infilling of the Holy Spirit. I continued to lead my congregation in the Holiness doctrine. In 1915 we changed our name to the Church of God in Christ USA.

I was a church leader for over fifty years and remained active until I had to retire due to illness. I attended my last convention in 1944. There, I was elected senior bishop and president emeritus of the national convention for life.

William J. Seymour
(1870–1922)
Pentecostal Minister

(WILLIAM recounts how he spread the Holiness doctrine throughout the United States.)

WILLIAM

My name is William J. Seymour. Some people call me the most influential black leader in American religious history. In 1900 I moved from Louisiana to Cincinnati, Ohio, where I joined the Church of God Restoration Movement. It was also called the Evening Light Saints. This church was part of the Holiness movement, which maintained the doctrine of the imminent return of Christ. We believed that after the acceptance of Christ and the baptism of the Holy Spirit that there was immediate conversion, sanctification, faith, and healing.

I was ordained as a minister in the Church of God in 1902. I spent the next three years traveling as an evangelist. In 1905 I settled in Houston, Texas. That summer I served as a temporary replacement for Lucy Farrow, the niece of abolitionist Frederick Douglass, and a Holiness minister. It was Lucy Farrow who encouraged me to contact Charles Parham, a white evangelist who ran a Bible school in Texas. Parham taught that speaking in tongues was a sign of the working of the Holy Spirit. Parham allowed me to attend his school, but I wasn't allowed to sit in the classroom with the white students because of Texas's segregation laws. I had to listen through an open door or window. I didn't support this view on racism, as I believed a sign of the return of Christ was racial integration. However, I did learn of glossolalia, or speaking in tongues, through Parham.

In 1906 I moved to Los Angeles, California. I was invited to preach at a church established by Julia M. Hutchins. She was expelled from a Baptist church in that city because of Holiness beliefs. When I incorporated glossolalia into the Holiness doctrine, she became upset and locked me out of her church. However, I believed that God was still working in my favor. I was offered the opportunity to hold services in the home of Mr. and Mrs. Asberry on North Bonnie Brae Street. Although I preached about the gift of speaking in tongues, I didn't experience it until 1906. It began April 9 when my preaching caused one of my members to start speaking in tongues. This powerful emotionalism among members continued for three days. On April 12 I was overcome while preaching and began speaking in tongues. News quickly spread about what transpired. Before long so many people came that we had to relocate. We found an unused building owned by the African Methodist Episcopal Church. It was a warehouse and livery stable located at 312 Azusa Street. We scrubbed and cleaned the building, then we filled it as best we could with self-made furniture. We nailed two boxes together for the pulpit and attached planks to empty barrels for pews.

Our church drew national attention and was called the Azusa Street Revival. On April 18, 1906, the *Los Angeles Times* ran an extensive news story about our church's activities and emotional services. The article appeared the exact day of the San Francisco earthquake. Many people felt this disaster had been predicted by our church. Shortly afterward, more than one thousand pamphlets were circulated that connected the earthquake, the church, and the impending end of the world. Numerous people consider the San Francisco earthquake a significant factor in the rise of Pentecostalism on a national level. By May the Azusa Street revival drew more than one thousand people per day and news reporters came from all over the United States.

My ministry flourished. In September 1906 our church's newspaper, the *Apostolic Faith*, was published. In 1907 we became the Pacific Apostolic Faith Mission in Los Angeles. Throughout 1909 we held three services per day and conducted prayer meetings twenty-four hours per day.

I achieved my mission of a completely integrated religious community. I saw the spread of Pentecostal teachings by religious leaders who visited my church. I also witnessed the growth of new Pentecostal churches around the United States.

Nannie Burroughs
(1879–1961)
Baptist Reformer

(NANNIE shares her role in reforming the Baptist Church.)

NANNIE

I'm Nannie Burroughs. I was concerned about the lack of significant participation of women in the worship service and our role in the church. I knew we could do more than usher and work in the kitchen.

At the 1906 National Baptist Convention, I proposed to have a national Women's Day. Women's Day would be a special Sunday when women could speak and take a leadership role in Baptist churches nationwide. Women's Day has become a significant event in the Baptist denomination.

I was also concerned about women improving their role in society. In 1909 I opened the National Trade and Professional School for Women and Girls in Washington, D.C. It stressed Christian womanhood, professional and practical skills, as well as a classical education. I am proud to say that I helped uplift the status of women in the church and in the community.

MILITARY

African Americans in the Military

(SPEAKER commemorates the bravery of African Americans in the U.S. military.)

SPEAKER
African Americans have fought in every war in which the United States has been involved. They fought for freedom abroad when they didn't have freedom in America. They had to fight racism within the military, then take off their uniforms and fight racism at their doorsteps. Despite all this, they have always answered every call to defend the nation and the values it professed. They were decorated and unsung heroes who fought and died for the American dream.

Tuskegee Airmen

Two of the Tuskegee Airmen

(SPEAKER gives a brief account of the Tuskegee Airmen's military success.)

SPEAKER

The Tuskegee Airmen were composed of four all-black squadrons that fought in World War II. Because of segregation in the U.S. military, the black cadets weren't allowed to train with the white cadets; instead, they received their training in Tuskegee, Alabama, in 1941.

The first pilots graduated three months after the bombing of Pearl Harbor, yet the government refused to deploy them outside the United States until 1943. Racism was a major issue in the military and this bias almost cancelled the program. However, their commander, Benjamin O. Davis Jr., provided testimony that preserved the program. Benjamin Davis Jr. later became the first African American U.S. Air Force general.

In 1944 the airmen merged with three other black squadrons and formed the 332nd Fighter Group. They became an escort unit and provided protection to bombers on 200 missions. In their 1,578 combat missions, they shot down 111 enemy planes, destroyed 150 more on the ground, and sank a German destroyer. The Tuskegee Airmen participated in combat missions in Africa, France, Germany, Sicily, the Balkans, and Italy. Members of the airmen won over one hundred Distinguished Flying Crosses and three Distinguished Unit Citations as a group.

Daniel James "Chappie" Jr.
(1920–1978)
Pilot, U.S. Air Force General

(CHAPPIE describes how he became the first African American four-star general in the U.S. Air Force.)

CHAPPIE

My name is Daniel James Jr., but you can call me Chappie like most of my friends. I'm a soldier and an airplane pilot. I always wanted to fly, but during the early years of my military career, black Americans were excluded from pilot training. Fortunately, the NAACP put so much pressure on the government that they gave in and formed the all-black Tuskegee Airmen program. I graduated from that unit and became a second lieutenant in the Army Air Corps. Even though we completed the program and were army officers, one hundred of us were arrested for protesting against the policy of "white officers only" clubs in the service.

I flew with the Tuskegee Airmen during World War II. We shot down enemy planes and protected the bombers we were escorting. I flew missions in both the Korean and Vietnam Wars. I was the first black four-star general in the U.S. Air Force. I was able to succeed, because I stuck to my personal eleventh commandment, "Thou shall not quit."

Doris "Dorie" Miller
(1919–1942)
U.S. Navy Sailor

Dorie Miller

(DORIE *explains the acts that earned him the Navy Cross.*)

DORIE
Abandon ship! Abandon ship! I'll never forget that cry. It was December 7, 1941, the day the Japanese bombed Pearl Harbor in

Hawaii. I'm Dorie Miller. On that day I was aboard the USS *Arizona*. I was down in the galley working as a mess man, or cook, when my ship was attacked. I ran to the deck only to see the ship in flames. I instinctively grabbed an antiaircraft gun and started firing. I shot down four enemy planes before we were ordered to abandon ship. I watched as the *Arizona* sank. I was hailed a hero and was awarded the Navy Cross on May 27, 1942.

It's ironic because I didn't have experience using artillery. The military was still segregated and had separate training programs for Negroes. We weren't trained to operate sophisticated equipment. We were trained to be cooks and to perform other menial jobs. Sadly, limited opportunities and segregation existed in the armed forces just like in other parts of our society. We were not as fortunate as you are now. Black people back in the day, as you like to say, learned to survive and find a way to overcome obstacles. I believe that you have to take advantage of life, not let life take advantage of you.

Colin L. Powell
(1937–)
U.S. Army General

Colin Powell

(SPEAKER *highlights landmarks in Colin Powell's career in the U.S. military.)*

SPEAKER

Colin Powell was born in New York City to Jamaican immigrants. He graduated from City College where he majored in geology. Powell was a second lieutenant in the U.S. Army in 1962 and was sent to Vietnam. On his second tour of duty, Powell was injured in a helicopter crash but managed to save others from the burning aircraft. In 1971 he was a major and received a political appointment in the Nixon administration.

Colin Powell had an exceptionally successful military career. He was a four-star general and the military assistant to the Defense Secretary in 1983. He helped coordinate the U.S. invasion of Grenada, helped plan air raids in Libya, and commanded U.S. troops in Germany for six months. Later, he was assigned to the National Security Council, where he was an advisor for military involvement in the Persian Gulf.

In 1989 President George H. Bush appointed Colin Powell chairman of the Joint Chiefs of Staff. In 2001 President George W. Bush appointed him Secretary of State. His prestigious career and high personal standards have earned him the respect and love of his countrymen and race.

Henry Simmons Newport
(1936–2001)
U.S. Army Major

(HENRY describes his success in the U.S. military.)

HENRY

My name is Henry Simmons Newport. I was born in a hospital near Sodus Point, New York, which is where I was raised. My family had been the only African American family in the village since the early 1800s. I was happy during my years there and had numerous friends.

I never let color stop me from setting goals and doing the things I enjoyed. I was an Eagle Scout, a volunteer fireman, and served in the U.S. Coast Guard."

After graduation I attended Fordham University. When I graduated in 1959, I became the first African American in the history of the university to graduate from the ROTC with distinguished military honors. I served in the Vietnam War and retired from the military with the rank of major.

African American Military Firsts

(Fourteen speakers consecutively come to center stage and highlight African Americans' accomplishments in the military.)

SPEAKER 1
In 1778 the 1st Rhode Island Regiment was formed. It was the first and only all-black unit to fight in the Revolutionary War.
*(*SPEAKER 1 *moves to stage right.)*

SPEAKER 2
In 1861 Nicholas Biddle became the first black person to be wounded in the Civil War.
*(*SPEAKER 2 *moves to stage right.)*

SPEAKER 3
In 1865 Michael Augustine Healy became the first African American to be appointed to the U.S. Revenue Service, which later became the U.S. Coast Guard.
*(*SPEAKER 3 *moves to stage right.)*

SPEAKER 4

In 1867 the Buffalo Soldiers became the first all-black unit in the regular army.

(SPEAKER 4 moves to stage right.)

SPEAKER 5

In 1877 Henry O. Flipper became the first African American to graduate from the U.S. Military Academy at West Point, New York.

(SPEAKER 5 moves to stage right.)

SPEAKER 6

In 1940 Benjamin O. Davis Jr. became the first African American general in the U.S. Army.

(SPEAKER 6 moves to stage right.)

SPEAKER 7

There were 926 black pilots known as the Tuskegee Airmen. They received their training in the Army Air Force Aviation Cadet program, which was established by Congress in 1941.

(SPEAKER 7 moves to stage right.)

SPEAKER 8

On August 21, 1943, Harriet M. West became the first African American female major in the Women's Army Corps, or WAC.

(SPEAKER 8 moves to stage right.)

SPEAKER 9

Leonard Roy Harmon served in the U.S. Navy during World War II. In 1944 the navy fighting ship USS *Harmon* was named after him. It was the first time an African American was commemorated with this honor.

(SPEAKER 9 moves to stage right.)

SPEAKER 10

In 1945 Phyllis Dailey became the first African American female to serve as a nurse in the U.S. Navy.
(SPEAKER 10 moves to stage right.)

SPEAKER 11

In 1949 Wesley A. Brown became the first African American to graduate from the U.S. Naval Academy in Annapolis, Maryland.
(SPEAKER 11 moves to stage right.)

SPEAKER 12

Frank Peterson Jr. became the first black marine pilot and the first African American to win Marine Corps wings in 1952.
(SPEAKER 12 moves to stage right.)

SPEAKER 13

In 1965 Milton Olive III became the first African American to win the Medal of Honor in the Vietnam War.
(SPEAKER 13 moves to stage right.)

SPEAKER 14

In 1966 Merle J. Smith Jr. was the first African American to graduate from the U.S. Coast Guard Academy.

(Speakers exit stage.)

AVIATION AND ASTRONAUTICS

Elizabeth "Bessie" Coleman
(1896–1936)
Pilot

(BESSIE describes how she accomplished her goal of becoming a pilot.)

BESSIE
I'm Bessie Coleman, also nicknamed Queen Bee. I'm an airplane pilot, but this wasn't an easy goal for me to accomplish. No flight school in the United States would accept me because I was black. But I wouldn't let that discourage me. I moved to Paris, France, where I attended an aviation school. When I returned to the United States in 1921, I became the first black female pilot in this country. My dream was to get my pilot's license and open a flight school for black people. To earn money for the school, I performed stunts in air shows. However, I hated racism and refused to perform for segregated crowds. I also demanded that black people be allowed to attend my shows.

Albert Forsythe and Charles Anderson
(1919–1988) (1907–1996)
Pilots

Characters:
ALBERT, *male, retired pilot*
CHARLES, *male, retired pilot and flight instructor*

Costumes:
Present-day casual attire
Props:
Two chairs

(ALBERT *and* CHARLES *reminisce on their accomplishments in aviation.*)

ALBERT
Hey, Charles. I was just thinking back on my days of flying, and why I fell in love with planes. I loved flying from the first day I was in a plane. I loved it so much that I worked part-time to pay for pilot's license classes while I was in college. The classes cost me $5.25 for a twenty-minute lesson.

CHARLES
It was worth it, because we were the first black pilots to make a transcontinental round-trip flight.

ALBERT
That's right. We left Atlantic City, New Jersey, on July 17, 1933. Do you remember our plane, the Pride of Atlantic City? We flew without parachutes, landing lights, blind-flying instruments, or a radio. We were lucky to complete that flight in eleven days. In fact, we were lucky to make it at all.

CHARLES
Yep, I'll never forget that date, July 28. At that time, I had only been flying four years. Sometimes I think about how hard I had to fight to become a pilot. I had to teach myself to fly, because no flight school would accept a black applicant. But with practice, my skills got better and better.

ALBERT
They sure did. You became an ace pilot. It wasn't much later that you were hired to be the chief flight instructor for the Tuskegee Airmen, right?

CHARLES
That's right.

ALBERT
I remember when you started teaching there. I love to tell my grandkids that you took First Lady Eleanor Roosevelt for a flight.

CHARLES
That was one of the highlights of my career. In 1941 she came to visit our training site. She wanted to know if black people could really fly. I invited her to get in the plane with me and see. She did, and we flew for forty minutes. Her confidence in my skills helped pave the way for the government to validate the Tuskegee Airmen program.

ALBERT
That's right. That's why they call you the Father of Black Aviation.

(End scene.)

Willa Brown-Chappell
(1906–1992)
Pilot

(WILLA describes her trailblazing career in aviation.)

WILLA
I'm Willa Brown-Chappell. In 1934 I became the first black female in the United States to hold a commercial pilot's license. I also formed the

National Airmen's Association of America. It was the first group for black aviators in our country.

John W. Greene Jr.
(ca. 1915–?)
Pilot

(SPEAKER describes how John Greene Jr. became the first African American to open a private airport.)

SPEAKER

John Greene Jr. was his name. The year was 1940, and it was a historic year in the field of aviation. That was the year that Greene opened a private airport. It was a time when other airports were only open to whites. His was the first airfield in the state of Maryland that was owned and operated by an African American. Greene renamed the airfield Columbia Air Center. The U.S. Navy used the site as a training field during World War II. He had an all-black staff. Many of the personnel were former Tuskegee Airmen. Greene's staff was the only civil air patrol squadron in the Washington, D.C., area. His terminal offered a flying school, facilities for repairs, and a charter service. The business owned ten planes, five runways, and three hangars. John Greene believed that if opportunities weren't created for you, that you should create them for yourself. If you believe that, then the sky's the limit.

Perry H. Young
(1919–1998)
Pilot

(PERRY describes his success in the field of aviation.)

PERRY
My name is Perry Young. I flew for New York Airways. In 1957 I became the first African American to pilot for a regularly scheduled commercial airline. During World War II, I was assigned to help train an all-black unit that became a part of the Tuskegee Airmen.

Ruth Carol Taylor
(1933–?)
Flight Attendant

*(*SPEAKER *shares Ruth Taylor's success in aviation.)*

SPEAKER
In 1958 Ruth Carol Taylor became the first African American flight attendant in the United States. She was a flight attendant for Mohawk Airlines.

Marlon Green
(1929–2009)
Pilot

*(*SPEAKER *describes Marlon Green's struggles and successes within the aviation industry.)*

SPEAKER
Marlon Green was the first African American pilot hired by a major passenger airline. His battle to get hired wasn't easy. He retired from the air force with nine years of service and over three thousand hours of flying time. When Green lived in Colorado, he applied to ten different U.S. airlines for a job as a pilot but was denied every time. Green was sure the only reason he wasn't hired was because he was black. So when he applied at Continental Airlines, he deliberately omitted the section requesting racial identity; neither did he send the

two photographs their company wanted. A short time after Continental received his application, he was called for a flight test along with five white applicants. Even though he had more experience than anyone else, he wasn't hired.

Green decided enough was enough! He filed a discrimination complaint in Denver, Colorado, and won. But the airline fought back and was able to have his case overturned. However, he refused to accept the ruling. Green took his case to the U.S. Supreme Court. In April 1963 the Court ruled in his favor. In 1965 Continental Airlines hired him, and he became a pilot for them in 1966. Marlon Green's lawsuit not only brought him success, his case also created opportunities for other African American pilots to fly for interstate commercial airlines.

African American Astronauts

(NARRATOR and sixteen speakers consecutively come to center stage and share the history of African Americans in astronautics.)

NARRATOR
Are you brave and adventurous? How would you like to fly to the moon or walk in space? Are you willing to risk your life to help your country make positive discoveries beyond the realms of gravity? If so, you would probably like to be an astronaut. But, you not only have to be brave and adventurous, you also have to be very smart. Before the space program was created in 1959, NASA began recruiting individuals to train for space exploration. Every year NASA receives thousands of applications from people with very diverse backgrounds. As of July 2008, only 321 astronauts had been accepted. Of those 321, 16 were African American. The next speakers will tell you about these amazing African Americans and their contributions to the space program. *(NARRATOR exits stage.)*

SPEAKER 1

In June 1967 Robert Henry Lawrence Jr. became the first African American selected to be an astronaut. He was a major in the U.S. Air Force and had a PhD in physical chemistry. Unfortunately, Major Lawrence was killed during training in an F104 Starfighter on December 8, 1967. He never got the opportunity to fly aboard a space shuttle. However, thirty years later on the anniversary of his death, NASA recognized his achievements by inscribing his name on the Space Mirror Memorial at the Kennedy Space Center in Florida. *(SPEAKER 1 moves to stage right.)*

SPEAKER 2

Guion Bluford became an astronaut in 1978. He was a lieutenant colonel in the U.S. Air Force and earned a PhD in aerospace engineering. When Bluford applied to the astronaut program, there were 8,878 applicants, but only 35 were accepted. On August 30, 1983, he joined the crew of the orbiter *Challenger* and became the first African American in space. His primary responsibility was to launch a $45 million communications and weather satellite. *(SPEAKER 2 moves to stage right.)*

SPEAKER 3

Ronald McNair was accepted into the astronaut program in 1978. He was also a physicist. Unfortunately, he was one of the crew members aboard the space shuttle *Challenger* when it met disaster seventy-three seconds after airlift. *(SPEAKER 3 moves to stage right.)*

SPEAKER 4

Frederick Gregory joined the astronaut program in 1978. He is a colonel in the U.S. Air Force. Gregory has flown three shuttle missions and was the first African American space shuttle commander. *(SPEAKER 4 moves to stage right.)*

SPEAKER 5

Charles F. Bolden graduated from the U.S. Naval Academy and achieved the rank of major general in the U.S. Navy. He became an astronaut in 1980. Bolden was the first person to ride in the Launch Complex 39 side-wire baskets. NASA was reluctant to order the crew to use the baskets, which provided a rapid escape, because they were untested. He allowed himself to be a human guinea pig by testing them. He helped his country and perhaps helped save future astronauts' lives. *(SPEAKER 5 moves to stage right.)*

SPEAKER 6

Dr. Mae Jemison was a dreamer. For her, dreams could help you reach your goals. Jemison said, "The best way to make dreams come true is to wake up. I don't believe people should rob themselves of the opportunity to realize their dreams." Two of her dreams did come true. The first was to become a medical doctor; the second was to become an astronaut, which she accomplished in 1987. In 1992 Mae Jemison became the first African American female to fly in space. *(SPEAKER 6 moves to stage right.)*

SPEAKER 7

Bernard Harris was accepted into the astronaut program in 1990. In addition to being an astronaut, he's also a medical doctor and has a master's degree in biomedical science. Bernard Harris was the first African American to walk in space. *(SPEAKER 7 moves to stage right.)*

SPEAKER 8

Winston Scott is a retired captain and pilot of the U.S. Navy. He became an astronaut in 1992. He was a mission specialist aboard two flights to the International Space Station. During his career, he amassed a total of 240 days, 14 hours, and 34 minutes of space time. Winston Scott also made three space walks, which totaled 19 hours and 26 minutes. He orbited Earth 252 times and traveled 6.5 million miles in space.

(SPEAKER 8 *moves to stage right.*)

SPEAKER 9

Michael Phillip Anderson was a lieutenant colonel in the U.S. Air Force and became an astronaut in 1994. Colonel Anderson was one of the crew members aboard space shuttle *Columbia*, which exploded sixteen minutes prior to landing.

(SPEAKER 9 *moves to stage right.*)

SPEAKER 10

Robert Curbeam was accepted into NASA's astronaut program in 1994. He has a bachelor's degree in aerospace engineering and two postgraduate degrees: one in aeronautical engineering and a second in aeronautical and astronautical engineering. His career as an astronaut included three flights to the International Space Station. These flights involved 901 hours in space and seven space walks totaling 45 hours and 34 minutes.

(SPEAKER 10 *moves to stage right.*)

SPEAKER 11

Yvonne Cagle was a colonel in the U.S. Air Force and a physician. In 1996 she was accepted into NASA's astronaut training program and qualified as a mission specialist. As a doctor, Cagle has made contributions to the ongoing study of astronauts' health and space telemedicine. As a member of the NASA Working Group, she traveled to Russia and instituted international medical standards and procedures for astronauts.

(SPEAKER 11 *moves to stage right.*)

SPEAKER 12

Joan Higginbotham was accepted into the astronaut program in 1996. She has two master's degrees: one in management and the second in space systems. During her career at NASA, she participated in fifty-three space shuttle launches at the Kennedy Space Center in Florida. On December 9, 2006, she was one of seven crew members that flew a 12 day mission to the International Space Station. Her crew delivered a new group of astronauts and over two tons of equipment and supplies to the station.
(SPEAKER 12 moves to stage right.)

SPEAKER 13

Stephanie Wilson was accepted into NASA's astronaut training program in 1996. She has a master's degree in aerospace engineering. As an astronaut, she has flown on two space missions to the International Space Station. Her first flight was in 2006. Her crew tested new equipment that would increase space shuttle safety. In 2007 she flew on another mission to the space station, and her crew delivered a module that made it possible to add future station laboratories.
(SPEAKER 13 moves to stage right.)

SPEAKER 14

Leland Melvin was accepted into the astronaut program in 1998. He has a master of science degree in materials engineering. Melvin flew aboard the space shuttle *Atlantis* on February 25, 2008. It was the twenty-fourth shuttle mission to the International Space Station. The crew had to prepare the *Columbus* laboratory for scientific work. The shuttle traveled 5,296,832 statute miles and orbited Earth 203 times. It took 12 days, 18 hours, 21 minutes, and 40 seconds.
(SPEAKER 14 moves to stage right.)

SPEAKER 15

Benjamin Alvin Drew was selected for NASA's astronaut training program in the year 2000. He has a dual bachelor of science degree in physics and aeronautical engineering from the U.S. Air Force Academy and a master's degree in aerospace science. Drew is also a colonel in the U.S. Air Force. On August 8, 2007, he was one of seven crew members aboard the space transport shuttle *Endeavour* to fly to the International Space Station. The mission took 12 days, 17 hours, 55 minutes, and 34 seconds. It also flew a total of 5,274,977 miles. *(SPEAKER 15 moves to stage right.)*

SPEAKER 16

Robert Satcher was accepted into the astronaut training program in 2004. Not only is he a mission specialist, he's also a medical doctor and has a PhD in chemical engineering. In his private practice, he treated patients who suffered from cancer in their legs and arms. Satcher was concerned about the NASA astronauts. He was aware that one of the problems of living and working in space was bone loss. He became interested in finding ways to prevent that. His careers allowed him to achieve his goals. Dr. Satcher said, "I have always had an interest in service and in space. I am interested in exploration. To become an astronaut lets me do all three."

(Speakers exit stage.)

MEDICINE

Mary Mahoney
(1845–1926)
Nurse

(MARY explains how she became the first African American to graduate from a nursing school in the United States.)

MARY
I'm Mary Mahoney. I attended a sixteen-month nursing course at the New England Hospital for Women and Children. Forty women entered the program. It was very difficult, and only three of us were able to earn our diplomas. I graduated in 1879 and became the first Negro to graduate from a nursing school in the United States.

Daniel Hale Williams
(1858–1931)
Physician

Characters:
DR. DAN, *male, physician*
NURSE, *female, nurse*
Costumes:
Typical attire for a physician and nurse of the late 1800s
Props:
Desk, chair, desk lamp, stethoscope, file folder, newspaper

(DR. DAN *reviews files while sitting at his desk at Provident Hospital in Chicago in 1893.*)

Scene 1

NURSE
Excuse me, Dr. Williams. Do you have a few minutes?

DR. DAN
Of course. Come in, and call me Dr. Dan just like everyone else.

NURSE
Dr. Dan, I just wanted to thank you for giving me the opportunity to become a nurse. If you hadn't opened your training school at Provident Hospital for nurses, a lot of Negro nurses would never have been able to pursue this career.

DR. DAN
I'm glad you appreciate it. I knew young ladies like you needed a place where they could train, because the white hospitals wouldn't admit them. I had the same problem when I was an intern. No hospital in Chicago would allow me to use their facility because I was black.

NURSE
Well, thank you again. I have to make my rounds. Have a good night.

(End scene.)

Scene 2

NURSE
(DR. DAN *reads files*. NURSE *rushes in.*)

Dr. Dan! Come quickly! A man has been stabbed in the chest. It looks as though he may bleed to death. *(Both rush off behind a small curtain where the hospital bed is located.)*

DR. DAN
(Speaking behind the curtain.)
Nurse, get my surgical equipment. I'll have to open his chest immediately and sew up his wound.

(End scene.)

Scene 3

(DR. DAN asleep at his desk; he awakens when he hears NURSE come in.)

NURSE
(Holding a newspaper.)
Good morning, Dr. Dan. I didn't mean to wake you; I just wanted to check on you. I know you're tired. The surgery took over three hours. Would you like some coffee?

DR. DAN
No, thank you. I'm fine. I want to check on the patient. How's he doing?

NURSE
Mr. James Cornish is resting well. You saved his life. Dr. Dan, you may not know it, but the word has already spread about the operation.
(Hands him the newspaper.)
Look at the headline of this Chicago newspaper: "Sewed up His Heart." Everywhere, people are hailing you as a miracle surgeon. You are the first doctor in the world to successfully perform an open-heart

operation. Not everyone wants to give you credit though. The medical world doesn't want to believe you're a Negro. They say a black man isn't smart enough to perform that kind of surgery.

DR. DAN
I stopped worrying a long time ago about how the world judged me. My goal isn't to win the approval of my colleagues, it's to save lives. The truth will speak for itself. Let's check on Mr. Cornish.
(Both go behind the curtain to check on the patient.)

(End scene.)

Charles R. Drew
(1904–1950)
Physician, Scientist

(DR. DREW explains how he designed a way to preserve blood.)

DR. DREW
I'm Dr. Charles Drew. I found a way to preserve blood. I researched the four blood types and discovered that none of them could be stored for seven days without spoiling. I experimented with plasma, which is blood without its red cells. I created a way of separating plasma from red blood cells so that the cells could be stored and shipped long distances.

My discovery came at a critical time. It was the beginning of World War II. England was fighting Germany. The British had thousands of casualties but couldn't preserve banked blood on the battlefields. The United States was asked to help, and my colleagues selected me to be the medical supervisor of the program.

In 1941 I encouraged the American Red Cross to establish a blood bank in the United States. I initiated the use of refrigerated bloodmobiles, which the Red Cross still uses today. This was also the year I became furious with the U.S. War Department. The department ordered that blood be segregated by race. They cited, "It isn't advisable to collect and mix Caucasian and Negro blood." I protested and resigned my position as director of the Red Cross blood bank program. They knew scientifically that blood can't be classified according to race. The war department continued this practice of racism until 1949. I told my peers, "In the laboratory I have found that you and I share a common blood; but will we ever share a common brotherhood?" I ask you, America, will we ever share a common brotherhood?

Mrs. Rosa
(1911–1982)
Midwife

(MRS. ROSA *gives a brief history of the role of African Americans in midwifery.*)

MRS. ROSA

My name is Mrs. Rosa. I'm not well-known outside of Polk County, Florida, which is where I live. I work as a midwife in my black community in Winter Haven. I've probably delivered more babies than some doctors in our town. I didn't go to nursing school, but I have had midwifery training.

As a black woman, I can trace my profession back to Africa. Midwives brought their knowledge of caesarean and natural childbirth deliveries with them from the mother country. They also knew how to use various vegetables and herbs to help heal mothers after giving birth. Enslaved midwives were highly valued; they delivered babies for white and black women. Midwives continued to serve expectant mothers even after the Civil War. For example, there was Mattie D. Brewer, who was born in Tennessee in 1882. She delivered more than one thousand babies. She performed her last delivery when she was eighty-one years old. There was also Marie Jones Francis from Dublin, Georgia. She was considered an expert in premature childbirth. I can't forget about Julia M. Shade, who became a midwife in 1925 in Mississippi. She is recorded as having delivered over four thousand babies. Midwives have been a vital part of our communities and culture. We have delivered babies for women who couldn't afford a doctor or weren't allowed in the white hospitals. Even today in the mid-1960s, many women prefer to deliver at home with a midwife, rather than deliver in a hospital. I'm proud to be a midwife, and I'm proud to be a part of this piece of black history.

Ben Carson
(1951–)
Physician

*(*SPEAKER *recounts how Dr. Carson successfully separated conjoined twins.)*

SPEAKER
Dr. Carson is a pediatric neurosurgeon. On September 7, 1987, he led a team that performed the first successful separation of conjoined twins. The children were joined together at the head. It took twenty-two hours of surgery, but Dr. Carson was able to save their lives. He's among the most highly respected doctors in his field.

ONE MINUTE POETRY

Arthur Ashe

(SPEAKER *describes Arthur Ashe's success in tennis.*)

SPEAKER
Tennis pro Arthur Ashe did something that had never been done
He was the first African American male to win a grand slam at
Wimbledon

Crispus Attucks

(SPEAKER *shares Crispus Attucks's role in the Revolutionary War.*)

SPEAKER
When the colonists' cry for independence was struck
The first to die for our liberty was Cripsus Attucks

Jim Beckwourth

(JIM *highlights his success as an American pioneer.*)

JIM
I'm Jim Beckwourth
I'm a mountain man of great fame
I discovered a pass in the Sierra Mountains
That still bears my name

Mary McLeod Bethune

(MARY shares her contribution to education.)

MARY
I'm Mary McLeod Bethune
I wanted to do more than just teach
So I founded a school in Daytona Beach
With only a dollar and a half and sales from pies
My dream to build a college was realized

Sarah Boone

(SARAH highlights her invention.)

SARAH
My name is Sarah Boone, in case nobody knows
I invented the ironing board
I made it easier for you to iron your clothes

Ralph Bunche

(RALPH highlights his role in African American history.)

RALPH
I'm Ralph Bunche
I was a U.S. ambassador who used negotiations
To try to bring peace among the world's nations
For my expert diplomacy and numerous tries
I was the first African American to receive the Nobel Peace Prize

George Washington Carver

(GEORGE shares his contribution to African American history.)

GEORGE

I used the peanut, sweat potato, and sandy red clay
To make many items that are still used today
I made over three hundred discoveries
That helped save the South's economy

Bessie Coleman

(BESSIE shares her achievement in aviation.)

BESSIE

I'm Bessie Coleman
I flew in the wild blue yonder
As the crowd yelled my name
I was the first black American female
Licensed to fly an airplane

Charles Drew

(DR. DREW describes his contribution to medicine.)

DR. DREW

I'm Dr. Charles Drew
I saved thousands of lives
And received many thanks
I learned how to preserve blood
And set up numerous blood banks

W. C. Handy

(W. C. shares his contribution to music.)

W. C.

Many of you have heard of me
To others it may be news
I'm W. C. Handy
Also known as the Father of the Blues

Matthew Henson

(MATTHEW shares his contribution to exploration.)

MATTHEW

I'm Matthew Henson
I was an explorer and the first person to reach the North Pole
Others failed because the climate was too harsh and too cold

Michael Jordan

(SPEAKER shares Michael Jordan's accomplishments in basketball.)

SPEAKER

Basketball was the game Michael Jordan loved to play
He set many records and is a legend in the NBA

Mary Mahoney

(MARY shares her accomplishments in nursing.)

MARY
I'm Mary Mahoney
I take great pride because I was the first
Black person in America to graduate as a nurse

Dorie Miller

(DORIE shares his contribution to Peal Harbor.)

DORIE
I'm Dorie Miller
I was a sailor in the Navy for the USA
I want to tell you about one frightening day
It happened in 1941 on the seventh of December
It was an experience I'll always remember
My ship was bombed by Japanese planes
There was smoke everywhere and it burst into flames
I grabbed an antiaircraft gun and I let the bullets rip
I shot down four enemy planes before abandoning ship

Garrett Morgan

(GARRETT shares his success as an inventor.)

GARRETT
I'm Garrett Morgan
My invention is used day and night
I'm the inventor of the first traffic light

Constance Baker Motley

(CONSTANCE shares her success as a lawyer and a judge.)

CONSTANCE

I'm Constance Baker Motley
I'll work hard every day to achieve a victory
I won nine cases before the Supreme Court for the NAACP
In all my civil rights cases I fought hard and refused to budge
I was the first black female appointed as a federal court judge

Jackie Robinson

(JACKIE shares his role in baseball.)

JACKIE

I'm Jackie Robinson
I loved baseball
It was my claim to fame
I was the first Negro in modern times
To integrate the game

Harriet Tubman

(HARRIET shares her role in the Underground Railroad.)

HARRIET

I'm Harriet Tubman
I escaped from slavery in Maryland near the eastern shore
Afterward I went back nineteen times
And freed over three hundred more

Madam C. J. Walker

(MADAM WALKER shares her success as an entrepreneur.)

MADAM WALKER
I'm Madam C. J. Walker
By selling my products for black women's hair care
I may have been our country's first black millionaire

President Barack Obama

(SPEAKER *pays homage to Barack Obama.*)

SPEAKER
From Hawaii there came a man
Who made us believe "Yes, we can"
He proved that being black
Doesn't have to hold you back
We're proud to have Barack Obama represent
Our great nation as its president

PIONEERS, COWBOYS, AND EXPLORERS

York
(ca. 1730–1832)
Explorer

(YORK describes how he was essential to the Lewis and Clark expedition.)

YORK
The United States acquired a vast territory from France with the Louisiana Purchase in 1803. The government hired explorers Lewis and Clark to explore that land and find a route to the Pacific Ocean. I was an explorer on that expedition too. My name is York, and I was William Clark's slave. He took me with him. I proved essential to the party, because I could speak several languages and was an expert woodsman. I had a good relationship with the Indians we encountered. They were impressed with my stature. I was six feet tall, weighed two hundred pounds, and very agile for a man my size. Sometimes I entertained the Indians with athletic stunts. Most of them had never seen a black man before. Often they would rub my skin to see if the color would come off. The Flathead Indians took my color for a symbol of bravery. They were courageous warriors and painted themselves black when they went into battle. Many of the Indians saw me as the leader of the group, because I was the person who communicated most

with them regarding trading. It was a long, hard two-year journey, but I was glad to play an important part in American history.

Buffalo Soldiers

Buffalo Soldiers

(Fictional character QUENT BAKER *describes the Buffalo Soldiers' bravery and patriotism.)*

QUENT BAKER

My name is Quent Baker. I'm a member of the Negro troops known as the Buffalo Soldiers. We were former Union cavalry and infantry regiment soldiers in the Civil War. The Indians gave us the name Buffalo Soldiers, because our skin was dark and our hair looked curly like the buffalo's. Those of us who were enlisted first couldn't be over 5 feet 5 inches tall or over 150 pounds; the army wanted the horses to have more speed and to be able to run for longer distances.

We patrolled the Indian Territory along the western frontier. We were stationed in some of the worst outposts in the army. Many of our assignments were in isolated areas to keep us from living near the white settlers we were required to protect. Despite this unfairness, our bravery could not be denied. We not only protected the lands on the frontier, but some of us also fought alongside Teddy Roosevelt's Rough Riders in the Spanish American War. We Buffalo Soldiers did what was required of us and did it well.

Stephen Bishop
(ca. 1820–1857)
Explorer

(SPEAKER highlights Stephen Bishop's contributions to the exploration of Mammoth Cave.)

SPEAKER

Stephen Bishop was brought to Mammoth Cave in 1838 with his owner, Franklin Gorin. His exact age when he arrived is unknown; however, it is believed that he was between sixteen and eighteen years old.

When Gorin bought Mammoth Cave in South Central Kentucky in 1838, his objective was to increase the tourist trade by expanding the already known passages. Little did he know, Mammoth Cave would come to be known as the longest cave system in the world, with nearly four hundred miles of labyrinths.

In addition to Stephen Bishop's guide duties, the task of exploring the cave was assigned to him, along with two other slave guides. Bishop exceeded expectations for both of these duties. Nearly every day, Bishop would venture into the cave alone. He found numerous miles of unexplored regions. He found a section that was so small in width that he named it Fat Man's Misery. He discovered another section that could only be reached by crawling through river sediment and over protruding limestone. This trail led to a chamber where he could stand erect. He dubbed the room the Great Relief Hall. He was the first to cross the immense vertical passage known as the Bottomless Pit. He is also credited with discovering Mammoth Dome and Cleveland Avenue. Bishop's explorations also made him the first person to discover the existence of the eyeless and colorless fish that lived in one of the cave's rivers.

Stephen Bishop was emancipated in 1856 but died a year later. Like the mysteries of the cave, his death was also a mystery; it was attributed to unknown causes.

George Washington Bush
(ca. 1790–1863)
Pioneer

(GEORGE explains how he became a pioneer in the state of Washington.)

GEORGE

I am George Washington Bush. I was born a free man in Pennsylvania but became a pioneer in the West. I wanted to own land and give my family a home of their own. I moved my family to Missouri, bought a farm, and started raising some cattle. We thought we were permanent homesteaders, but Missouri passed a new law that denied Negroes the right to become residents of their state. We gathered our belongings, joined a wagon train, and headed farther west. We moved to Oregon in 1844, which was a free territory. Although slavery was forbidden there, Oregon passed a law preventing black people from owning property. I ended up moving my family to what later became the state of Washington and staked a claim to 640 acres of land. My family and I were able to live the rest of our lives on that land; we never gave up on our dream. Remember, your dreams will only come true if you stay true to your dreams.

Benjamin "Pap" Singleton
(1809–1892)
Pioneer

(PAP explains how he encouraged African Americans to move to the West.)

PAP

I'm Benjamin Singleton, but you can call me Pap like most people
do. Horace Greeley told Americans, "Go west, young man." He was
mostly talking to white citizens. But he wasn't the only one who
believed that west was best. I advised Negroes to do the same thing.
The period after the Civil War didn't bring former slaves the rights and
protection we needed. It was even worse when Reconstruction ended.
We were lynched, beaten, and kept in poverty. The little rights that
were given to us were almost completely taken away.

I printed and passed out thousands of posters encouraging Negroes to
move to the frontier. The biggest migration came in 1879. There were
so many of us that relocated to the Western Territory that we were
called Exodusters. We settled as far west as Oklahoma. We were able
to build numerous independent all-black towns with schools, churches,
banks, and officials. Always remember, if life doesn't provide you the
opportunities you want, sometimes you have to take a risk and step out
on faith. That's what we did. And for most of us, it meant a better life.

Willie Kennard
(1832–?)
Marshal

(WILLIE *tells how he became a respected marshal in Yankee Hill,
Colorado.)*

WILLIE

My name is Willie Kennard. I was a marshal in the mining town of
Yankee Hill, Colorado. It was a job nobody wanted. I read an article
in the newspaper about a town needing a lawman, so I went there to
get the job. I found the mayor and some of the councilmen sipping
coffee in a local café. When I told them I wanted the job, they thought
I couldn't handle it and decided to give me a test. They told me I had

to prove I could handle responsibility; they also wanted a good laugh. They sent me to arrest the town's most dangerous villain, Barney Casewit. Casewit had killed one marshal and made another one leave town. The crowd followed me to a saloon where I found him playing poker. Everybody expected to see me turn tail and run or get shot.

I told Casewit that he was under arrest and to put up his hands and come peacefully. He and his buddies thought it was funny until they saw the way I had my guns tied down. They stopped laughing, because they knew I wasn't joking. Casewit was a bully, and he knew if he surrendered to a black man, nobody would ever fear him again. He made the mistake of going for his guns. Before his guns could clear his holsters, I shot his revolvers out of his hands. Two of his friends tried to help him, but I shot them between the eyes before they could get their pistols out. Casewit surrendered and was hanged. What people thought was going to be a joke on me turned out to be a joke on them, especially Casewit. I got the job and the town's respect.

Nat "Deadwood Dick" Love
(1854–1921)
Cowboy

Nat Love

(NAT *describes his success as a cowboy.*)

NAT

My name is Nat Love. I was born a slave in 1854. When I was fifteen years old, I won a horse in a raffle. I sold the horse, paid a few bills, and gave part of the money to my widowed mother and my sisters. Then I headed to Dodge City, Kansas, to fulfill my dream of becoming a cowboy. I wandered throughout the West. I got real good at scouting and branding cattle. I was also good with my pistols and became known as a gunfighter.

In 1876 I was in Deadwood, South Dakota, during a Fourth of July celebration. The town was having rodeo and shooting contests. I won the handgun and rifle contests and set a record in the bronco-riding and rope-throwing matches. I beat the other cowboys so bad that folks gave me the name Deadwood Dick.

Mary Fields
(1832–1914)
Stagecoach Driver

(MARY describes her job as a stagecoach driver.)

MARY

I'm Mary Fields. I'm also known as Stagecoach Mary, because I drive a stagecoach. Makes sense, doesn't it?
(Laughs)
I bet a lot of you didn't even know there were black cowboys and pioneers, let alone a female driving a stagecoach. A lot of black people like me who were born into slavery moved west after the war. I settled here in Montana. I know driving a stage isn't an ordinary job for an ordinary woman, but I ain't no ordinary woman. I'm not dainty and prissy like some women; never have been, never wanted to be. I stand tall for a woman, 6 feet if you need to know. I'm strong as almost any man and able to handle anything that comes my way. One night I was

driving my stage and a pack of wolves attacked the horses. I got down and beat the devil outta those critters! You should've seen them big bad wolves running away like scared puppies. I didn't let nobody or nothing stop my stagecoach.

I used to live in the convent with the nuns, but they kicked me out. I don't hold that against them. To put it nicely, I wasn't lady enough for them. I loved to hang out at the saloon, smoke my cigars, and drink my liquor. I used to make a little money on the side by betting cowboys a silver dollar that I could knock them out in one punch. I would bust out laughing as they fell on the floor.
(Laughs)
I don't know why they let me hit 'em, but me and the dentist were happy.

(Turns to the right and shades her eyes with her hands.)
Well, I better get to movin'. I see my passengers are boarding. I believe in leaving on time and arriving on time. Come out west and see me. Take a ride in my stagecoach. I'll give you the ride of your life.

Bill Pickett
(1870–1932)
Cowboy

Bill Pickett

(BILL describes his career as a cowboy and steer wrestler.)

BILL

My name is Bill Pickett. I've always been a cowboy. I was born and raised in Texas. I quit school in the fifth grade to work as a ranch hand. I loved that kind of rugged life. When I was a teenager, I learned the skill of bulldogging. For you tenderfoots who don't know what bulldogging is, it's a sport where you jump off a horse's back and grab a steer by the horns and wrestle him to the ground. Now that's what you really call grabbing the bull by the horns. But I added an extra flare to the sport. When I wrestled the bull, I would bite his lip and throw both hands in the air. That big ol' bull stayed on the ground right where I put him. The crowd went wild. In 1905 I signed on with the 101 Rodeo Show, and it wasn't long before I was an international star. I was the first Negro to be inducted into the Rodeo Hall of Fame.

Outlaws

(SPEAKER *identifies infamous African American outlaws of the West.*)

SPEAKER

Most of the African Americans who traveled west wanted to escape the South's Jim Crow laws and make a better life for themselves. Most were willing to work hard to earn an honest living; however, there were some who tried the easy way out and broke the law.

There were several notorious black outlaws known throughout the West. One was a cattle rustler named Isom Dart. He would steal cattle before they could moo. Another outlaw was a handsome young man named Cherokee Bill. As his name implied, Bill was part Native American. The ladies found him charming and the men found him dangerous. Bill would commit his crimes then run to safety in the Indian Territory. During his short life, he was known to have killed at least fourteen men. He was eventually caught and hanged when he was twenty years old. When asked on the gallows if he had any final words, Cherokee Bill said, "I came here to die, not to make speeches." Ben Hodges was another outlaw. He was a con man who could con you into giving him the gold in your mouth, then sell the teeth back to you. Hodges even conned the president of the National Bank in Dodge City out of thousands of dollars.

These men were dishonest and often dangerous. However, like other outlaws during this period, they became colorful characters in the West.

Matthew Henson
(1866–1955)
Explorer

Matthew Henson

(MATTHEW describes how he was a part of the first crew to reach the North Pole.)

MATTHEW

I'm Matthew Henson. I was an arctic explorer who reached the North Pole. I've always been adventurous and learned to be independent at an early age. I became an orphan when I was only eight. I signed onto a merchant ship as a cabin boy when I was a little older. I spent the next six years sailing the seas. Afterward, I moved to Washington, D.C. That's where I met Robert Perry. He hired me to accompany him on an expedition to explore the possibility of linking the Atlantic and Pacific

Oceans by building a canal through Nicaragua. We shared a long association and a goal: we wanted to be the first people to reach the North Pole. Our first six attempts were unsuccessful because of severe weather and subzero temperatures. In 1908 we made our seventh attempt. We traveled to Greenland, then to Ellesmere Island, where we waited for the sea to freeze. When the sea was frozen over, we set off for the North Pole. In my notes I documented that "we [traveled] 18 to 20 hours out of every day [because] we couldn't carry food for more than 50 days. On April 6, 1909, two of my Eskimo assistants and I reached the North Pole, built an igloo, then waited for Perry to meet us to verify his calculations. When he arrived, he and I planted the United States flag."

For years my participation in the expedition was ignored or given only a little credit because of my race. Our country eventually acknowledged my participation in that historic event.

AMENDMENTS AND CIVIL RIGHTS ACTS

Thirteenth Amendment

(SPEAKER *defines the Thirteenth Amendment.*)

SPEAKER
(*Wears a sandwich board that displays the Thirteenth Amendment.*)
I am the Thirteenth Amendment to the Constitution. I was passed in 1865 shortly after the end of the Civil War. I was the amendment that ended slavery in the United States and all of its territories.

Civil Rights Act of 1866

(SPEAKER *defines the Civil Rights Act of 1866.*)

SPEAKER
(*Wears a sandwich board that displays the Civil Rights Act of 1866.*)
I represent the Civil Rights Act of 1866. I am the law that gave African Americans citizenship. I made it illegal for states to pass laws known as black codes, which took away black people's rights.

Fourteenth Amendment

(SPEAKER *defines the Fourteenth Amendment.*)

SPEAKER
(Wears a sandwich board that displays the Fourteenth Amendment.)
I am the Fourteenth Amendment to the Constitution. I was passed in 1868. I was the amendment that made African Americans citizens of the United States. I provided constitutional backing for the Civil Rights Act of 1866.

Fifteenth Amendment

*(*SPEAKER *defines the Fifteenth Amendment.)*

SPEAKER
(Wears a sandwich board that displays the Fifteenth Amendment.)
I am the Fifteenth Amendment. I was passed in 1870. I gave African American males the right to vote.

Civil Rights Act of 1875

*(*SPEAKER *defines the Civil Rights Act of 1875.)*

SPEAKER
(Wears a sandwich board that displays the Civil Rights Act of 1875.)
I am the Civil Rights Act of 1875. My law was intended to make public places and accommodations open to all people, regardless of their race. Unfortunately, in 1883 the U.S. Supreme Court ruled that I was unconstitutional.

Civil Rights Act of 1957

*(*SPEAKER *defines the Civil Rights Act of 1957.)*

SPEAKER
(Wears a sandwich board that displays the Civil Rights Act of 1957.)

I am the Civil Rights Act of 1957. I was created by Congress to investigate charges that people were being denied the right to vote because of their race, color, religion, or national origin.

Twenty-fourth Amendment

(SPEAKER defines the Twenty-fourth Amendment.)

SPEAKER
(Wears a sandwich board that displays the Twenty-fourth Amendment.)
I am the Twenty-fourth Amendment to the Constitution. I was passed in 1964. Before I became a law, many African Americans in the South could not vote, because they couldn't afford the poll tax. I made charging a tax to vote illegal.

Civil Rights Act of 1964

(SPEAKER defines the Civil Rights Act of 1964.)

SPEAKER
(Wears a sandwich board that displays the Civil Rights Act of 1964.)
I am the Civil Rights Act of 1964. I outlawed discrimination in projects that were federally funded. I also made discrimination in hiring and in public places illegal.

Voting Rights Act of 1965

(SPEAKER defines the Voting Rights Act of 1965.)

SPEAKER
(Wears a sandwich board that displays the Voting Rights Act of 1965.)

I am the Voting Rights Act of 1965. I made it illegal for states to use tests or other devices to deny people the right to vote in any local, state, or federal election.

Civil Rights Act of 1968

Lyndon Johnson signs the Civil Rights Act of 1968

*(*SPEAKER *defines the Civil Rights Act of 1968.)*

SPEAKER
(Wears a sandwich board that displays the Civil Rights Act of 1968.)
I am the Civil Rights Act of 1968. I made discrimination in housing illegal.

JURISTS AND JUDGES

William Hastie
(1904–1976)
Judge

(WILLIAM *recounts when he became the first black federal judge in the United States.*)

WILLIAM
I'm William Hastie. In 1937 I became the first black federal judge in the United States.

Fred Gray
(1930–)
Attorney

(SPEAKER *highlights Fred Gray's major legal battles.*)

SPEAKER
Fred Gray is a brilliant attorney and a highly successful civil rights lawyer. Jim Crow laws prevented him from being admitted to a law school in Alabama, where he was born and raised. Gray made a personal commitment to himself when he was in college, "To become a lawyer, return to Alabama, and destroy everything segregated I could find."

Gray has actively worked for over forty years on that quest. At age twenty-four, with less than a year's experience, he took the case of Rosa Parks when she was arrested for violating the city's segregation laws in Montgomery, Alabama. Her arrest triggered a bus boycott that resulted in the U.S. Supreme Court Case *Browder v. Gayle*. Gray successfully argued the case before the Court. The Court ruled that segregation on city buses in Montgomery was illegal.

In 1973 Gray also represented the families of victims of the Tuskegee Syphilis study. He brought a $1.8 billion class action suit against many individuals and organizations that took part in the experiment. The study involved six hundred impoverished African American males who, unknowingly, were used as long term subjects to study the effects of syphilis when left untreated. Gray called for the survivors of the study and family members of the deceased victims to be awarded $3 million each. The case was resolved out of court. The government paid each survivor $37,500 and heirs of the victims $15,000 each. Gray received approximately $1 million for his legal costs.

Fred Gray is credited with winning other important civil rights cases in Alabama. He successfully argued another U.S. Supreme Court case *Gomillion v. Lightfoot* in 1960. It was the basis for the "one man, one vote" premise. He represented the freedom marches in Alabama in the 1960s and provided counsel for the freedom walkers and freedom riders who needed legal intervention to ensure protection on their march from Selma to Montgomery. This manifested into the Voting Rights Act of 1965. His lawsuit *Lee v. Macon* resulted in a statewide mandate requiring all public schools and institutes of higher learning in Alabama to desegregate.

Gray has been a leader in changing American society in the areas of segregation and racial discrimination in housing, voting, and jury duty. He also implemented positive changes in the national judicial system.

In 2000 he was inducted into the International Society of Barristers. In 2001 he was president of the Alabama Bar Association.

James Benton Parsons
(1911–1993)
Judge

(JAMES explains how he became the first African American judge of the U.S. District Court of the Northern District of Illinois.)

JAMES

My name is James Benton Parsons. In 1961 I was appointed as a judge to the U.S. District Court of the Northern District of Illinois. I became the first African American to be appointed to this position in the continental United States.

Thurgood Marshall
(1908–1994)
Judge

Thurgood Marshall

(THURGOOD shares highlights from his career as a lawyer and a U.S. Supreme Court judge.)

THURGOOD

"Hear ye, hear ye. The court is now in session. The Honorable Thurgood Marshall presiding." I still recall the first time I heard those words as a judge. Oh, I've heard it numerous times as a lawyer, but the difference is too great to describe. To become a judge is a dream for many attorneys, but to be appointed a U.S. Supreme Court justice is the peak of any lawyer's career. I was excited and nervous, but confident. I was confident, because I was given the opportunity to carry out our country's philosophy of blind justice at a higher level. I intended to make decisions that could guarantee the rights of all citizens, especially the poor and people who faced discrimination in their daily lives. Justice should not be based on color or income.

I know how it feels to be a victim of discrimination. After graduating from the historically black college Lincoln University in Pennsylvania, I applied to the University of Maryland School of Law, which is in my home state. I was denied admittance because I was black. I was disappointed, because I knew I qualified for admission. I didn't let that stop me from achieving my goal of becoming a lawyer. I applied to another historically black college, Howard University School of Law in Washington, D.C. After graduating from Howard in 1933, I moved back to Baltimore and began a private practice.

I had a long, fulfilling career. I agreed to serve as local counsel for the NAACP. The pay wasn't very much. I was paid $5 per day for court appearances, investigations, and research and $25 a year for postage and stationery. But I didn't work for the money; I worked to fight for people's rights. One of my first assignments for the NAACP was to help organize picket lines to force white businessmen to hire black salespeople. I also tried to help organize African American schoolteachers in an attempt to receive the same pay as white teachers. During this same period, I was trying to persuade the Maryland congressmen to support a federal antilynching bill. I stayed busy. There were so many issues that needed attention. I had to prepare for many different kinds of cases. It seemed there was no end to the problems we were facing. Fortunately, I was successful in most of my cases.

The case of *Murray v. Maryland* in 1936, which I won with NAACP lawyer Hamilton Houston, was very rewarding. It challenged the University of Maryland School of Law's discrimination policy against African Americans. It was the same school that refused to admit me. It's ironic, isn't it? In 1938 I was able to convince the governor of Texas to provide protection for black Americans who served jury duty. There was also the case of the twenty-five black men who were charged with attempted murder in Tennessee. They defended themselves against a white mob that came into the black section of town and began shooting into their homes. I was able to get twenty-three of the twenty-five men acquitted.

In 1940 I began serving as director-counsel for the NAACP's Legal Defense and Educational Fund. I argued thirty-two major cases before the Supreme Court of the United States for the NAACP. I won twenty-nine of those thirty-two cases. Let me give you some examples of our battles. In 1944 in the case *Smith v. Allwright*, I was able to convince the Court to outlaw white-only primary elections. In 1946 there was the case of *Morgan v. Virginia*. It was the first victory for the NAACP that involved cases of segregated seating in interstate public transportation. The *Shelly v. Kraemer* case in 1948 brought another victory for our organization. This ruling made restrictive covenants, which were housing agreements that prevented the sale of homes to blacks, illegal. Perhaps my most famous case was *Brown v. Board of Education of Topeka* in 1954. The Court's decision in this case made segregation in public schools illegal.

My people weren't just discriminated against in the United States, they faced racism abroad too. It's shameful, but much of the discrimination occurred within the U.S. military. In 1951 I had to fly to Japan and Korea to investigate the court-martial involving thirty-two African American soldiers. By the time I arrived, half of them had already received the death sentence or a life term in prison. The remainder of the soldiers had sentences that ranged between ten to fifty years of hard labor. After investigating, I proved that one man was hospitalized at the time of the crime and the others who had been accused of desertion had been on duty. Through me, the NAACP was able to get many of the sentences either reversed and or reduced.

My hard work caught the attention of President Kennedy. He nominated me to be a judge on the Second Circuit Court of Appeals. I was confirmed on September 11, 1962. I handed down more than 150 opinions and never had a single one reversed by a higher court.

My career continued to rise. In 1965 President Johnson appointed me Solicitor General of the Department of Justice. I won fourteen of the nineteen cases I argued for the Justice Department. The highest point in my career came in 1967. That was the year President Johnson appointed me to the U.S. Supreme Court. I served twenty-four years on the bench. Now it's 1991. I'm retiring and clearing out my chambers. It's been a long, hard-fought career. So many things have been accomplished, yet there are still so many things to do. I'm looking for someone to whom I can pass the gavel. Can I pass it to you? Will you be a champion for civil rights? Will you be a lawyer concerned with justice and the rights of all citizens? More importantly, will you take advantage of all the cases we won for your benefit? Will you make education, schooling, voting, and other civil rights a priority in your life? I hope so. Never let justice retire.

Constance Baker Motley
(1921–2005)
Judge

Constance Motley

(CONSTANCE describes how she became the first female African American federal judge.)

CONSTANCE

My name is Constance Baker Motley. In 1966 I became the first female African American federal judge. I was appointed to the U.S. Circuit Court of the Southern District of New York. My appointment made me the highest paid African American woman in government. Prior to serving as a judge, I worked as a lawyer with the NAACP. I'm proud to say I won some very difficult cases. Perhaps my most famous case was against the University of Mississippi, when I represented James Meredith. This case made it possible to break down the segregation barriers in southern universities.

JOURNALISM

John Russwurm
(1799–1851)
Journalist, Newspaper Publisher

(JOHN explains why he published the first African American newspaper in the United States.)

JOHN

I'm John Russwurm, and I'm a newspaper journalist. My coeditor Reverend Samuel Cornish and I published the first Negro newspaper in the United States. There were many Negroes who were growing concerned, because there were very few newspapers that spoke on our behalf. Also it was difficult to find a newspaper that advocated for an end to slavery. We needed to make sure our issues were heard. On March 16, 1827, our first edition of *Freedom's Journal* was published. The immediate reason we established the paper was to respond to an antiblack publication in New York City, which defended slavery and ridiculed our race.

Our first issue boldly stated our objectives: immediate emancipation of all slaves, equal political and civil rights for free blacks, opposition to racist publicity, and truthful information about Africa. Our paper lasted less than two years, because many black people were illiterate, or because they didn't have enough money to support the paper. During our period of publication, however, we devoted ourselves to focusing on foreign and domestic news that was of interest to Negroes.

Robert S. Abbott
(1870–1940)
Journalist, Newspaper Publisher

(ROBERT *explains how he became a successful newspaper publisher.*)

ROBERT

My name is Robert Abbott. I'm the founder of the *Chicago Defender* newspaper, the paper I labeled the *World's Greatest Weekly*. I'm from St. Simon, Georgia. I've been to college and lived in a lot of places prior to settling in Chicago. I always dreamed of establishing a newspaper, even as a young boy. I didn't get much encouragement, and many people made fun of my vision.

When I was a student at Hampton Institute in Virginia, I took my stepfather's advice and learned the printing trade. I was glad that I listened to him, because this skill enabled me to start my newspaper. In 1896 I migrated to Chicago and obtained a law degree. I wandered throughout the Midwest for several years before I realized that I could defend more people in public print than in the courtroom.

With some borrowed money and a small amount of my capital, I used a folding card table and a kitchen chair and set it up as my office in my landlady's house. It was there on May 5, 1905, that I started the *Chicago Defender*. The first copies consisted of three hundred four-page-handbill sheets, which were printed on my employer's press. They contained local news and news clips from other papers. I went from door to door and to every barbershop, poolroom, drugstore, and church. I peddled my paper for two cents a copy.

In 1910 I hired my first employee, J. Hockey Smiley. He helped the *Defender* gain a national following. Smiley incorporated "yellow journalism" into the publication to increase sales. We used red ink to capture the reader's attention and to highlight horrible events. We also used sensationalistic headlines and graphic images to inform readers of the atrocities of lynchings, assaults, and other acts of violence. We had a media advantage, because we were located in the North. This gave us more opportunity to express the concerns and issues of the race. I say "the race," because we never used the term Negro or black in our paper. We referred to our people as "the race," "race man," or "race woman." We were militant in our editorials and didn't bite our tongues to comment on injustice. We also advocated for integration in sports and fought for antilynching laws.

We were the first paper of our race to have over 100,000 subscribers. We were widely read all over the South. However, we often had to smuggle the paper across the Mason-Dixon Line, because hate groups like the Ku Klux Klan would try to confiscate it. Also, other whites outside of the Klan would threaten our readers. To sneak the *Defender* into that region, we used black Pullman porters and entertainers to transport them for us. We were also the first paper of our race to have a health column and a full-page comic strip.

When I look back at my youth, when owning a newspaper was just a vision in my head, I remember how my friends mocked me. I had enough faith in myself not to let that hinder me. I don't look back in bitterness. I actually find it humorous, because now they're buying my paper. As I always say, "Success is the best revenge."

Claude A. Barnett
(1889–1967)
Journalist, Reporter

(CLAUDE *explains what prompted him to establish the Associated Negro Press.)*

CLAUDE

My name is Claude A. Barnett. I was born in Sanford, Florida. I'm the founder of the Associated Negro Press, located in Chicago, Illinois. In 1919 I established this news agency as an avenue to inform Negroes about worldwide issues relating to them. For years my news line was the only source in the United States that was primarily devoted to collecting and disseminating black news from all corners of the globe.

Prior to my innovation, news for our race wasn't spread any farther than the circulation range of local newspapers. I organized a body of news correspondents located across the country to report national news and events each week to black newspapers. I also successfully fought to have black reporters assigned to the front lines of battle during World War II. My goal was to make sure that black news received the same coverage as all other media occurrences. I can proudly say I reached that goal.

John Howard Johnson
(1918–2005)
Magazine Publisher

(SPEAKER explains what prompted John Johnson to establish Ebony and Jet magazines.)

SPEAKER

John H. Johnson, like most of you, loved school. He also loved reporting the news. He became editor of his school's newspaper. He was able to attend college, which wasn't easy during that time. Most African American families were too poor to afford college, and there weren't many scholarships available to them. After college, Johnson sold life insurance, but his real interest was in the publishing industry.

Johnson didn't have much money, but he had a mother who believed in him. In 1942 she allowed him to use her furniture as collateral for a $500 loan. He used the money to start a publishing company. Johnson wanted to focus on black news and report on issues overlooked by the white media. His first magazine was *Negro Digest*. Within a week the first five thousand copies were sold out. In 1945 he published *Ebony*. It was a picture-style magazine. He wanted to show positive images of black people. In 1951 he published *Jet*. It was a weekly pocket-size magazine. Johnson later published *Tan* and *Ebony Jr*. Today his family business includes Fashion Fair Cosmetics. His company also sponsors the internationally renowned Ebony Fashion Show.

John Johnson went from a poor man with a $500 loan to a multimillionaire, whose assets totaled close to $150 million before his death in 2005. His philosophy was that people should surround themselves with positive people and be willing to work hard, but most of all he felt that one must always believe they can succeed. His favorite expression was, "Failure is not a word I accept."

Alice Dunnigan
(1906–1983)
Reporter

(ALICE recounts her success in the field of journalism.)

ALICE

I'm Alice Dunnigan. I was a reporter with the Associated Negro Press. I worked mostly in the political arena. I was born in Kentucky and graduated from Kentucky State College.

I was the first African American woman to become an accredited journalist to the White House and State Department. I was also the first African American female to have access to the Senate press galleries and to the House of Representatives. In addition, I was the first African American to cover a presidential campaign. In 1948 I covered Harry S. Truman's whistle-stop train trips on his campaign trail.

Ethel L. Payne
(1911–1991)
Journalist

(ETHEL *highlights her work as a journalist.*)

ETHEL

My name is Ethel Payne. I'm also known as the First Lady of the Black Press. I may not be well-known outside of the Chicago area; however, like so many others I played a part in black history too. I'm a journalist and worked for the *Chicago Defender,* a newspaper that represented the black voice. I covered the events of the civil rights movement. I knew it was important for black Americans to keep informed of the struggles taking place throughout our country from an objective and black perspective.

National Association of Black Journalists

(LAWILTAY *defines the National Association of Black Journalists to his father.*)

LAWILTAY
(On the phone talking to his father.)
Hello, Dad. Guess what? You don't have to worry about taking out that loan for my tuition now. I got a scholarship from the National Association of Black Journalists. My English teacher told me to apply to the organization. I didn't know much about it, but I looked them up and they really have it together. They were founded on December 12, 1975, by 44 male and female members. Now they have over

41,000 members. Their headquarters is at the University of Maryland at College Park. Anyway, they give out more than $100,000 in scholarship money to black students majoring in journalism, place fourteen to sixteen students in paid internships, and sponsor short courses for students at historically black colleges and universities. It's the largest organization of journalists of color in the United States and the largest of the four associations that make up UNITY.

(Pauses)

What is UNITY? It's the organization that is made up of the Asian American Journalists Association, the National Association of Hispanic Journalists, the Native American Journalist Association, and the Black Journalist Association.

(Pauses)

I'm glad I made you proud. I love you too. Good-bye.

POETS AND WRITERS

Colonial Voices: 1745–1775

Lucy Terry
(ca. 1730–1821)
Poet

(LUCY cites her contribution to poetry.)

LUCY
My name is Lucy Terry. In 1746 I wrote the poem "Bars Fight." It was about a battle between local Indians and white settlers on the outskirts of our town in Deerfield, Massachusetts. I'm considered the first black female to write a poem.

Jupiter Hammon
(1711–ca. 1806)
Poet

(JUPITER recalls how he became the first published black poet in America.)

JUPITER
My name is Jupiter Hammon. Even though I was enslaved, I learned to read and write. I loved to read, and my master allowed me to use his library. I also wrote poetry. My first poem was published in 1760. It was an eighty-eight-line poetry piece titled "An Evening Thought.

Salvation by Christ, with Penitential Cries." I was the first Negro to be published in America.

Phyllis Wheatley
(1753–1784)
Poet

Phyllis Wheatley

(PHYLLIS describes her success as a poet.)

PHYLLIS

My name is Phyllis Wheatley, and I'm a poet. I was the first African American woman who tried to earn a living by writing. I often used my poetry to express how I felt. Are you the same way? When I was about eight, I was kidnapped from Gambia, Africa, by slave catchers and brought to Boston. I was bought by the Wheatley family to work as a maid for the mistress of the house, but because I was sickly, I only had light household duties. I learned English quickly and was taught to read and write. When I was fourteen, one of my poems was published in a local newspaper.

The Wheatleys gave me my freedom when I was twenty, and I traveled to England with my book of poetry: *Poems on Various Subjects, Religious and Moral*, which was published in 1773. In 1776 I dedicated a poem to General Washington. He was so impressed that he invited me to his headquarters during the Revolutionary War.

I used my poetry to criticize whites who supported slavery and to give hope to people of my race. I proved to society that black people were just as intelligent as people of the white race.

ANTEBELLUM WRITERS: 1820–1860

James Pennington
(1807–1870)
Autobiographer, Nonfiction Writer

(JIM highlights his published works on early African American history.)

JIM

I was born Jim Pembroke on Maryland's Eastern Shore in 1807. I escaped from slavery and changed my name to James Pennington. In 1841 I published a textbook called *The Origin and History of the Colored People*. It was the first recorded history of Negroes. In 1849 I wrote my autobiography, *The Fugitive Blacksmith*. It was also one of the first slave narratives.

Frances Ellen Watkins Harper
(1825–1911)
Poet, Novelist, Essayist

(FRANCES highlights works from her career as a writer.)

FRANCES

My name is Frances Harper. I was born in Baltimore, Maryland to a free black family, but I was orphaned when I was three. When I moved to Pennsylvania as an adult, I became active in the Underground Railroad and began to tour the country and speak out against slavery.

In 1854 I published *Poems of Miscellaneous Subjects*. It sold over ten thousand copies. I continued to write poetry, essays, stories, and novels. My work focused on racism and the oppression endured by females.

Harriet Jacobs
(1813–1897)
Autobiographer

(HARRIET shares the history behind her autobiographical slave narrative.)

HARRIET

Hello, my name is Harriet Jacobs. I changed my name to Linda Brent when I wrote my autobiography, because I was an escaped slave. My book, *Incidents in the Life of a Slave Girl*, was published in 1860. It was a narrative based on my life. It documented the seven years I hid from my master in a crawlspace in my grandmother's attic. My master would not free me, nor would he let anyone buy my freedom. He was determined to have me for himself, and I was determined not to allow him to touch me. I ran away after I could no longer tolerate his advances. Like most slave narratives, the purpose was to expose the brutality of slavery. I used my autobiography to disclose how Negro women suffered additional personal abuse from their masters.

THE PROGRESSIVE ERA: 1890–1920

Charles Chesnutt
(1858–1932)
Poet, Essayist, Novelist

(CHARLES shares his award-winning achievements in writing.)

———

CHARLES

I'm Charles Chesnutt. I was born in Cleveland, Ohio, but moved to Fayetteville, North Carolina, when my parents returned to their home state. I've written poems, novels, essays, and a biography of Frederick Douglass. I spent seventeen years in North Carolina. I experienced both the problems of Southern Reconstruction in Fayetteville and the rise of the black middle class in Cleveland. My life in the South provided some of the material for many of my short stories and novels.

My first literary works were published in 1887. One of these stories was *The Goophered Grapevine*. It was one of my conjure tales, which focused on black magic. In 1899 I published two more stories, *The Conjure Woman* and *The Wife of His Youth and Other Stories of the Color Line*. The stories in this collection explored the issues caused by racial prejudice. In 1901 I published *The Marrow of Tradition*. It was my second novel. I published my last novel in 1905. It was titled *The Colonel's Dream*.

I was considered a pioneer for writers of the Harlem Renaissance of the 1920s. Just like me, the renaissance writers destroyed the myth of racial progress by showing the true black experience. In 1928 I received the Spingarn Medal in honor of my works.

Paul Laurence Dunbar
(1872–1906)
Poet, Novelist, Editor

Paul Laurence Dunbar

(PAUL highlights works from his career as a writer.)

PAUL

I'm Paul Laurence Dunbar. I was born in Dayton, Ohio. I was the
only black student in my class. I became class president and class
poet. I published my first poem when I was sixteen. I also published a
newspaper called the *Tattler* for the Negro community. I wrote dialect
poems, and I'm credited as being the founder of the school of black
dialect. I used this dialect to preserve oral storytelling as an art form. I
was aware of the importance of portraying both the joys and hardships
of Negro life. My first book of poems, *Oak and Ivy*, was published
in 1893. My next book was *Majors and Minors*. I felt my readers,
who were mostly white, didn't appreciate what I considered my best
works. They wanted me to write poems that validated the stereotype
of Negroes, which portrayed them living a contented life on Southern
plantations.

I always had poor health. I suffered from tuberculosis, and in 1899 I
developed pneumonia. I continued to write, even though I knew my
illness was incurable. I wrote four short stories and four novels. I

feel that I have accomplished a lot in my life. Even though I was the son of runaway slaves and couldn't afford to go to college, I became successful. People dubbed me the Poet Laureate of the Negro Race.

Angelina Weld Grimke
(1880–1958)
Poet, Playwright

(ANGELINA highlights her published plays and poems.)

ANGELINA
My name is Angelina Grimke. I was born in Boston, Massachusetts in 1880. My poetry and short stories have been featured in *The Poetry of the Negro, Opportunity, New Negro Poets and Their Poems, Caroling Dusk*, and the *Crisis*. My play *Rachel: A Play in Three Acts* was performed in 1916 in Washington, D.C. It was written for the NAACP for the purpose of gathering support to protest the racist movie *Birth of a Nation. Rachel* was one of the first antilynching plays in America.

Carter G. Woodson
(1875–1950)
Nonfiction Writer

(CARTER shares his achievements in nonfiction writing.)

CARTER
I'm Carter Woodson. I'm known as the Father of Black History. This is because I was determined to make sure black people had a recognized place in U.S. history. My life was dedicated to the pursuit of truth about black people in our country. I was one of the few people who tried to understand slavery from the slave's point of view. I didn't focus on the black person as a victim of racism like many white researchers had done.

In 1913 my associates and I founded the Association for the Study of Negro Life and History. The purpose was to educate everyone, especially black people, about the Negro's achievements and history. In 1916 I published *The Journal of Negro History.* I spent years researching hundreds of articles on slavery, black labor, culture, and history.

Many of my notable works were published in the 1920s and 1930s. For example, in 1921 *The History of the Negro Church* was published; in 1922 *The Rural Negro*; in 1933 *The Miseducation of the Negro Prior to 1861*; and in 1937 *The Negro History Bulletin.* I also established Negro History Week in February of 1926. I chose February, because that was the birth month of Frederick Douglass and Abraham Lincoln. Today I am proud to say Black History Week has expanded to Black History Month. But don't just celebrate black history in February; celebrate black history and black people's achievements every month.

HARLEM RENAISSANCE WRITERS: 1920–1935

Langston Hughes
(1902–1967)
Poet, Novelist, Playwright

Langston Hughes

(LANGSTON highlights works from his career as a writer.)

LANGSTON

I'm Langston Hughes. I was born in Joplin, Missouri, in 1902. I grew up in Kansas and Ohio and lived with my grandmother, Mary Langston, until I was twelve. Her first husband, John Leary, was killed in a fight in Harpers Ferry, Virginia, in the rebellion against slavery led by John Brown. My grandmother would tell me stories about black heroes, and at night she would put my grandfather's bloodstained bullet-ridden shirt from John Brown's raid around me.

My father was absent in my life, and I never got over my resentment toward him. I also resented the fact that my mother gave me away. These feelings were reflected in a lot of my stories. I began writing poetry when I was a teenager. I moved to Washington, D.C., and met a popular poet who encouraged me to develop my talents. I later moved to New York City to attend Columbia University. I chose that school because it was in Harlem. In 1921 the NAACP's *Crisis* magazine published my poem called "The Negro Speaks of Rivers." That lyric earned me the title Poet Laureate of Harlem. I published my first book of poems, *The Weary Blues*, in 1926. I used jazz and blues to create new poetic forms that would express the vital life of urban blacks. The following year, I published my second book, *Fine Clothes to the Jew*. My first novel, *Not Without Laughter*, was published in 1930.

In 1934 I published *The Ways of White Folks*. It was a collection of short stories. In 1943 I wrote a humorous column for the *Chicago Defender*. It was about the views of a character named Jesse B. Simple. The Simple stories were later collected into five books. They became some of my most popular works. I've authored a number of children's stories, short stories, and biographies and edited numerous anthologies. I also founded the Harlem Suitcase Theater.

My work always celebrated ordinary black people. My poetry identified with everyone in every walk of life.

Claude McKay
(1890–1948)
Poet, Novelist

Claude McKay

(CLAUDE shares his achievements in writing.)

CLAUDE

I'm Claude McKay. I was born in Sunny Ville, Jamaica. In 1912 I left my native Jamaica to move to the United States, because I saw it as a golden land of education. I enrolled at Tuskegee Institute in Tuskegee, Alabama. I only stayed there two months then transferred to Kansas State College. This experience of life in the South left me disillusioned and showed me that blacks in the United States didn't have the same opportunities as whites.

I wrote two books of poetry: *Songs of Jamaica* and *Constab Ballads*. They were published in 1912 in Jamaica. They were inspired by my love for my homeland and written in Jamaican dialect. In 1914 I moved to New York to begin a literary career. *The Seven Arts* literary magazine published two of my sonnets in 1917. Shortly after that, I had other works published. I've been labeled an angry poet because I'm best known for my poetry that is militant, like "If We Must Die." It encourages blacks to fight against injustice. In 1922 I published *Harlem Shadows*. It is considered my most important collection of

poems. In 1928 I wrote my first novel, *Home to Harlem*. It was the first
of three thematically related novels. It won the Harmon Foundation
Gold Award for Literature.

I traveled extensively in Russia, Germany, France, England, and
Morocco. I enjoyed living among the masses. These travel experiences
influenced the title of my 1937 autobiography, *A Long Way from Home*.
When I retired from writing in my later years, I dedicated a lot of my
time to helping young people. I joined the Catholic Youth Organization
in Chicago as a means to aid them.

Anne Spencer
(1882–1975)
Poet

(ANNE highlights the themes in her poetic works.)

ANNE
My name is Anne Spencer. I was born Annie Bethel Bannister in 1882
in Henry County, Virginia, but I spent my early childhood in West
Virginia. Later, my mother had me return to Virginia to attend school.
I enrolled in Virginia Seminary in Lynchburg. After graduation, I made
Lynchburg my permanent home.

I was one of the early Harlem Renaissance writers. I was discovered
by James Weldon Johnson. It was James who gave me the name Anne
Spencer. He said it had a more sophisticated tone than Annie. Even
though I didn't live in Harlem, numerous famous black writers and
well-known personalities visited my Lynchburg home.

Between 1920 and 1931, I had at least twenty poems published
in a variety of magazines and anthologies. Some of those poems
are "Before the Feast of Shushan," "At the Carnival," "White

Things," "Lady, Lady," "The Wife Woman," "Letter to My Sister," "Translation," "Lines to a Nasturtium," and "Dunbar."

Jean Toomer
(1894–1967)
Novelist

(JEAN highlights his success as a novelist.)

JEAN

My name is Jean Toomer. I was born in Washington, D.C., in 1894. I became famous after writing the novel *Cane* published in 1923. It established me as one of the most talented of the Harlem Renaissance writers. I got the inspiration to write *Cane* after teaching in a segregated school in Sparta, Georgia. The Negro folk songs and the beautiful landscape sparked my imagination. I tried to capture both the beauty and ugliness of poverty and racial oppression. I divided *Cane* into three parts. The first section is set in rural Georgia. The characters encounter tragedy and frustration, but their lives are touched by beauty, despite it all. The second segment is set in the urban areas of Washington, D.C. and Chicago. These characters in the city find their lives filled with materialistic corruption. The final third of the book focuses on a black intellectual who returns to the South and searches for his roots unsuccessfully. I chose not to be very active in the literary world after *Cane*. I retired to spend a quiet life with the Quakers in Pennsylvania.

Alain Leroy Locke
(1885–1954)
Poet, Essayist

(ALAIN highlights his achievements in writing.)

ALAIN

My name is Alain Locke. I was born in Philadelphia, Pennsylvania. I was the first black Rhodes Scholar. I developed a deep interest in Africa while studying in Europe. I founded the African Union Society. It was an organization that promoted communication among black leaders and improved the condition of blacks in the United States, Africa, and the Caribbean.

When I returned to the United States in 1911, I toured the South for six months. The following year, I accepted a position as an English professor at Howard University. Following World War I, I earned my PhD from Harvard University. I became one of the leading intellectuals of the emerging Harlem Renaissance.

In 1925, when I returned from another trip to Africa, I had a conflict with Howard University's white president. I was fired, although both alumni and students protested my dismissal. I published a book that same year, which was a collection of poems, essays, stories, and artwork titled *The New Negro: Voices of the Harlem Renaissance*. My book emphasized the fact that a new Negro now existed, who now endorsed a proud consciousness of the black race and resisted the past stereotypes. My published philosophy was believed to define the new Negro movement, which was later called the Harlem Renaissance. It also made me a key spokesman and leader of this movement. In 1928 I returned to Howard's faculty. The university now had its first black president. He and I worked closely together and he encouraged me to establish an African American studies program.

I've written countless books, essays, and articles. Among them are *Plays of Negro Life: A Source-Book of Native American Drama, The Four Negro Poets,* and *When Peoples Meet: A Study in Race and Culture Contacts.*

Zora Neal Hurston
(1901–1960)
Novelist, Short Story Writer, Autobiographer

Zora Neal Hurston

(ZORA highlights works from her career as a writer.)

ZORA

I'm Zora Neal Hurston. I was born in Eatonville, Florida. Eatonville was an all-black town that was rich in Southern folklore. I was fascinated by these tales and incorporated folklore into my stories.

I studied writing at Howard University and later received a scholarship to study anthropology at Barnard College. I continued to collect folklore after college. In 1934 I published *Jonah's Gourd Vine*. In 1935 I published a folklore collection called *Mules and Men*. In May 1925 I gained literary recognition when my short story "Spunk" was published in *The New Negro: Voices of the Harlem Renaissance,* which introduced the birth of the new Negro and the Harlem Renaissance. In 1942 I published my autobiography, *Dust Tracks on a Road.* In 1943 I became the first black person to appear on the cover of the *Saturday Review of Literature.* I continued my theme of black folklore in my stories, essays, and various articles. I told it and wrote it like it was. I was the first black person to use regional black dialect as a complicated language of narration.

I was an independent woman and writer. During the Harlem Renaissance, I received a great deal of criticism from several of my contemporary male authors. They called my work lyrical symbolism. These prominent writers were more interested in what they called resources in naturalism. In other words, they focused on the practice of describing the actual circumstances in literature. I didn't let their writing styles influence me to change my writing style. Despite their criticism, I became the most acclaimed black female writer since Phyllis Wheatley.

I was the first novelist to successfully showcase a black woman's search to find a voice and overcome male-dominated oppression in literature. I suppose I symbolized women's liberation, before it became popular. My message to you is, when faced with criticism, don't change for other people. The only true success is the success that is within you.

Countee Cullen
(1903–1946)
Poet, Novelist

(SPEAKER shares Countee Cullen's contributions to poetry.)

SPEAKER
Countee Cullen was one of the most popular poets of the Harlem Renaissance. He was born Countee LeRoy Porter. His place of birth is not certain. It may have been New York City, Baltimore, Maryland, or Louisville, Kentucky. His parents are also unknown. He was possibly raised by his grandmother for a while, and later taken in by the pastor of a large church in Harlem. His initial poetry was published while he was still a high school student.

Cullen was known to be a fast writer and published books in rapid succession. He is classified as a traditional poet; almost all of his poetry is written with mixed meters, rhyme schemes, and standard verse. Perhaps most influential was Cullen's view that art is blind to race. He never wanted to be labeled a Negro poet. He let it be stated that he wanted to be known as a man of literature. The irony is, however, that he continually found himself writing about the African American race. His poems "Heritage," "From the Dark Tower," and "Incident" all focus on his concerns involving race. The titles of his volumes of poetry also strongly suggest his concern with racial themes for example, *Color*, *Ballad of the Brown Girl*, and *Copper Sun*. In 1932 he wrote his only novel, *One Way to Heaven*. It depicted the aspect of living in Harlem. Cullen believed black people should be presented in a positive manner in order to successfully advance their position in life.

Rudolph Fisher
(1897–1934)
Novelist, Short Story Writer

(RUDOLPH *highlights works from his career as a writer.*)

RUDOLPH

I'm Rudolph Fisher. I was born in Washington, D.C. I published my first short story in the *Atlanta Monthly* while I was still a medical student. Most of my stories focus on the conflict between the Southern black migrant's dream of Northern urban life and the harsh realities of the city. My themes incorporate humor and sympathy. I published two novels in addition to my short stories. My novel *The Conjure Man Dies*, published in 1932, was the first detective novel written by an African American.

Arna Bontemps
(1902–1973)
Poet, Novelist, Editor

(ARNA shares his contributions to writing.)

ARNA

I'm Arna Bontemps. I was born in Alexandria, Louisiana. I moved to New York City during the Harlem Renaissance, where I began to perfect my writing with the prominent authors of that day. I have written poetry, essays, and more than a dozen books for children and young adults. A few of my works are *Anyplace But Here*, *God Sends Sunday*, and *100 Years of Negro Freedom*. My most popular novel is *Black Thunder*, published in 1936. It was a historical narrative about slavery told through the eyes of a slave. Some of my poems are "The Day Breakers," "A Black Man Talks of Reaping," and "Southern Mansion." I coedited *The Poetry of the Negro 1746–1949* with Langston Hughes. I was also the editor of *American Negro Poetry*.

James Weldon Johnson
(1871–1938)
Poet, Autobiographer, Essayist

James Weldon Johnson

(JAMES highlights his published works.)

JAMES

I'm James Weldon Johnson. I was born in Jacksonville, Florida. My mother encouraged my creativity. When I was seventeen, I worked for a white doctor who opposed racism. He gave me books and discussed them with me. He also encouraged me to write poetry. I moved to New York City in 1902. I became a part of the theater community. I also became active in civil rights activities. In 1925 and 1926, my brother and I edited two volumes of Negro spirituals. In 1927 I wrote numerous essays highlighting the accomplishments of Negroes in the arts. In 1929 I wrote an entry on black poetry for the *Encyclopedia Britannica*. I published my last volume of poetry in 1935. Among my published works are *Fifty Years and Other Poems, God's Trombone, St. Peter Relates an Incident*, and my autobiography, *Along This Way*. In addition to poetry and essays, I wrote lyrics for musical shows and hit songs. Even though I've written prose and poetry on various subjects, I'm best remembered for cowriting the lyrics and music for "Lift Every Voice and Sing" with my brother J. Rosamond Johnson. It was adopted by black people as the black national anthem.

WORLD WAR II, COLD WAR, AND POST WAR WRITERS: 1938–1960

Richard Wright
(1908–1960)
Short Story Writer, Novelist

Richard Wright

(RICHARD shares the impetus for his successful novels and short stories.)

RICHARD

My name is Richard Wright. I'm an author. I'm going to tell you a story, so listen carefully. Once upon a time, there was a little black boy who lived in the South. When he was four, he accidentally set his house on fire. He was beaten until he lost consciousness and nearly died. His father was a heavy drinker and deserted the family when he was six. His mother was destitute. She couldn't afford to support her children and had to put them in an orphanage for a short time.

His family later moved to Arkansas and lived with relatives. It wasn't long before they were forced to move. A white man murdered his uncle, because he wanted his uncle's business. His mother was under a lot of pressure and suffered a stroke. The family then moved to Jackson, Mississippi, to live with his grandmother. They were extremely poor, with barely enough to survive. The little boy didn't get along with his grandmother. She was extremely religious and disapproved of his desire to become a writer. When he turned seventeen, he left home and moved to Memphis, then to Chicago.

Did you like that story? Most people only like stories that have a happy theme. But this is a true story. It's my story. I was the little boy that experienced that sad childhood. This harsh childhood in the South and living as a black man in America influenced the themes of most of my writings. In 1938 I published *Uncle Tom's Children*, a collection of short stories. It focused on discrimination in the South. In 1940 I wrote *Native Son*, my most famous novel. The book sold over 200,000 copies in less than three weeks. It gave me national acclaim and established me as a leading author. I wrote a number of other stories. My most painful was my autobiography, *Black Boy*, which I wrote in 1946. I migrated to France with my wife and daughters in 1947 and continued to write. I remained there the rest of my life. I became pessimistic about racial change in the United States. However, I kept the issue alive through my novels by trying to make America conscious of itself.

Robert Hayden
(1913–1980)
Poet

(ROBERT highlights works from his career as a poet.)

ROBERT
I'm Robert Hayden. I was born in Detroit, Michigan, in 1913. Two of my volumes of poetry are *Heart Shape in the Dust* and *Ballad of Remembrance*. I have won numerous awards for my poems about black history and black historical figures. I've written about figures such as Harriet Tubman, Frederick Douglass, Nat Turner, and Malcolm X. In

1976 I became the first black person to serve as Poetry Consultant to the Library of Congress.

Margaret Walker
(1915–1998)
Poet, Novelist

(MARGARET highlights her successful published works.)

MARGARET

I'm Margaret Walker. I was born in Birmingham, Alabama. I grew up in a "talking" family. This exposure to oral history became a significant factor in my life. I had a unique style of presenting racial consciousness and protest, but my main goal as a writer was to express black optimism and strength. My first volume of poems, *For My People*, won the Yale Younger Poets Series Award. In 1937 the title poem was published in *Poetry* magazine and was an instant sensation. In 1966 I published *Jubilee*, a historical novel based on the stories my grandmother recounted of a slave family.

Ralph Ellison
(1914–1994)
Novelist, Essayist

Ralph Ellison

(RALPH shares the influences that made him a great writer.)

RALPH

I'm Ralph Ellison. I was born in Oklahoma City, Oklahoma, and attended Tuskegee Institute in Alabama. I loved to read. I read everything I could find. I also loved to listen to other people's stories and tell tales that I made up. At first I wanted to be a lawyer, but after moving to New York and meeting Langston Hughes and Richard Wright, I was encouraged by them to write a short story and contribute to a Harlem literary magazine. Between 1938 and 1944, I published a large number of short stories. In 1945 I decided to write a novel based on history, black identity, and heroism. I began writing *The Invisible Man*. It took me over five years to complete it. It was about a black man who moved to New York, who hoped to improve his condition in life. The book was influenced by sermons, spirituals, blues, and folklore. *The Invisible Man* received the National Book Award in 1953. I published *Shadow and Act* in 1964. It was a collection of essays focusing on literature, folklore, jazz, and blues as they relate to black and white culture. My collection of essays, *Going to the Territory*, deals with my experiences in New York in 1936. Some of my other works are *Flying Home: and Other Stories* and *Juneteenth: a Novel*. I believed in writing with a purpose. I felt that black American writers should create work that would raise the consciousness of its readers.

Gwendolyn Brooks
(1917–2000)
Poet

Gwendolyn Brooks

(GWENDOLYN shares her accomplishments as a poet.)

GWENDOLYN

I'm Gwendolyn Brooks. I was born in Topeka, Kansas, but raised
in Chicago, Illinois. My writings were influenced by the works of
Langston Hughes. He made me realize the importance of writing about
African American life. Many of my poems focus on black heritage
and self-discovery. I published my first book of poems, *A Street in
Bronzeville*, in 1945. It won me national recognition. For my next
volume of poetry, *Annie Allen*, I won the Pulitzer Prize for poetry in
1950. I was the first African American poet to win that award. Some of
my published books are *Maud Martha, Bronzeville Boys and Girls, The
Bean Eaters, Selected Poems, Riot, Family Pictures,* and *Aloneness*. In
1972 I published *Report from Part One: An Autobiography*. I served
as poet laureate of the state of Illinois for eighteen years. I changed
that position from one of solely a ceremonial position to one of input
in schools, halfway houses, and prisons. I also served as a poetry
consultant to the Library of Congress in 1985.

Frank Yerby
(1916–1991)
Novelist

(FRANK highlights his achievements in writing.)

FRANK

My name is Frank Yerby. I was born in Augusta, Georgia, in 1916. Originally, I wrote romance novels with settings in the antebellum South, but I'm known as a historical novelist. I spend countless hours of in-depth research for my novels. I have authored thirty-three novels. Some of them are *The Vixens, Pride's Castle, The Old Gods Laugh, Western: A Saga of the Great Plains*, and *McKenzie's Hundred*. In 1946 I published *The Foxes of Harrow*. It was a best seller. Later that year, Twentieth Century Fox purchased the book to make it into a movie. The title was shortened to *Foxes*. This made me the first African American to have a Hollywood studio purchase a book and transform it into a screenplay.

James Baldwin
(1924–1987)
Essayist, Novelist, Playwright

(JAMES highlights his published works.)

JAMES

I'm James Baldwin. I was born and raised in Harlem, New York. I'm not bragging, but I've always had a gift for writing. When I was in elementary school, I wrote the school song and was editor of my high school newspaper. I moved to Paris, France, in 1948 and lived there until 1957. It was in Paris that I wrote my first novel, *Go Tell It on the Mountain*, in 1952. It received critical acclaim.

One of the major themes in my fiction is the black family. Three of my books of essays are *Notes of a Native Son, Nobody Knows My Name*, and *The Fire Next Time*. These works identify me as a writer and spokesperson for black people's concerns. Some other books are *Giovanni's Room, Another Country*, and *Going to Meet the Man*. I've also had two successful plays: *Blues for Mr. Charlie* and *Amen Corner*.

Chester Bomar Himes
(1909–1984)
Novelist, Short Story Writer, Autobiographer

(CHESTER shares the experiences that led to his career in writing.)

CHESTER

My name is Chester Himes. I was born in Jefferson City, Missouri, in 1909 to upper-middle-class parents. My family later moved to Cleveland, Ohio. It was there that my parents divorced. I enrolled in Ohio State University but was expelled for a prank that proved not to be very funny.

Although I was born into an upper-middle-class family, this didn't prevent me from entering a life of crime. When I was nineteen, I was convicted of armed robbery and sentenced to a twenty-year prison term. The sentence was more years than I had lived. I witnessed a lot of horror during the time I was in prison. Some of those experiences I later used as a format for my novels. I began writing short stories while incarcerated. They were published in a national magazine.

Following my parole, I wanted to become a professional writer. I moved to Los Angeles in 1940. My goal was to be a screenwriter, but I couldn't get a job with a studio because I was black. I ended up working in the war-manufacturing industry. During the four years I was there, I witnessed a lot of racial discrimination and violence in the workplace. These things influenced me to write my first published novels: *If He Hollers Let Him Go* and *Lonely Crusade*. They were about the wave of black immigrants drawn to jobs in the Los Angeles defense industries.

Mary Elizabeth Vroman
(1923–1967)
Novelist, Screenwriter, Short Story Writer

(MARY highlights her achievements in writing.)

MARY

I'm Mary Vroman. I was born in Buffalo, New York, but grew up in the West Indies. My writing career has been diverse. I taught school for twenty years in Alabama, Illinois, and New York. I always wanted to make a difference in my students' lives. My teaching experiences influenced me to write "See How They Run." It's set in rural Alabama and focuses on the main character, an idealistic black third-grade teacher. I won the Christopher Award for inspirational magazine writing for my story. The story describes the teacher's rewarding relationship with her disadvantaged students while teaching in the segregated South. It was also published in the July 1952 issue of *Ebony*. In 1953 I wrote the movie script for the motion picture *Bright Road*. I became the first African American female member of the Screenwriters Guild. I've written three books: *Esther* in 1963; *Shaped to Its Purpose*, a fifty-year history of my sorority Delta Sigma Theta, in 1965; and *Harlem Summer*, which was published in 1968.

Lerone Bennett Jr.
(1928–)
Poet, Historian, Editor

(SPEAKER highlights Lerone Bennett's published works.)

SPEAKER

Lerone Bennett Jr. was born in Clarksdale, Mississippi. Bennett has written numerous stories and poems, but he's probably best known for his writings based on the historical research of black Americans. Between 1962 and 1972 his published works included *Before the Mayflower*, *What Manner of Man*, and *Black Mood*. He also wrote *Black Power U.S.A.: The Human Side of Reconstruction, 1867–77*; *Pioneers In Protest*; and *The Challenge of Blackness*. Lerone Bennett was also senior editor of *Ebony* magazine.

ERA OF PROTEST AND SOCIAL CHANGE: 1960–1979

Dudley Randall
(1914–2000)
Poet

(DUDLEY highlights his published poetry.)

DUDLEY

I'm Dudley Randall. I was born in Washington, D.C., in 1914. I was gifted as a poet since early childhood. I wrote my first poem when I was four years old. By the time I was thirteen, some of my poetry had been published in the *Detroit Free Press*. My work connected earlier black writers to writers of the 1960s. In 1963 I wrote "Ballad of Birmingham." It was about the tragic deaths of little girls during the bombing of Sixteenth Street Baptist Church in Birmingham, Alabama. In 1968 I published *Cities Burning*, which reflected the ongoing racial and political climate in our country. In the early 1970s my poetry focused on promoting black pride and nationalism.

I published over eighty poems during my career, but I think my biggest accomplishment was in 1965 when I founded Broadside Press. Broadside Press was at the forefront of independent black publishing companies. In 1966 we had our first publication. It was *Poem Counterpoem*. *Poem Counterpoem* was a collection of ten poems written by Margaret Danner and me. The poems were of the same theme and were printed on opposite pages. Although Margaret Danner and I were established writers, Broadside provided an avenue of exposure for unknown poets as well. It emerged into the most significant black press in the United States.

Lorraine Vivian Hansberry
(1930–1965)
Playwright

Lorraine Hansberry

(LORRAINE highlights works from her award-winning career as a playwright.)

LORRAINE

When I was in elementary school, my family tried to move into an all-white neighborhood. The residents didn't want us to move in. We were threatened and evicted by a court order. My father wouldn't accept being denied the right to live wherever he chose. He took his case all the way to the U.S. Supreme Court. The Court ruled in our favor in 1940. Although we won the case, the neighbors were still angry and continued to protest.

In 1950 I moved to New York City and began my writing career. I started by writing for Paul Robeson's magazine *Freedom*. I wrote about poverty, false imprisonment of black people, and civil rights issues. I also wrote reviews regarding books, art, and local theater productions. Later, I wrote the play *A Raisin in the Sun*. It was a drama relating to my experience. It was about a black family that tried to move into an all-white neighborhood. I had difficulty finding producers to read my script, because I was unknown and a black female. Also there was concern that there wouldn't be an audience for a serious black drama. I decided to raise $100,000 to produce it myself. As a result, more people invested in the production than in any prior Broadway play. *Raisin in the Sun* ran for nineteen months and was made into an award-winning movie. It won the New York Drama Critics' Circle Award for Best American Play for the 1958 to 1959 season. In 1974 the musical version won a Tony Award. It was also translated into thirty languages. I was the first black woman to have a Broadway production. My second play, *Sidney Brustein's Window*, opened in 1964. I also wrote the text for *The Movement*. It was a collection of photos documenting the civil rights movement.

I believe writers should use their talents to bring about social change and advocate for civil rights. I also believe that everyone can overcome hardships and despair if they have the desire to do so.

Ishmael Reed
(1933–)
Novelist, Poet, Publisher

(SPEAKER shares Ishmael Reed's achievements in writing.)

SPEAKER

Ishmael Reed was born in Chattanooga, Tennessee. He and his mother moved to Buffalo, New York, when he was four. He was a cofounder of the *East Village Other* newspaper and the Yardbird Publishing Company. Reed's work mixes western literary forms with segments of African American traditions. Some of his novels are *The Free-Lance Pallbearers*, *Mumbo Jumbo*, *The Last Days of Louisiana Red*, and *Flight to Canada*. He has written a number of books of poetry. Reed's first volume of poetry, *Conjure*, was nominated for the National Book Award. He uses his poetry to create satires and parodies to attack the middle and upper classes for their vices and excuses. Ishmael Reed's novels are purposely controversial and identified for their sharp satire. The accomplishments of his powerful pen are almost too monumental to cite; however, as of 1995 he published nine novels, five books, four plays, and four collections of essays. He also authored three television productions.

Sonia Sanchez
(1935–)
Poet

(SPEAKER shares Sonia Sanchez's many contributions to poetry.)

SPEAKER

Sonia Sanchez was born Wilsonia Benita Driver in 1935 in Birmingham, Alabama. Her poetry emphasizes African American pride and identity. In her writings she incorporates the use of urban African American vernacular. Her work also supports strong family relationships and lashes out at all forms of ignorance.

Regarding her writings, Sanchez says, "I write to tell the truth about the black condition as I see it. Therefore I write to offer a black woman's view of the world." Her use of the black idiom began in her first volume of poetry, *Homecoming*, in 1969. In 1970 she published *We a BaddDDD People*. She highlighted the roles and struggles of black women in *A Blues Book for Blue Black Magical Women*. Some of her other books of poems are *It's a New Day: Poems for Young Brothas and Sistuhs* and *Three Hundred and Sixty Degrees of Blackness Coming at You*. Ms. Sanchez's poetry has been featured in numerous periodicals and anthologies, including *Natural Process*, *The Black Poets*, and *New Black Voices*. She has also published seven plays and a number of children's stories. In 2001 she was awarded the Robert Frost Medal in poetry. It is one of the highest national honors a poet can achieve.

Claude Brown
(1937–2002)
Autobiographer

(CLAUDE describes his success as a writer.)

CLAUDE

I'm Claude Brown. I was born in New York City. I wrote the book *Manchild in the Promised Land*. It was an autobiography describing my childhood and early life in Harlem. When I was ten years old, I joined a Harlem gang. At age eleven I was sent to a school for emotionally disturbed boys; later, I was sent to a reform school. None of these institutions changed me, and I continued committing crimes and selling drugs. When I was thirteen, I was shot in the abdomen by a local drug addict. It was after this incident that I decided to change my life. I finished high school and graduated from Howard University. It was during my first year at Howard that I submitted an article to the *Dissent* magazine about my youth. The publisher liked my piece and influenced me to expand it. This resulted in *Manchild in the Promised Land*, which was published in 1965. It was considered an American success story, because it documented how I rose from a life of poverty and crime to become a successful citizen. In 1976 I published *The Children of Ham*. It focused on the lives of thirteen Harlem residents and the trials of everyday life in Harlem.

Amiri Baraka
(1934–)
Poet, Playwright

*(*SPEAKER *shares Amiri Baraka's contribution to dramatic writing.)*

SPEAKER
Amiri Baraka was born Everett LeRoi Jones in Newark, New Jersey. He changed his name in order to establish more of a connection with his African heritage. He initially started his career as an avant-garde beat poet. He became more radical during the 1960s and was a significant factor in the black arts movement. He has also written several plays. His play, *The Dutchman*, won the *Village Voice's* Obie Award.

Baraka has researched and written a comprehensive study of African American music in the United States. His book *Blues People: Negro Music in White America*, published in 1963, highlights the development of black music in America since the beginning of slavery. He's published several volumes of poetry, including *Black Magic*, *Tales*, and *Preface to a Twenty-Volume Suicide Note*. He's also published essays and short stories.

Alex Haley
(1921–1992)
Novelist, Biographer, Editor

*(*ALEX *cites his works as a published author.)*

ALEX

My name is Alex Haley. I was born in Ithaca, New York, and raised
in Henning, Tennessee. I enrolled in college when I was fifteen years
old. I stayed in college for two years then returned home. My father
didn't think I was disciplined enough, and that I needed more maturity.
He convinced me to join the military. I spent the next twenty years
in the U.S. Coast Guard. Military opportunities were limited to black
Americans at that time, but I made it my career choice. While serving
in the Pacific Ocean during World War II, I began writing stories.
I received eight rejection letters before anyone accepted any of my
stories.

After I retired from the Coast Guard, I made writing my career. I
became senior editor of *Reader's Digest*. I also had a job with *Playboy*
magazine. I interviewed the famous and the infamous. Some of the
people I interviewed were Miles Davis, Martin Luther King, Jim
Brown, Sammy Davis Jr., Quincy Jones, and Cassius Clay—who
talked about his name change to Muhammad Ali. I'm sure my most
uncomfortable interview was with American Nazi Party leader George
Lincoln Rockwell. He kept a handgun on the table throughout the
entire session.

About six months before Malcolm X was assassinated, I completed
an interview with him. This interview led to our collaboration on *The
Autobiography of Malcolm X*, which was published in 1965. Malcolm
was killed the following February. *Playboy* published the memoir in
July of that same year. I'm best known for my epic *Roots: the Saga
of an American Family*. It took many years of extensive research to
complete the work. I completed the saga by tracing my family history
back to 1750 to an ancestor named Kunta Kinte. He was kidnapped in
Africa and enslaved in America. It was published in 1976. Later, it was
made into a twelve-hour television miniseries. The book sold millions
of copies and won the National Book Award in 1976 and a special

Pulitzer Prize in 1977. In 1979 a sequel TV miniseries was produced. It was called *Roots: the Next Generation*. My work inspired thousands of African Americans to research their family roots.

Nikki Giovanni
(1943–)
Poet

(SPEAKER shares Nikki Giovanni's contributions to the field of poetry.)

SPEAKER

Nikki Giovanni was born in Knoxville, Tennessee, and raised in Cincinnati, Ohio. Her poetry has been described as the poetics of self-discovery and black consciousness. Many of her poems were a reflection of her experiences during the 1960s, her connection to the black power movement, and her growth as a black woman. During the 1970s, her poetry shifted to a family theme but continued to incorporate racial pride. Giovanni has published almost twenty volumes of poetry. They include *Black Feeling, Black Talk, Black Judgment*; *My House*; *The Women and the Men: Poems*; and *Cotton Candy on a Rainy Day*. In 1972 Giovanni recorded *Truth Is on Its Way*. It was poetry recited to gospel music. That year *Truth Is on Its Way* was selected by the National Association of Radio and Television Announcers for Best Spoken Word Album. In 2004 she was nominated for a Grammy Award for her album *The Nikki Giovanni Poetry Collection*, and in 2008 she received an NAACP Image Award for Poetry.

Audre Lorde
(1934–1992)
Poet

(AUDRE shares her achievements in poetry.)

AUDRE

I'm Audre Lorde. I was born in New York City in 1934. My published works have appeared in *Journal of Black Poetry*, *Negro Digest / Black World*, *Transatlantic Review*, *Freedomways*, and *Women: A Journal of Liberation*. I'm included in the anthologies *Beyond the Blues*, *Sixes and Sevens*, *New Negro Poets: USA*, *New Black Poets*, and *The Black Woman*.

Eugenia W. Collier
(1928–)
Short Story Writer, Literary Critic

(SPEAKER highlights Eugenia Collier's achievements in writing.)

SPEAKER

Eugenia Collier was born in Baltimore, Maryland. She exhibited a talent for writing at an early age. When Eugenia was twelve, she won a writing contest sponsored by the *Afro-American Newspaper*. She coedited a two-volume anthology of African American works. She is a noted scholar. The *CLA Journal* and *Phylon* have published some of her critical writings. She was the editor for the anthology of literature for young people called *Impressions in Asphalt*. Her prizewinning short story "Marigolds" made its initial appearance in *Negro Digest* in 1969. Her first collection of short stories, *Rachel's Children*, was published in 1991.

Toni Morrison
(1931–)
Novelist, Essayist, Editor

(SPEAKER shares Toni Morrison's accomplishments in writing.)

SPEAKER

Toni Morrison was born Chloe Anthony Wofford in Lorain, Ohio. Prior to starting her writing career, she worked as senior editor at Random House Publishing Company. She used her position to promote books on black history and inspire young black writers. While there she edited *The Black Book*, which was about African American history. It contained photographs, newspaper articles, African American songs, and bills of sale for slaves.

From 1970 to 2008 Morrison wrote nine novels. She typically places her characters in a historical context and incorporates their lives into public events. Her first novel, *The Bluest Eye*, was published in 1970. Other novels include *Sula* and *Song of Solomon,* which won the National Book Critics' Circle Award. Song of Solomon was her first novel to have white characters. She also wrote *Tar Baby*, which was published in 1981. In 1988 she became the first African American female to receive the Pulitzer Prize for literature. She won for her novel *Beloved,* which was later turned into a movie. In 1993 she won the Nobel Prize in literature.

In 1986 she received the New York State Governor's Award for her play *Dreaming Emmett*. It was about Emmett Till, the fourteen-year-old African American boy who was murdered in Mississippi. In 2008 she was nominated for a Grammy Award for Best Spoken Word Album for Children.

Ernest Gaines
(1933–)
Novelist

(SPEAKER shares Ernest Gaines's contributions to the field of writing.)

SPEAKER

Ernest Gaines was born on the River Lake Plantation in Pointe Coupee Parish, Louisiana. He spent most of his childhood on an old slave plantation where his family had lived for five generations. Gaines spent much of his childhood working in the fields, fishing, and listening to stories and conversations shared among adults. He moved to California when he was fifteen but used his earlier experiences on the plantation to write some of his fiction.

Gaines wrote eight novels. His most famous work was *The Autobiography of Miss Jane Pittman*, which was published in 1971. It was later adapted into a made-for-television movie. He came a long way from his roots in Louisiana, where he worked for fifty cents a day. He rose from a field laborer to a writer in residence at the University of Southwest Louisiana. Gaines, like the characters in some of his stories, triumphed over adversity through strength and dignity. He has received numerous awards and recognitions for his literary work. In 1993 he won the National Book Critics Circle Award for fiction for *A Lesson Before Dying*. It was also nominated for a Pulitzer Prize. *A Lesson Before Dying* was later adapted for television, and in 1999 it received an Emmy Award for Best Film for Television.

Alice Childress
(1920–1994)
Playwright, Novelist

(SPEAKER highlights works from Alice Childress's writing career.)

SPEAKER

Alice Childress was born in Charleston, South Carolina. The goal of her life's work was to accurately depict African Americans. She wasn't afraid to challenge stereotypes. The characters in Childress's plays were usually blue-collar workers as well as artists, dancers, and teachers.

Childress was multitalented. In 1949 she wrote, starred in, and directed her first play, *Florence*. She wrote several other plays, including the Obie Award-winning *Trouble in Mind*. Her book *A Hero Ain't Nothin' but a Sandwich* won numerous awards and was made into a movie in 1978.

Ntozake Shange
(1948–)
Poet, Playwright

(SPEAKER shares the impetus behind Ntozake Shange's writings.)

SPEAKER
Ntozake Shange was born Paulette Williams in Trenton, New Jersey in 1948. When she was eight years old, her parents moved to St. Louis, Missouri. This was a culture shock for her. Unlike Trenton, all the schools were segregated, and she was confronted with a lot of racism and prejudice. Although Shange came from an upper-middle-class family, she was unhappy most of her childhood. She felt that no one expected much of her, because she was female and black. She decided to become a writer when her first two career choices of being a war correspondent or a jazz musician were dismissed by others. She graduated from high school in New Jersey then enrolled in Barnard College in New York. She was one of the few African American women at a predominantly white college.

Shange was a student during the civil rights protests. Demonstrations were springing up all around the country. The tense atmosphere and protests in the United States affected her so much that she tried to commit suicide several times. In 1971 she changed her name to

Ntozake Shange. She found that this gave her strength and helped
establish her identity. Ntozake Shange's name means "she who comes
with her own things," and she "walks like a lion."

She received national attention and instant success for her choreopoem
*For Colored Girls Who Have Considered Suicide When the Rainbow
is Enuf.* It became a Broadway production and was a mixture of
poetry, music, dance, and drama. All of her work heavily centers on
her personal experiences and the problems and frustrations of being
an African American woman. Regarding her writing, Shange says, "I
write about things that I know have never been given their full due."
She feels a deep commitment to be honest in her work and to highlight
these experiences.

CULTURAL CONSERVATISM: 1980–1999

Edna Lewis
(1916–2006)
Cookbook Writer

(EDNA highlights her published cookbooks.)

EDNA
Hi. I'm Edna Lewis. Do any of you like to cook?
(Scans audience.)
Oh, some of you do and some of you don't. I'll bet all of you like to
eat.
(Smiles)
I'm Edna Lewis. I was born in 1916 in Freetown, Virginia. I left
home when I was young and moved to Washington, D.C.; then, I
moved to New York City. It was in New York that I got my first job
as a professional cook in a popular restaurant. A lot of famous people

came to eat there. As luck would have it, I broke my leg and couldn't work for a while. It was during this time that I was encouraged to write a cookbook. I did so and later wrote more cookbooks. I'm going to give you their names so you can buy them and try out some of my specialties: *The Edna Lewis Cookbook, The Taste of Country Cooking,* and *In Pursuit of Flavor*. I also coauthored *The Gift of Southern Cooking* with Scott Peacock. In 1986 I was named in *Who's Who in American Cooking*, a cooking magazine. In 2003 I was inducted into the KitchenAid Cookbook Hall of Fame.

August Wilson
(1946–2005)
Poet, Playwright

(AUGUST shares many of his achievements in dramatic writing.)

AUGUST

I, August Wilson, was born in Pittsburg, Pennsylvania. I describe myself as a cultural nationalist. I began my literary career as a poet. While I was still a teenager, many of my poems were accepted at the University of Pittsburg. I began writing my first play in 1972; it was called *Jitney* and was about a gypsy cab station. After the production of *Jitney*, I decided to focus on playwriting. I always create at a continual pace. As soon as I complete one play, I don't get up until I've gotten an idea for another one. In my work I blend elements of African American history and culture. I use the theater as a device to raise the consciousness of black people. Four of my plays have been produced on Broadway: *Ma Rainey's Black Bottom, Fences, Joe Turner's Come and Gone*, and *The Piano Lesson*. Both *Fences* and *The Piano Lesson* won a Pulitzer Prize.

Alice Walker
(1944–)
Novelist

*(*SPEAKER *highlights Alice Walker's achievements in writing.)*

SPEAKER

Alice Walker is a very well-known author. She has written many books, but perhaps her best known work is *The Color Purple*, which she wrote in 1983. It was later made into a movie and received eleven Oscar nominations. The book also won a Pulitzer Prize and the National Book Award. Some of her other published works include *Possessing the Secret of Joy*, published in 1992; *Anything We Love Can Be Saved*, published in 1997; and *Now Is the Time to Open Your Heart*, published in 2004.

Alice Walker grew up very poor, but she didn't let poverty discourage her from being a successful writer. One has to learn that you can be poor in life but rich in talent. If you have such a talent, fulfill your dream and share your gift with others through your works as Alice Walker did.

Donald Crews
(1938–)
Children's Books Writer

*(*SPEAKER *highlights Donald Crews's children's stories.)*

SPEAKER

Children's book author Donald Crews was born in 1938 in Newark, New Jersey. The majority of his works focus on modern technology and travel vehicles. *We Read: A to Z*, published in 1984, was a unique book, because it focused on abstract ideas rather than the traditional

ABC word association. Some of his transportation themed books are *Freight Train, School Bus, Flying, Sail Away,* and *Truck.*

Rita Dove
(1952–)
Poet

(SPEAKER shares Rita Dove's contributions to poetry.)

SPEAKER

Rita Dove was born in Akron, Ohio. After she graduated from college, she studied in West Germany and traveled to Israel and southern Europe. Dove's concern for race and female issues was evident in her writing, but she didn't always make it her central theme. For this reason she has often been described as a quiet poet.

In 1985 she published a collection of short stories called *Fifth Sunday.* *Thomas and Beulah,* a collection of poems published in 1986, was a story of her grandparents' lives. She won a Pulitzer Prize for that work in 1987. Rita Dove's other collections of poems include *The Yellow House on the Corner, Museum,* and *The Other Side of the House.* In 1993 she became poet laureate of the United States. She was the youngest person and first African American to be appointed to that position.

Gloria Naylor
(1950–)
Novelist

(SPEAKER shares Gloria Naylor's achievements in writing.)

SPEAKER

Gloria Naylor was born in Harlem, New York. She was influenced by Toni Morrison, whose book *The Bluest Eye* showed her that women could be successful in the male-dominated world of writing. In 1983 Naylor published *The Women of Brewster Place*. The novel won an American Book Award. Later, it was turned into a television movie. Naylor published two other novels in the 1980s. Some consider her writings complex and multilayered, but she likes for her readers to use critical thinking and draw conclusions. Her novels depict the uniqueness of African American society.

Walter Mosley
(1952–)
Novelist

(SPEAKER *highlights Walter Mosley's published works.*)

SPEAKER

Walter Mosley grew up in South Central Los Angeles. This environment provided the setting for his novels. Mosley's work is credited with realistically portraying the street life of African American neighborhoods post-World War II. The popularity of his books can be attributed to his character Ezekiel "Easy" Rawlings, a black private detective in Watts. Equally popular is Easy's childhood friend, the cold-blooded, charming Raymond "Mouse" Alexander. In 1990 Mosley wrote his first novel, *Devil in a Blue Dress*, which was later made into a big-screen movie. His novels *Fallen Angels: Red Wind* and *Always Outnumbered* were made into television movies.

Mosley frequently incorporates the names of colors into his book titles and character names, for example, *Devil in a Blue Dress*, *A Red Death*, *White Butterfly*, *Black Betty*, *A Little Yellow Dog*, and *Bad Boy Brawly Brown*. He has written four nonfiction books and over twenty novels.

He has received many awards and honors, including the Anisfield Wolf Award, which is an honor given to writers who expand the appreciation and understanding of an American race of people. President Clinton acknowledged Walter Mosley as one of his favorite authors.

Maya Angelou
(1928–)
Poet, Playwright

*(*SPEAKER *highlights Maya Angelou's works in poetry and the arts.)*

SPEAKER
Maya Angelou was born Marguerite Johnson in 1928 but changed her name to Maya Angelou. She has been active in social issues and the arts all her life. When she was young, she was a dancer and even sang at the Apollo Theater in Harlem. Later, she broadened her career and became a playwright and actress.

In 1972 she received an Emmy for her screenplay *Georgia, Georgia*. It was also nominated for a Pulitzer Prize. She became the first African American female to have a screenplay produced. Maya Angelou's writings consist of novels, plays, children's stories, and poetry. She also wrote an autobiography, *I Know Why the Caged Bird Sings*. In 1993 President Clinton asked her to participate in his inaugural ceremony. Angelou wrote and recited her poetic piece "On the Pulse of Morning," which made her the first African American inaugural poet.

Maya Angelou's life has been rich, but she had to overcome many obstacles when she was young; however, she didn't use obstacles as an excuse to let life bypass her. She turned those obstacles into stepping stones and became one of the most successful writers in America.

Henry Louis Gates Jr.
(1950–)
Essayist, Editor

(SPEAKER highlights works that Henry Louis Gates Jr. wrote during his career as a writer.)

SPEAKER

Henry Louis Gates Jr. was born in Piedmont, West Virginia. He graduated with highest honors from Yale University. Gates wrote his doctoral dissertation on the critical perception of early black literature. He has been described as a literary archaeologist. Gates has received research grants, numerous awards, endowment grants, and scholarships for cultural and humanities research. He has authored a multitude of essays, reviews, and articles. Some of the books he's written are *Thirteen Ways of Looking at a Black Man*; *Colored People: A Memoir*; and *The Signifying Monkey: A Theory of Afro-American Literary Criticism*. He collaborated with Cornel West to publish *The Future of the Race* in 1996. Gates also coedited *Africana: The Encyclopedia of the African and African American Experience* and *African American Lives*. In 1999 he was elected to the American Academy of Arts and Letters.

Tyler Perry
(1968–)
Playwright, Screenwriter

(SPEAKER shares Tyler Perry's success in dramatic writing.)

SPEAKER

Tyler Perry rose to fame as Madea. This character—created and portrayed by Perry—is a brash, outspoken, domineering, well-intentioned female who doesn't bite her tongue.

Tyler Perry was born Emmitt Perry Jr. in 1968 in New Orleans, Louisiana. In 1992 he moved to Atlanta, Georgia. He worked and saved nearly $12,000 to produce his first play. Initially, it had an unsuccessful run, but in 1998 the play found an audience and became a success. Since then his productions have become multimillion-dollar ventures. A few of his plays are *Diary of a Mad Black Woman*, *I Can Do Bad All By Myself*, *Madea's Family Reunion*, and *Madea Goes to Jail*.

In addition to his plays he also wrote the book *Don't Make a Black Woman Take Off Her Earrings: Madea's Uninhibited Commentaries on Love and Life*. Recently he expanded into television by writing and directing *Tyler Perry's House of Payne*, a sitcom television series. Perry has found success on the big screen as well. In 2005 his first movie was released, *Diary of a Mad Black Woman*. It was produced for $5.5 million and grossed $50.6 million. Since 2005 he has found success with his follow-up movies, including *Madea's Family Reunion, Madea Goes to Jail,* and *I Can Do Bad All By Myself*. In 2008 Perry opened a movie studio in Atlanta, Georgia, which made him one of few African Americans to ever own a production studio.

NEW MILLENNIUM WRITERS: 2000–2010

Jawanza Kunjufu
(1953–)
Nonfiction Writer

(SPEAKER shares Jawanza Kunjufu's success in writing.)

SPEAKER
Dr. Jawanza Kunjufu was born in Chicago, Illinois, in 1953. His books and lectures focus primarily on the education of black youths, health care, uplifting the community, and child rearing, with special attention

to the black male. Dr. Kunjufu has written over twenty books. They include *Countering the Conspiracy to Destroy Black Boys*, *Motivating and Preparing Black Youth to Work*, and *To Be Popular or Smart: The Black Peer Group*. He founded African American Images, which is a consulting and publishing company. He also wrote the movie *Up Against the Wall*. It addressed the problems facing contemporary black males. The goal of the movie was to take a black boy through positive and negative peer pressure to see if he could survive and become a responsible young man.

Bebe Moore Campbell
(1950–2006)
Novelist, Journalist, Playwright

(BEBE shares her achievements in writing.)

BEBE

I'm Bebe Campbell. I was born and raised in Philadelphia, Pennsylvania. I was the author of four best sellers: *Brothers and Sisters*, published in 1994; *Singing in the Comeback Choir*, published in 1998; *What You Owe Me*, published in 2001; and *72 Hour Hold*, published in 2006. My novel *Your Blues Ain't Like Mine* won the NAACP's Image Award for Literature. I also wrote my memoir, *Sweet Summer: Growing Up With and Without My Dad*. My concern regarding mental health led me to write my first children's book, *Sometimes My Mommy Gets Angry*. It was about a little girl who coped with being raised by her mentally ill mother. It won the National Alliance for the Mentally Ill Outstanding Literature Award in 2003. My first play, *Even with the Madness*, made its debut in New York in June 2003. My career as a journalist included writing articles for the *New York Times*, *Washington Post*, *Ebony*, *Essence*, and *Black Enterprise*. My essays and excerpts have appeared in numerous anthologies.

Eric Jerome Dickey
(1961–)
Novelist

(SPEAKER highlights Eric Jerome Dickey's published works.)

SPEAKER
Eric Jerome Dickey was born in 1961 in Memphis, Tennessee. Dickey is a multitalented writer. He has written comedic material during his career as a comedian, screenplays, and short stories. However, he's probably best known for his *New York Times* best-selling novels. His novels typically portray contemporary African American life. Dickey's main characters are grifters, assassins, and ex-convicts. He's written several crime novels that include international characters and settings that range from the United Kingdom to the West Indies. He wrote twenty-two novels between 1996 and 2008. A few of them are *Sister, Sister*; *Liars Game*; *Drive Me Crazy*; *Chasing Destiny*; *Pleasure*; and *Dying for Revenge*.

Thomas Dexter "T. D." Jakes
(1957–)
Nonfiction Writer

(SPEAKER highlights T.D. Jakes's published nonfiction works.)

SPEAKER
Bishop T. D. Jakes was born in South Charlestown, West Virginia. He is a bishop, author, motivational speaker, and entrepreneur. He has authored over thirty books, a number of which have been on the *New York Times* best-seller list. His books focus on motivation, inspiration, and redesigning one's life. Some of his books are *God's Leading Lady*; *The Lady, Her Lover, and Her Lord*; *His Lady*; *He-Motions*; and *Maximize the Moment*. His book *Woman, Thou Art Loosed!* was a

best seller in print, video, and CD. It was also an award-winning stage production and was made into a motion picture. Black Entertainment Television televises his sermons live every Sunday. He is the recipient of a Grammy Award, the Quill Award, and several NAACP Image Awards.

Tavis Smiley
(1964–)
Nonfiction Writer

(SPEAKER shares Tavis Smiley's achievements in writing.)

SPEAKER
Tavis Smiley was born in Gulfport, Mississippi, in 1964. By 2008 he authored eight books. His writings, like his commentaries, focus on African American heritage and social and political issues. His books include *The Covenant in Action; Never Mind Success—Go for Greatness!: The Best Advice I've Ever Received*; and *What I Know for Sure: My Story of Growing Up in America*. Tavis Smiley also hosts a talk show. *Newsweek* named him as one of the "twenty people changing how America gets its news."

Zane
(1967–)
Novelist

(SPEAKER shares Zane's achievements in writing.)

SPEAKER
Kristina Laferne Roberts is better known by her pen name Zane. She was born, educated, raised, and currently resides in the Washington, D.C. area. It is also the setting for many of her books. Her novels are intended for adult readers and focus on black professionals. She began

her writing career in 1997, which started as a hobby after her children went to bed at night.

Zane was self-motivated and began by posting her work on the internet. It wasn't long before she amassed a large following. She has become one of the most successful writers of contemporary fiction. Zane expanded her career by signing a deal with Cinemax for a television series beginning in October 2008.

AFRICAN AMERICAN ORGANIZATIONS

Early Social Organizations

Prince Hall
(1735–1807)
Prince Hall Masons Founder

(PRINCE describes the challenges he faced when founding the Prince Hall Masons.)

PRINCE

My name is Prince Hall. I'm the founder of the first Masonic lodge
for Negroes. It was the first social organization for black people in
this country. Let me tell you something about myself. I was a free man
living in Boston, Massachusetts, and a Methodist minister. I believed
all free men should have equal responsibilities and privileges. One
of those privileges should have been the right to join any existing
organization, but this was not the case. I wanted to join the Masons
that the colonists had established in Boston. I petitioned them, but
they refused my application because I was black. I was determined to
have a formal social outlet for Negroes. I contacted the British soldiers
stationed in the city, who also had a lodge. Some may find that unusual,
because the British soldiers were despised by the colonists; yet, they
were the ones who befriended me. In 1775 fourteen black men and I
established African Lodge No. 1 under the British Masons.

During the Revolutionary War, I fought on the side of the colonists. We black patriots hoped independence from England would mean freedom to all people, but slavery was not abolished. Even Negroes who were free continued to face discrimination after the United States gained its liberty. After the war ended in 1783, I submitted an application to my countrymen a second time and was refused. I had to return to the British for a permanent license. In 1787 the Freemasons of London approved my application. We were chartered as African Lodge Number 459. It was under this charter that I became the provincial grand master of North America. In 1791 I began organizing other black lodges in Philadelphia, Pennsylvania, and Providence, Rhode Island. My lodges became known as Prince Hall Masons or Prince Hall Grand Lodge.

Members of the Masons represented respectability and prestige. Because as Masons we had achieved a level of social status, I felt we had an opportunity to help the less fortunate members of our race. For example, when three black men were kidnapped in Boston in 1788 to be sold as slaves, I petitioned the state legislature to intervene. After much pressure, Governor Hancock finally negotiated their release. I also wanted to help Negroes become educated, so when Boston failed to provide schools for black children, I opened a school in my home.

I never promoted bitterness or hatred. I encouraged all my brother Masons to treat everyone fairly. In my famous "Charge delivered to the African Lodge" speech I wrote, "Give the right hand of affection and fellowship to whom it justly belongs [and] let their color and complexion be what it will . . . for they are your brethren."

Arthur J. Riggs and Benjamin "B. F." Howard
(1855–1936) (?–1918)
Founders of the Improved Benevolent Protective Order of the Elks of the World

Characters:

ARTHUR, *male, cofounder of the IBPOEW*

BENJAMIN, *male, cofounder of the IBPOEW*

Costumes:

Casual attire of the early 1900s

Props:

At director's discretion

(ARTHUR and BENJAMIN discuss the struggles they faced when founding the IBPOEW.)

BENJAMIN

I think I see my good friend Arthur Riggs. Hello Arthur. Over here. *(Waves to ARTHUR.)*

ARTHUR

(Comes over and shakes BENJAMIN's hand.)

Hello my friend. How have you been?

BENJAMIN

I've been doing very well. But I've been worried about you, especially after all the trouble they put you through.

ARTHUR

I know. I often think back on the days when we were trying to get our Elks organization founded.

BENJAMIN

I was living in Covington, Kentucky, and you were living just across the Ohio River in Cincinnati.

ARTHUR

A lot of slaves escaped by that river. Fortunately, I was one of them.

BENJAMIN

Yes, you were fortunate. I remember when we realized a need for a social and fraternal organization among Negroes. In 1897 we tried to establish an inclusive order within the white Benevolent Protective Order of Elks of the World, but our request for membership was denied. We were determined to form a chapter that would also admit qualified Negroes. We knew that the first thing that needed to be done was to get a copy of the BPOE's secret ritual book, and you took care of that.

ARTHUR
(Laughs)
To this day, nobody knows how I got a copy. The white order was outraged, to put it mildly. They accused me of stealing a copy from a passenger on the train, because I was a Pullman porter. I prepared myself for their backlash. I consulted an attorney. Thank goodness my lawyer discovered that the ritual had never been copyrighted. And you know what happened next. I immediately submitted that ritual for copyright. That copyright allowed us to hold our first meeting on November 11, 1898.

BENJAMIN

I'll never forget all the trouble that ritual book caused. I know you remember what happened once the BPOE members learned we had it.

ARTHUR

I sure do. First they threatened us. Then they organized. Next thing you know, they barged into our meeting, tried to take our book and have all of us arrested. What right did they have to stop a Negro Elks lodge from being established?

BENJAMIN

Well, according to them, they were here first and Negroes had no right to use the BPOE ritual book.

ARTHUR

(Laughs)

That's right; but do you remember the looks on their faces when I pulled out my book, my copyrighted, signed, and sealed-by-Uncle-Sam book? I told them, "Look at this. If I hear another word about a Negro Elks lodge, I will put the entire white lodge in jail for infringing on my copyright." They knew they couldn't beat us legally, so they tried intimidating our Negro members, especially me. I guess they saw me as the ringleader. Did I ever tell you that on one of my train routes as a porter—while passing through Birmingham, Alabama—some white Elks members pulled me off the train and threatened to lynch me on my next trip to Birmingham, unless I gave up our charter? Naturally I agreed, because I knew I was never going to return to Birmingham. But that wasn't the end of things. I was boycotted. My family suffered, because I couldn't hold a decent job. I had to leave Cincinnati, get an alias name, and go into hiding. I'm glad you were there to keep things going.

BENJAMIN

Well, I did run the organization while you were in hiding, but I didn't do it alone. I got help from the fraternal chapter of the black Knights of Pythias. We were able to establish our first chapter of Black Elks in Cincinnati in 1899. Our new title was the Improved Benevolent

Protective Order of Elks of the World. The white Elks reluctantly accepted the fact that we were a permanent organization. But there still was resentment. They especially resented our use of the BPOE's seal. New York State even passed a law in 1906 making it illegal for non-BPOE members to wear the seal. Our grand exalted ruler, Armand W. Scott, turned this into an opportunity to mend the relationship between the two groups. He ordered our black members to wear the IBPOEW pin and not the pin of the BPOE. This slight difference of initials seemed to have made an acceptable difference.

ARTHUR

I'm glad we were able to reach a mutual agreement between our organizations. You and I can be proud that we were the founders of the Improved Benevolent Protective Order of the Elks of the World.

(End scene.)

J. Finley Wilson
(1881–1952)
Grand Exalted Leader of the IBPOEW

(J. FINLEY describes how he helped expand the IBPOEW.)

J. FINLEY

I'm J. Finley Wilson. I was born in Tennessee but left home when I was thirteen. I was adventurous. I traveled west and worked with Buffalo Bill in Arizona and Colorado. It was in Colorado that I joined the IBPOEW. Arthur Riggs and B. F. Howard conceived the idea for the organization in 1897. There had been a lot of hostility toward our organization by the white Elks, but we were able to work out our differences. In 1918 the BPOE officially terminated its opposition. However, we had only grown moderately. Our membership was 36,306 in 1921 when I was elected exalted grand ruler. I put all my energy into reviving the IBPOEW and making it grow.

I traveled over fifty thousand miles my first year in office. It paid off, because the membership increased to 51,491, and I established eighty-five new lodges. Under my leadership, we incorporated the Elks scholarship program in 1925. In 1927 we established the famed Elks Oratorical Contest. We also established the systematic health survey among Negroes. During World War II, we aided our country by sponsoring drives for the Allied Relief Fund, and we set up a Victory Book Campaign in which we donated books to servicemen. The IBPOEW also bought and sold defense bonds and stamps. We sold over $2 million worth in New York City alone.

In 1952 we had $450,000 in net assets and $181,390 in cash. We aided thousands of young Negroes through our scholarship program and our oratorical contests. I'm proud to say that I helped the IBPOEW become the largest Negro organization in the world.

GREEK-LETTER FRATERNITIES AND SORORITIES

Alpha Phi Alpha Fraternity Inc.

(SPEAKER describes Alpha Phi Alpha's founding and present-day social initiatives.)

SPEAKER
Alpha Phi Alpha Fraternity Inc. was founded on Cornell University's campus on December 4, 1906. Alpha Phi Alpha was the first African American Greek-letter fraternity in the United States. It was established by seven students who met to discuss their concerns regarding campus life. They knew there was only a handful of black students on campus,

and that the numbers were slowly decreasing. For example, six of the university's black students in the 1904 to 1905 class didn't return for the following term. The founders of Alpha Phi Alpha realized that the social environment contributed to this poor retention rate. This prompted them to form a social and academic support group for the remaining students.

Black students were excluded from the white fraternal organizations on campus. These seven young men were aware that fraternities and sororities provided students with housing, study groups, and a common social environment to bond and identify with others. With this in mind, they decided to make the group more permanent and purposeful. On December 4, 1906, the idea of creating a fraternity was born. Thus, the Seven Jewels of Alpha Phi Alpha, as they dubbed themselves, established Alpha Phi Alpha Fraternity. They chose the colors old gold and black and based their principles on "manly deeds, scholarship, and love for all mankind."

In 1907 they established a second chapter at Howard University and continued to expand to other campuses. In 1911 they founded their first alumni chapter. To maintain an information flow with the new chapters on the various campuses, they created the *Sphinx* magazine. They also began to hold annual conventions to set policy and to strengthen brotherhood and fraternal bonds. In 1922 the fraternity focused on aiding African American students by implementing a tutoring program and providing financial aid for education.

Alpha Phi Alpha continues to be active in the community and has established national partnerships with a number of outreach agencies. They also work with Habitat for Humanity, which provides the needy with affordable housing. Today the fraternity has over 175,000 members throughout the United States.

Alpha Kappa Alpha Sorority Inc.

(SPEAKER recounts Alpha Kappa Alpha Sorority's founding and proliferation.)

SPEAKER
In the fall of 1907 on the campus of Howard University, Ethel Hedgeman inspired eight of her fellow classmates to found a sorority for Howard's students. On January 15 these nine women came together to define the sorority. They chose Alpha Kappa Alpha as the name, By Culture and By Merit as the motto, salmon pink and apple green as the colors, and a green enameled ivy leaf with the letters AKA as the symbol. Howard University's administration approved their petition that same month. They became the first African American sorority in the United States.

Internal conflict began in the fall of 1912 when new members wanted to change the sorority's name, colors, motto, and symbols. When the founders denied these requests, the dissenters withdrew and began Delta Sigma Theta Sorority. Urged to ensure the perpetuation of Alpha Kappa Alpha, the founding members incorporated the sorority on January 29, 1913. Soon after, they began to charter chapters on different campuses, and in 1918 the sorority held its first national conference in Washington, D.C. In 1921 they published the first issue of the *Ivy Leaf* magazine.

Alpha Kappa Alpha members made an early commitment to take an active role in cultural issues. During the Great Migration, when thousands of African Americans were moving from the South to the North, the sorority worked in the Traveler's Aid Society to help migrants adjust to Northern life. They also advocated for women to attain voting rights and participated in women's suffrage marches. Today the organization has over 250,000 members around the world.

Kappa Alpha Psi Fraternity Inc.

*(*SPEAKER *describes Kappa Alpha Psi Fraternity Inc.'s founding and proliferation.)*

SPEAKER
Elder Diggs was a student at Indiana University and one of the founders of Kappa Alpha Psi Fraternity. Frustrated with discrimination on campus, which prevented black males from using social facilities, Diggs decided to form a support group to help alleviate the isolation. On January 5, 1911, he and nine other students formed Kappa Alpha Nu, which was the precursor to Kappa Alpha Psi. It was chartered and incorporated four months later by the state of Illinois.

Before concentrating on expansion, Kappa Alpha Nu wanted to create a solid foundation that would reflect the principles and goals of the new fraternity. Once they were comfortable with a constitution, motto, coat of arms, and ritual book, they sought to expand to new campuses across the United States.

They quickly began to fulfill their motto, Achievement in Every Field of Human Endeavor. They began to hold annual social events that were open to all students of Indiana University and the local community. On February 8, 1913, Kappa Alpha Nu chartered Beta chapter at the University of Illinois. They continued to grow quickly. Between 1914 and 1918 they established chapters from the Atlantic to the Pacific. In 1914 Kappa Alpha Nu decided to change its name to Kappa Alpha Psi, a name which they felt would better distinguish them as a Greek-letter fraternity.

Along with expansion, they also concentrated on building solidarity and reaching out to the local community. In 1921 they published the *Kappa Alpha Psi Journal*, which was a publication that kept members up-to-date with issues that related to the fraternity. In 1922 they approved a social program called Guide Right. It was their first service program aimed at alleviating social issues around the nation.

Kappa Alpha Psi has continued to achieve in every field of human endeavor. It has reached many communities through the Kappa Alpha Psi Foundation and has awarded numerous fellowships to its college members.

Omega Psi Phi Fraternity Inc.

(SPEAKER briefly highlights Omega Psi Phi Fraternity's founding and expansion.)

SPEAKER
Omega Psi Phi Fraternity was founded at Howard University by three students—Edgar Love, Oscar Cooper, and Frank Coleman—who called themselves the Three Musketeers. Prior to Omega Psi Phi's founding, Alpha Phi Alpha was the only fraternity on Howard's campus. The founding brothers of Omega felt it was time for a black fraternity to be established on a black campus. They asked professor and scientist Ernest Just to be their advisor.

On November 17, 1911, the three men met with Ernest Just to create a name, concepts, and goals for their new organization. They came up with the motto Friendship is Essential to the Soul. They decided that friendship, manhood, perseverance, and uplift would be their four principles. Thus, Omega Psi Phi Fraternity was officially formed. After they drafted the constitution, they submitted their proposal to the administration. It was a difficult time for the fraternity to request a charter. This was a period when many of the colleges in the country feared that fraternities and sororities caused division within the student body. The university rejected Omega Psi Phi's initial request.

Howard University didn't realize the determination and seriousness of these three males. Love, Cooper, and Coleman began to post index cards that publicized their new fraternity all over the campus. This angered the administration. The president announced in a speech before the students that Omega Psi Phi Fraternity did not exist. This action resulted in the men implementing phase two of their plan. They personally lobbied the faculty and spoke with the president directly. After much persuasion and time, the administration approved the students' request; however, they were only allowed to exist on Howard University's campus. The administration also made changes to their constitution. Displeased with the compromises they had to make, the young men worked to combine their objectives with the faculty's concerns. After numerous meetings, the university finally granted the request to expand nationally.

Omega Psi Phi took their time expanding. In 1912 they started looking at letters of interest from different colleges around the country. They became incorporated in 1914 and founded their second chapter on the campus of Lincoln University in Pennsylvania.

In 1926 the fraternity became more community active. They took out a lifetime membership with the Association for the Study of Negro Life. They continued supporting numerous African American organizations. In 1940 the Omegas voted to make their major programs focus on socioeconomic issues rather than on social or cultural affairs. Today Omega Psi Phi has over 750 chapters and continues to improve the lives of families around the world.

Delta Sigma Theta Sorority Inc.

(SPEAKER *describes Delta Sigma Theta Sorority's founding and* initiatives.)

SPEAKER

Delta Sigma Theta Sorority's roots are found in Alpha Kappa Alpha Sorority. In 1912 twenty-two of Alpha Kappa Alpha's undergraduate members decided to change the sorority's name, colors, motto, and symbols. They also wanted to focus more on political and social issues, such as civil rights and voting rights. When recent Alpha Kappa Alpha graduate Nellie Quander found out about these proposed changes, she was infuriated. She rallied other graduate members who opposed the changes. The undergraduates were given an ultimatum, either keep the sorority's name and symbols or leave the sorority. The dissenting members did not relent, and on January 13, 1913, Delta Sigma Theta was formed.

One of the Delta's first political activities was participation in the Women's Suffrage March in 1913. Their participation made their commitment to political and social issues known in two ways: first, they overlooked Howard's rule that forbade them to participate in the march; second, instead of walking behind the white females, which was protocol for black women, they marched at the women's sides.

As the sorority grew, the Deltas continued their mission of activism. They awarded academic scholarships to youths and created one of the country's first bookmobiles as part of their national library project. They loaded buses with books and took them to isolated areas in the South, where African Americans didn't have access to reading materials. They also participated in the civil rights movement by helping to pay the bail for student protesters.

Delta Sigma Theta Sorority Inc. still prides itself on being proactive in women's and social issues. Today they have over 200,000 members on campuses and in communities around the world.

Phi Beta Sigma Fraternity Inc.

(SPEAKER highlights Phi Beta Sigma Fraternity Inc.'s founding and expansion.)

SPEAKER
Langston Taylor was a high school student from Memphis, Tennessee. During the summer of 1910, he met a recent graduate of Howard University, who impressed him with the glamour of campus fraternity life. Taylor, who had already made plans to enroll in Howard, decided that he wanted to establish another fraternity on the campus.

By the fall of 1913, he realized that founding a new fraternity would be a challenge, and that he would definitely need help. He recruited two other male students for assistance. The Great Three, as they were called, cemented the foundation for Phi Beta Sigma Fraternity. In November 1913 they met at a member's home and decided to initiate the first pledge line. New initiates would provide the numbers the men needed to move forward in solidifying Phi Beta Sigma Fraternity. When the group met in January 1914 in Washington, D.C., they incorporated the motto Culture for Service and Service for Humanity and elected officers. On January 9, 1914, Phi Beta Sigma was officially formed.

They took the next step of submitting a charter to Howard University in order to be recognized by the institution. The deans in charge of the approval procedure took three months to inform them that they had been approved. The fraternity's primary focus was on expansion, but they were met with resistance on some of the historically black college campuses. Many of the administrators were trying to ban new and existing Greek organizations; however, they were able to establish chapters on the campuses they selected. It was reported that Kappa Alpha Psi contacted Phi Beta Sigma regarding a possible merger to expand the two organizations. The Sigmas considered the offer and decided to respectfully decline.

During the 1920s, Phi Beta Sigma became proactive in local, national, and international issues. For example, they supported an antilynching law. They also voiced opposition to the United States' intervention in Haiti. As the fraternity grew, they made it a priority to support African American businesses, an issue that remains of great importance to their organization. They also boast being the only black fraternity that officially supported and helped to organize the 1995 Million Man March.

Today Phi Beta Sigma's initiatives are numerous. They have joined with organizations such as the American Cancer Society and the March of Dimes, which works to prevent premature births. Presently, they have grown to approximately 150,000 members worldwide.

Zeta Phi Beta Sorority Inc.

(SPEAKER shares Zeta Phi Beta Sorority's founding and social agenda.)

SPEAKER
Zeta Phi Beta was founded when Arizona Cleaver was asked by Phi Beta Sigma member Charles Taylor about forming a sister organization to their fraternity. Leaver took the request under consideration.
She knew Howard University already had two existing sororities, Alpha Kappa Alpha and Delta Sigma Theta. She wasn't sure if the administration would approve another. She decided to pursue the possibility of a new sorority.

Fourteen young ladies attended the initial meeting. Of the fourteen who attended, only five followed through or met Zeta's standards.

On January 16, 1920, they became the five founders of Zeta Phi Beta Sorority. It became the third African American sorority in the United States. They drafted a constitution based on Phi Beta Sigma's. This alliance made them the only official brother and sister organizations bound by a constitution.

In the coming years, the sorority grew steadily. In 1920 Zeta Phi Beta held their first national convention in conjunction with Phi Beta Sigma. In 1923 they became incorporated under the laws of Washington, D.C. It was also during these early years that the sorority began their tradition of Finer Womanhood Week. They also expanded to campuses from New York City to Atlanta and solidified their organization by electing national officers. In the 1930s they became associated with the NAACP and the National Negro Congress. In 1948 they became the first Greek-letter organization to charter a chapter in Africa.

Zeta Phi Beta also concentrated on community-based projects. They established the Prevention and Control of Juvenile Delinquency project. They created a non-Greek auxiliary called Amicae, or Friends of Zeta. This group assisted the sorority in their community-based projects. Zeta Phi Beta has chartered hundreds of chapters around the world. Their priorities and goals can be summed up in their motto, Scholarship, Service, Sisterhood, and Finer Womanhood.

Sigma Gamma Rho Sorority Inc.

*(*SPEAKER *shares Sigma Gamma Rho's founding and social initiatives.)*

SPEAKER
Sigma Gamma Rho Sorority was founded by seven undergraduate students at Butler University. Their mission was to create a sorority that emphasized service and achievement for black people. On November

12, 1922, the seven women founded Sigma Gamma Rho Sorority. It was the only African American sorority to be founded on a white campus.

This was a disadvantage for the new sorority. They were founded in Indiana, which was where the Ku Klux Klan had one of its strongest bases of operation. This was a bitter environment for a black organization that wanted to exist and expand. The first few years, Sigma Gamma Rho focused on organizing and expanding, rather than holding national conventions. They used this period to form their motto, pledge, slogan, coat of arms, and hymn. They didn't hold their first national convention until 1925. They were finally able to become incorporated as a national sorority on December 30, 1929, by the state of Indiana.

Although Sigma Gamma Rho is the smallest black sorority, their activism matches all others. Since the early years of its existence, they have been involved in the fight for women's rights. They have also strived to create better African American leaders. In the field of education, Sigma Gamma Rho developed literary contests that provided books for young black students. Today through programs like Operation Big Book Bag, they provide encyclopedias, thesauri, notebooks, paper, and other necessary school supplies to children in homeless shelters, hospitals, and other centers that assist children in need. Their National Marrow Donor program recruits and educates African American potential donors in order to reduce the amount of deaths associated with bone marrow diseases. Today Sigma Gamma Rho Sorority has over ninety thousand members nationwide.

Iota Phi Theta Fraternity Inc.

(SPEAKER *describes Iota Phi Theta Fraternity's founding and expansion.*)

SPEAKER

During the 1960s, African Americans across the nation were growing more and more dissatisfied with traditional leaders. Young adults were becoming more proactive regarding civil rights issues. This new consciousness was the basis for the foundation of Iota Phi Theta Fraternity Inc.

On November 19, 1963, the Twelve Honorable Founders established Iota Phi Theta Fraternity on the campus of Morgan State University in Baltimore, Maryland. Their fraternity was unique from other college chapters in that they were three to five years older than their undergraduate peers. Some were former military men, and some were married and had families. Most of them had known each other the majority of their lives, and many of them had full-time jobs in addition to their school courses. Their perspective on fraternities also differed. They considered the act of hazing pledges to be senseless and immoral, especially since black Americans were fighting and dying for their civil rights.

Although Iota Phi Theta had a strong foundation, the fraternity didn't grow rapidly in the early stages. Several factors contributed to this. First, the members lived off campus. This made it harder for undergraduate students to identify and connect with them. Second, their fraternity wasn't a member of the Pan-Hellenic Council like the other African American Greek-letter organizations. Membership in the council established legitimacy in the Greek world. These two main factors kept the fraternity small and local. However, 1967 proved to be a year of change. A group of undergraduate campus men became the first pledges. They were dubbed the Pied Pipers. This stimulated student interest and created a major change in Iota's image. The Pied Pipers decided to expand the fraternity. They focused on campuses on the Eastern Seaboard. In 1968 Iota Phi Theta became incorporated.

They expanded their organization from regional to national. They also continued to add graduate chapters.

Since their inception, Iota Phi Theta Fraternity had a mission of being in the forefront of the African American struggle. One of their first protest acts was to boycott a segregated mall in Baltimore. They also worked to promote programs to improve the black community. They supported numerous organizations, such as the NAACP and the United Negro College Fund. They also established a youth alliance national program that addressed the needs of black youths.

Today, Iota Phi Theta has continued to address concerns in the black community. Some of their programs are Iota Minority Political Mobilization, which aims to educate the black community on politics; and Afya Njema, which addresses health concerns of critical importance to African Americans. Iota Phi Theta has approximately 250 chapters that extend as far as the Republic of Korea.

HOLIDAYS, CELEBRATIONS, AND COMMEMORATIVES

Martin Luther King Day
January

(SPEAKER shares the origin of Martin Luther King Day.)

SPEAKER
Martin Luther King Day is celebrated the third Monday in January. It commemorates slain civil rights leader Martin Luther King Jr., who was born January 15, 1929. The day became a federal holiday in 1986, when it was signed into law by President Reagan. However, it wasn't observed by all fifty states until the year 2000. Some of the traditional celebrations for this day include parades, speakers, church services, and special programs in the African American community.

National Freedom Day
February

(SPEAKER gives the origin of National Freedom Day.)

SPEAKER
National Freedom Day was founded by a former slave named Major Richard Robert Wright Sr. He started the holiday, because he felt that there should be a day to celebrate freedom for all Americans. February 1 was selected because it marked the date in 1865 that President Lincoln signed the Thirteenth Amendment, which abolished slavery.

On June 30, 1948, President Truman signed a bill proclaiming February 1 National Freedom Day.

Black Love Day
February

(SPEAKER describes the origin and purpose of Black Love Day.)

SPEAKER
Black Love Day was established by Ms. Ayo Kendi in 1993. It is celebrated February 13, the day before Valentine's Day. It was initially organized in northeast Washington, D.C. In 1994 the mayor of D.C. proclaimed Black Love Day as an official day of recognition, observance, and celebration. It is designed to create a spirit of reconciliation, forgiveness, and atonement. It is also intended to demonstrate "love for the creator, the self, the family, the community, and the black race."

African Americans should practice the following five tenets: (1) display the akoma, which is a symbol of patience, suffering, goodwill, and endurance, (2) greet others with the phrase "nya akoma," which means "get a heart; be patient," (3) read *Black Love*, which is a book of poetry (4) purchase from black businesses, and (5) celebrate love with family, friends, and companions.

Black History Month
February

(SPEAKER explains the origin and purpose of Black History Month.)

SPEAKER
Black History Month is an extension of Negro History Week. It was started in 1926 by Carter Woodson, the Father of Black History.

Woodson's purpose, as continued today, was to recognize the achievements of African Americans. He chose February, because it was the birth month of Frederick Douglass and Abraham Lincoln. The celebration runs throughout the month. Festivities include programs that highlight outstanding African Americans, parades, special church services, speakers, and carnivals. Many black people dress in traditional African garments.

Crispus Attucks Day
March

(SPEAKER *shares the origin and purpose of Crispus Attucks Day.*)

SPEAKER
To honor the black Revolutionary War patriot, the black abolitionists in America began Crispus Attucks Day in 1858. It began as a day to remember the patriotism of Attucks, who was the first person to die for our country's freedom. On April 25, 1947, Crispus Attucks Day became a legal holiday in New Jersey. March 5 of each year is designated as Crispus Attucks Day in that state.

Harriet Tubman Day
March

(SPEAKER *recounts how Harriet Tubman Day became a holiday.*)

SPEAKER
Harriet Tubman Day is commemorated on March 10 each year. Tubman died March 10, 1913. In 1990 President George H. Bush proclaimed March 10 Harriet Tubman Day. The state of New York also established it as a holiday in 2003.

Black Marriage Day
March

*(*SPEAKER *explains the origin and purpose of Black Marriage Day.)*

SPEAKER
Black Marriage Day was founded by Nisa Muhammad. It is usually celebrated the fourth Sunday in March. The purpose is to celebrate the institution of marriage within the black community. The basic concept is that marriage is an integral part of the community, not solely a commitment between two people. This premise is based on the theory that in communities where marriages are successful, property values go up and crime rates go down. Schools are better, and people live healthier. It is further believed that communities have a charge to support and encourage the institution of marriage.

Richmond, Virginia, Emancipation Day
April

*(*SPEAKER *describes Emancipation Day in Richmond, Virginia.)*

SPEAKER
Emancipation Day in Richmond, Virginia, was first celebrated on April 3, 1866. It wasn't a celebration of the Emancipation Proclamation issued by President Lincoln, but a celebration of the fall of Richmond, the capital of the Confederate States of America. African Americans in Richmond continued to celebrate this day until the early twentieth century.

Paul Robeson Day
April

*(*SPEAKER *shares the origin of Paul Robeson Day.)*

SPEAKER
Paul Robeson was an actor, singer, and civil rights activist. Paul Robeson Day is an African American observance commemorated on his birthday, April 9.

Jackie Robinson Day
April

(SPEAKER shares the origin of Jackie Robinson Day.)

SPEAKER
Jackie Robinson entered the Major League on April, 15, 1947. Major League Baseball began Jackie Robinson Day on April 15, 1981, at Shea Stadium to recognize Robinson's impact on Major League Baseball. All the players, coaches, and managers donned Robinson's number forty-two. Fourteen other ball parks celebrated with the same tribute. Jackie Robinson Day continues to be celebrated by the Major League.

Washington, D.C., Emancipation Day
April

(SPEAKER shares the purpose and origin of Emancipation Day in Washington, D.C.)

SPEAKER
Emancipation Day in Washington, D.C., is celebrated on April 16 each year. It commemorates the day that President Lincoln signed the Compensated Emancipation Act, which was April 16, 1862. Approximately 3,100 slaves were freed in the nation's capital. Slave owners were paid up to $300 for each person, and slavery was abolished in Washington, D.C.

African American Women's Month
April

(SPEAKER *describes the purpose of African American Women's Month.*)

SPEAKER
African American Women's Month is observed the entire month of April. It's a cultural affair that seeks to recognize the contributions of African American women.

Malcolm X Day
May

(SPEAKER *shares the origin of Malcolm X Day.*)

SPEAKER
Malcolm X Day is celebrated in most major American cities in the United States on the third Sunday in May. It has a very large festival in Washington, D.C., where over seventy-five thousand people gather at Anacostia Park.

National Tap Dance Day
May

(SPEAKER *shares National Tap Dance Day's purpose and origin.*)

SPEAKER
May 25 has been chosen as National Tap Dance Day by the United States Congress. The date was selected because it is the birthday of Bill "Bojangles" Robinson.

Juneteenth
June

(SPEAKER explains Juneteenth's origin and purpose.)

SPEAKER

"The people of Texas are informed that in accordance with a Proclamation for the Executive of the United States, all slaves are free. This involves an absolute equality of rights and rights of property between former masters and slaves, and the connection heretofore existing between them becomes that between employer and free laborer." This was General Order Number 3 read to African American Texans by Union general Gordon Granger on June 19, 1865, in Galveston, Texas. Even though the Emancipation Proclamation went into effect January 1, 1863 liberating all persons in the Confederate states, blacks in Texas were still enslaved. When African Americans learned they were free, there was immediate jubilation and prayer. Texas was the last state where slavery existed.

The Juneteenth celebration began in Galveston, Texas, in 1865. In 1980 Juneteenth became an official Texan holiday. Today, twenty-nine other states and Washington, D.C. recognize June 19 as an official holiday. It is the oldest national holiday commemorating the abolishment of slavery. In 1997 the U.S. Senate adopted a joint resolution recognizing Juneteenth as the actual independence day for African Americans. Celebrations have incorporated emphasis on education and African American achievements. Traditional foods include barbecue, soul food, and red soda pop.

Marcus Garvey Day
August

(SPEAKER shares Marcus Garvey Day's purpose and origin.)

SPEAKER

Marcus Garvey was born on August 17, 1887. He was the founder of the Universal Negro Improvement Association and the African Communities League. Garvey was also a journalist, orator, and entrepreneur. The celebration of Marcus Garvey's birthday began in 1993 in Toronto, Canada. Terry Brown was prompted to begin this celebration. He collaborated with the African Culture Restoration Association and 150 supporters. This holiday's purpose is to celebrate Garvey's lifelong work and to commemorate him for inspiring a black nationalist movement. Today's celebrations are national and international. Commemorative events are usually planned for the weekend closest to his birthday.

Jerry Rescue Day
October

(SPEAKER gives the origin of Jerry Rescue Day.)

SPEAKER

Jerry Rescue Day is celebrated in Syracuse, New York, as a freedom holiday. It began on October 1, 1851, when a group of white citizens freed a slave named Jerry and sent him to Canada to live as a free man.

Harambee
October

(SPEAKER shares Harambee's origin and purpose.)

SPEAKER

Harambee is an East African word meaning "unity" or "let's pull together." The African American community of Dallas, Texas, began the celebration in 1974. It is in recognition of black culture and meant to be a safe alternative to Halloween. Equally important, the black citizens of that city didn't feel that Halloween had any significance to African Americans. In its initial year in 1974, more than three thousand people of many diverse backgrounds attended the celebration. Today, it is typically celebrated during the last week in October and includes authentic African foods, dance performances, films, and art exhibits.

Umoja Karamu
November

(SPEAKER describes Umoja Karamu's origin and purpose.)

SPEAKER

Umoja Karamu was created by Dr. Edward Sims Jr. in 1971. It begins on the fourth Sunday in November and lasts five days. It is celebrated in a similar manner to Thanksgiving. The purpose is to "instill solidarity, black values, and appreciation for black heritage into black families." The five-day celebration is highlighted with historical readings, feasts, prayers, and libations to honor dead ancestors.

Five colors are used to represent five periods in the life of African Americans:

- Black represents black families before slavery
- White represents the scattering of black families during slavery
- Red symbolizes blacks' liberation from slavery
- Green highlights the significance of the struggles for civil rights and equality
- Gold directs celebrants to hope for the future

Junkanoo
December

(SPEAKER gives the origin of Junkanoo.)

SPEAKER

Enslaved Bahamians who were brought to Miami to work on the railroads in the Florida swamplands started Junkanoo. During the Christmas season, slaves had to take care of their masters' holiday needs before they could plan for themselves. They didn't get the opportunity to celebrate Christmas until December 26. Their Junkanoo festivities lasted one week and didn't end until New Year's Day.

Junkanoo continues to be celebrated in Miami. The main attraction of Junkanoo is the battle of the bands. The competition is so intense that some bands will secure a hiding place months in advance of the occasion to practice and make their costumes. When it's time for Junkanoo, the bands play their drums and blow whistles while performing in grand parades. Prizes are awarded to the most elaborate, crowd pleasing band.

Kwanzaa
December 26–January 1

(SPEAKER shares Kwanzaa's meaning and purpose.)

SPEAKER

Dr. Maulana Karenga, a professor of African culture, created Kwanzaa in 1966. He noticed seven ideas that kept reappearing in African culture. He put those ideas into a seven-day holiday, beginning on December 26 of each year. The seven-day observance has seven principles that apply to each day individually:

- December 26 is Umoja, which emphasizes unity and community
- December 27 is Kujichagulia, which emphasizes self-determination
- December 28 is Ujima, which emphasizes collective work and responsibility
- December 29 is Ujamaa, which emphasizes cooperative economics
- December 30 is Nia, which emphasizes purpose
- December 31 is Kuumba, which emphasizes creativity
- January 1 is Imani, which emphasizes faith

Watch Night
December

(SPEAKER explains Watch Night's origin and purpose.)

SPEAKER

Watch Night was originally a religious and political celebration. On December 31, 1862, black people gathered in their churches and homes to wait for the stroke of midnight. At midnight they would hear the announcement that the Emancipation Proclamation had become law. The proclamation declared that all people living in Confederate states were free. At the stroke of midnight, there were nationwide prayers, singing, dancing, shouting, and jubilant celebrations.

Today, most African American churches hold Watch Night services to celebrate the blessing of seeing a new year. However, in many cases the original purpose has been diluted or incorporated into the service through songs, prayers, and general thanksgiving.

BLACK CERTAINLY IS BEAUTIFUL

BEAUTY PAGEANTS

Miss America

(TAYLOR *shares the history of African Americans in the Miss America pageant.*)

TAYLOR

My name is Taylor. I'm planning to represent my state in the Miss America contest. Today any female, regardless of color, has the opportunity to become Miss America. It took a long time for our country to publicly acknowledge that black is beautiful. For example, did you know it took sixty-three years for the Miss America contest to crown an African American? Let me give you a little of the pageant's history.

The Miss America pageant was founded in 1921 in Atlantic City, New Jersey. In 1923 the first black women appeared in the Miss America pageant in a musical number as slaves. The pageant sought contestants who would portray the "all-American girl." To ensure that, the contest had what was called rule number seven. Basically, this rule stated on the application form that one must be of good health and of the white race.

However, African American women did eventually compete. Let me give you a brief history of the beautiful women who graced the pageant's runway. Cheryl Brown was Miss Iowa in 1970. She was the first African American female to compete for the title of Miss America. Lencola Sullivan competed in 1980 as Miss Arkansas. She was the first black female to become one of the top five finalists. In 1984 African Americans finally had their year. Vanessa Williams competed as Miss New York, and Suzette Charles competed as Miss New Jersey. For the first time ever, two African Americans were the top finalists. Vanessa Williams became Miss America, and Suzette Charles was first runner up. Due to controversy, Vanessa Williams lost her crown that same year, and Suzette Charles became Miss America.

Six years later, Debbye Turner, who represented Missouri, became Miss America. In 1991 Marjorie Vincent represented Illinois and earned the crown. In 1994 Kimberly Akin became Miss America for the state of South Carolina. And last but not least, Ericka Dunlap represented Florida and won Miss America in 2004. As you can see, many beautiful women came before me, and I hope to wear the crown proudly just as they did.

Miss USA

(MORGAN *shares the history of African Americans in the Miss USA pageant.)*

MORGAN
My name is Morgan. I've been going to charm classes and learning all about the Miss USA pageant. I've also been studying hard in school, because one day I hope to wear the crown like the beautiful and intelligent black women who came before me.

Now, I'm in a rush because I'm on my way to class, but for those of you who don't know, I'll give you a brief history lesson on African Americans in the pageant. Let's start with the dynamic Miss Michigan

Carol Gist. In 1990 she became the first African American woman ever to be crowned Miss USA. Not too long after her in 1993, Kenya Moore from Michigan graced the stage as the second African American Miss USA. Shauntay Hinton won the crown in 2002 as Miss District of Columbia. Five years later, Rachel Smith—who was Miss Tennessee—became Miss USA. Crystle Stewart represented Texas and won the competition in 2008. Now, if I don't hurry, I'll be late to class. In the nearby future, if you hear "and the winner is . . ." don't be surprised to see me wearing the crown.

Miss Black America

(RIHANA briefly shares the history of the Miss Black America pageant.)

RIHANA
My name is Rihana. One day I would like to be Miss Black America. The pageant's history is inspiring. J. Morris Anderson began the Miss Black America contest on August 17, 1968. The pageant had a twofold purpose. First, it was to protest the national Miss America pageant, because it lacked black participants. Second, it was to provide a positive image of black women by giving them the opportunity to showcase their intelligence, talents, and beauty. The contest was, and continues to be, open to females between eighteen and twenty-nine years old. Many of the contestants have become successful in the field of entertainment. The very first winner was Sandra Williams. However, one of the most popular former contestants is Oprah Winfrey. She competed as Miss Tennessee in 1971.

I'm looking forward to the day I can compete. Who knows, maybe the pageant will give me the same confidence it gave Oprah Winfrey, who eventually became one of the most successful and respected black women in America.

Miss Black USA

(DESTINEE describes Miss Black USA's history and purpose.)

DESTINEE

My name is Destinee. I'm completing an entry form for the Miss Black USA contest. Many people don't know much about the pageant, so just in case you're one of those people, I'm going to tell you a little about it. The Miss Black USA Scholarship Pageant was founded in 1986 by Karen Arrington. Now, don't confuse Miss Black USA with Miss Black America. The major difference between the two is why they were founded. Miss Black America was founded in 1968 during the civil rights movement. The founder wanted to provide a platform that would display the intellect and beauty of the black woman, since the Miss America pageant didn't allow black participants at the time. Miss Black USA, on the other hand, was founded eighteen years later with the specific purpose of awarding scholarships to the winners. According to the Miss Black USA Scholarship Pageant, its mission is to "provide educational opportunities to outstanding young women of color and to develop the whole woman, body and spirit." That's what I call the total package.

Now I have to get back to this entry form. If I win, I can follow in the footsteps of the pageant's first winner, Tamiko Gibson. I want to be a news anchor just like she was. Well, we'll see what happens. I'm going to go mail it off now. Wish me luck!

SUPERMODELS

Naomi Sims
(1948–2009)
Fashion Model, Entrepreneur

(SPEAKER *describes Naomi Sims's trailblazing career in modeling.*)

SPEAKER

Naomi Sims is considered by many to be the first black supermodel. Naomi Sims was born in Oxford, Mississippi on March 30, 1948. While she was still young, her mother moved the family to Pittsburgh, Pennsylvania. It was in Pittsburgh that Sims's mother became very sick, and Sims had to enter foster care. As a child she was often made fun of, because she was much taller than her classmates. It was during this difficult period that she decided she would become successful.

After high school in 1966, she moved to New York City to attend the Fashion Institute of Technology, which had awarded her a scholarship. It was there that her classmates encouraged her to begin a career in modeling. After many rejections from modeling agencies because of her dark skin, Sims took her career into her own hands. She approached photographers directly in hopes of getting them to photograph her. Finally, in August of 1967 she received her break. A photographer from the *Times* placed her on the cover of their fashion section, Fashions of the Times.

After her feature in the *Times*, she was disappointed that her career didn't take off right away. Modeling agencies continued to refuse her as a client. Desperate for income and looking for an opportunity to break into the industry, Sims approached former model Wilhelmina Cooper, who had just opened a modeling agency. Cooper agreed to hire her to distribute magazines. Although this wasn't a modeling job, Sims was able to make valuable connections.

By the end of 1968, she was earning near $1,000 per week and had been hired to represent AT&T in a national television campaign. Her greatest accomplishment in 1968, however, was being featured on the cover of *Ladies Home Journal*. Not only was she the first African American woman on the magazine's cover, she was also the first African American woman on the cover of any American magazine.

Her modeling career began to blossom quickly; however, she became more interested in the business side of the beauty industry. She started her own wig line for African American women and expanded her company to include cosmetics and fragrances. Within five years, her company was earning more than $5 million annually.

Naomi Sims will always be remembered as the first African American woman to grace the cover of an American magazine. But she was also an entrepreneur who used her intellect to build one of the most successful beauty lines ever created by an African American woman.

Beverly Johnson
(1952–)
Supermodel, Actress, Writer

Characters:
DEE, *female fictional character, middle-aged woman,* DIANE'*s friend*
DIANE, *female fictional character, middle-aged woman*
Costumes:
Present-day exercise attire
Props:
Weights, yoga mat, picture of Beverly Johnson

(DEE and DIANE *discuss the success of Beverly Johnson.)*

DEE

One, two, three, four—this is hard work, but I guess a girl's gotta do, what a girl's gotta do.

DIANE

I know. If I lift this weight one more time, my arm will fall off!

DEE

(Stops exercising and picks up a picture of Beverly Johnson.)
I know, me too. But I keep looking at my inspiration photo. Beverly Johnson is my inspiration. I've been reading her book *Beverly Johnson's Guide to a Life of Health and Beauty.*

DIANE

Girl, it's a little late to be trying to get into modeling.

(Both laugh.)

DEE

I'm not trying to become a model like her, although I could if I wanted to.
(Laughs)
But I wouldn't mind being as fit as her. We saw her at a charity ball recently, and my husband said, "How come you don't look like that? You're the same age as her." I told him—well, never mind what I told him. It wasn't very nice. So when I bought her book, it inspired me to work out and get healthy.

DIANE

I once read how her friends at college suggested that she try modeling. She took a risk and followed up on their suggestion. She ended up landing a job with *Glamour* magazine. Apparently that jump-started her career.

DEE

But the highlight came in 1974 when she became the first black model to be featured on the cover of *Vogue* magazine. After that, she was on over five hundred magazine covers. Within the year that she appeared on *Vogue*, fashion designers in the United States started using African American models. She opened a lot of doors for so many beautiful, talented young ladies.

My husband even noticed the difference in me since I've been working out and using some of her beauty tips. She helped him notice how gorgeous I am. He calls me Diva Dee. Beverly caused the fashion world to say what so many have been saying all the time, black is beautiful.

DIANE

Well, I know that's right, cuz I'm definitely beautiful.
(Laughs)
Well, break time's over. Let me work the other arm. I don't think this one will move any more.

DEE

(Puts down the picture and starts exercising again.)
One, two, three, four, five . . .

(End scene.)

Tyra Banks
(1973–)
Supermodel, Talk Show Host, Actress

Characters:

WENDY, *female fictional character, high school student,* MELISSA's *older sister*

MELISSA, *female fictional character, middle school student*

Costumes:

Present-day casual attire

Props:

Computer, computer desk, two chairs

(MELISSA *and* WENDY *discuss Tyra Banks's success as a model and media mogul.*)

MELISSA

You're always on the internet. What are you looking at?

WENDY

I'm looking at information on Tyra Banks. I want to go on her *America's Next Top Model* show. It could be the start of my career, but Mama thinks I'm too young to seriously consider a modeling career. You have to help me talk her into it.

MELISSA

She might be right. It's a lot of pressure. You'll be competing with girls from all over the country. Do you think you can handle that much competition?

WENDY

Competition doesn't scare me, and I'm not too young. Look at this. Tyra was the same age as me when she started her career.

MELISSA

Wow! It says she was only a junior in high school. Look! Look! It says she's modeled in London, Paris, Tokyo, and New York. I guess while other girls were getting excited about the prom, Tyra was getting excited about her next modeling assignment.

WENDY

I read that her first week in Paris, she mesmerized the designers so much when she took the runway that they booked her for twenty-five shows. She was also the first African American model on the cover of *GQ*, *Sports Illustrated* swimsuit issue, and the *Victoria's Secret* catalog. Since she retired from modeling in 2005, she's done some acting, music videos, created her *America's Next Top Model* reality show, and won an Emmy for her daytime program, *The Tyra Banks Show*. Now you see why I need your help convincing Mama that I'm not too young to begin a modeling career. I could be a multimillionaire like her by the time I'm thirty-five.

MELISSA

Mama, come here!

WENDY

Thanks for calling her for me.

MELISSA

I'm not calling her for you. I'm calling her for me. I want to be a model too.

(End scene.)

FICTIONAL CHARACTERS HIGHLIGHTING HISTORY

The Quilt Makers

Characters:
DORA, *female fictional character, elderly woman,* SARAH's *younger sister*
SARAH, *female fictional character, elderly woman*
Costumes:
Present-day casual attire
Props:
Two chairs, table, partial quilt, quilting supplies

(SARAH and DORA discuss the history and importance of quilt making.)

SARAH
Dora, hand me some of that yellow for a star.

DORA
I thought I was supposed to be making the star.

SARAH
Well, I changed my mind. I want to make it myself.

DORA

Sarah, you always want to do everything yourself. You act like Grandma didn't teach me how to make quilts too.

SARAH

She taught both of us, but I learned better.

DORA

Don't nobody think that but you. I wish my granddaughters wanted to learn to quilt. I tried to tell them that quilting is part of our heritage. Every woman's family has made quilts since slavery times.

SARAH

We had to. We were too poor to afford store-bought blankets.

DORA

The only way young girls these days would buy a quilt is if it was a designer brand. The only thing they have time for is shopping at the mall.

SARAH

My niece doesn't even have time for that. She sits at the computer and shops on that bBay.

DORA

Is it eBay or bBay? You don't know anything about computers, do you?

SARAH

No. And neither do you.

DORA

I can't argue with that. Remember when we used to have quilting bees? It was a time when colored women would get together and share feelings and socialize.

SARAH

How many times I have to tell you we ain't colored anymore. We're African Americans. And it wasn't socializing that we were doing, it was gossiping.
(Both laugh.)

DORA

It takes too long to say African American, but I'll say it just to shut your mouth. I get tired of you calling me old-fashioned. I'm not old-fashioned, I'm traditional.

SARAH

We have to find a way to get the younger generation interested. If we don't teach them, it may be a lost art in our family forever. This isn't something we do just because we don't know how to work the remote control. We're the last ones in our family who know how to quilt. We're getting old, you know.

DORA

Speak for yourself. I'm not getting older, I'm getting better.
(Waves her hand and snaps fingers.)
Holla at your girl.

SARAH

I have to holler. You can't half hear. And stop saying everything those young folks say. Pretty soon you'll be speaking Ebonics.

DORA

Don't be a hater.

(Laughs)

As much as it hurts me to agree with you, we do have to find a way to get them interested.

SARAH

I remember Grandma Austin telling us about her great-grandmother who was a slave. She talked about how the slaves would help each other escape by hanging quilts on clotheslines or fences. They would use different kinds of cloth to tell each other which way to go. Different patterns were used as a warning signal.

DORA

They had one called the drunkard pattern, because a drunk man can't walk straight. They would also design strips in a zigzag fashion. That meant don't travel in a straight path. Go left and right when you're running. A star meant keep going north.

SARAH

Grandma made it north to freedom. She found a job and saved her money to buy her baby sister's freedom. She swears those quilts were her divine guide. I bet the young people would be interested in family stories like that.

DORA

Let's have a quilting bee and invite all the women in the family over. We'll make quilts and tell family stories. I know they'll love them. Any idea how to get everybody here?

SARAH

Yeah. We'll get the little boy down the street to post it on Bmail.

DORA
Good idea!
(They try to do a creative handshake like youths.)

(End scene.)

Macon County Farmer

(Fictional character MR. JACKSON *describes the pain he felt as a victim of the Tuskegee Syphilis Study.)*

MR. JACKSON
Good day to y'all. I'm somebody who was treated like a nobody. I'm just a dirt farmer from Macon County, Alabama. I was involved in a scientific experiment, but I'm not a scientist. I was a victim. I was one of the farmers that the American Medical Society tricked and lied to about the painful and sometimes deadly disease syphilis.

We were the perfect guinea pigs. All of us were poor and black, and many of us were illiterate. Thirty-six percent of us black sharecroppers in the county were infected with syphilis. When government doctors found out how bad the health conditions were, they came down here. But it wasn't to help us. They came to study us. We didn't know what was wrong with us. We just knew we were sick. The health officials told us we had "bad blood."
(Pauses)
Bad blood they called it. The doctors didn't tell us it was syphilis, or that we could go blind, crazy, pass it on to our wives, or even die from the disease.
(Shakes his head.)
Dr. Clark from the venereal disease division headed the project. He wanted to observe the syphilis disease as it passed through our bodies untreated to see how it progressed. He wanted to disprove the theory

that syphilis was less deadly to black people than to whites. He even convinced the medical director at Tuskegee Institute, the black college founded by Booker T. Washington, that this study would bring prestige to the college.

Dr. Clark retired in 1933, but another doctor named Vonderlehr took over the experiment. Dr. Clark wanted to study us for a few years, but Vonderlehr wanted to study us indefinitely. He even wanted our bodies after we died. He took about four hundred men who were in the latter stages of the disease for diagnostic tests. He got cooperation from Tuskegee Institute, where the autopsies were to be done. He did a lot of underhanded things that kept us suffering. He convinced the local health officials and area doctors to agree to refuse treatment to any of us who came for help. They even had a black nurse, Ms. Eunice Rivers, working with them. Her job was to give us pills for our "bad blood" and keep us away from any place that would give us help. The pills weren't more than aspirin and some kind of tonic. They say she actually liked some of us, but I don't see how. She watched us suffer and never said a word. Seems like everybody knew what was going on but us.

In the late 1930s, there was a nationwide campaign to fight venereal disease, but they wouldn't let us get any treatment from the mobile units in Macon County. That's not the worst part. When penicillin was discovered and proved effective against syphilis, no one would give it to us.

(Angry)

They experimented on us for forty years! When the study was finally stopped in 1972, at least twenty-eight and maybe as many as a hundred of us human guinea pigs had died from the disease. You won't read about us in most of your social studies books. America was embarrassed, because we were the most shameful experiment in our country's history.

Chain Gang Charlie

(Fictional character CHARLIE *recalls the chain gang system's horrors and injustices.)*

CHARLIE

How y'all do? I'm Charlie Simmons, but most people call me Chain Gang Charlie. That's because I was on the chain gang when I was in prison years ago. Before y'all judge me, let me tell you know-it-alls something. The only real crime I committed was the crime of being black. I was a poor colored man living in the South. I was a free spirit. I liked to wander and meet different ladies and see different places. I didn't have much, but I didn't need much. Wasn't nobody but me. I would pick up work when I had to, you know, enough to get by. I wasn't lazy, but I was tired of hard work. My daddy was born a slave. When slavery ended, we had to sharecrop. That wasn't much better. I left the farm and started drifting.

One day, I wandered into this town. I wasn't hurting anybody, just looking around and minding my own business. Next thing I knew, the local sheriff grabbed me and arrested me for vagrancy. When I went to court, I told the judge that I was only passing through, but he didn't care. He sentenced me to five years hard labor on the chain gang. You see, after the Civil War the South needed free labor, so they created this legal system that targeted black men. It was set up to give us long prison terms for any kind of misdemeanor, so they could work us as long and hard as they wanted.

Sometimes, if you went to court and didn't have the money for the fine, a white man would volunteer to pay it for you, whether you wanted him to or not. The court would lease you out to him to work off the fine. The fine might've only been three or $4, but you would have to work for that man for three years or more. In other words, you became his property.

The chain gang was worse than being leased out. The guards chained us together all day to keep us from escaping. We had to build roads, clear ditches, or do any other kind of backbreaking job they saw fit to make us do. Just like in the slave days, we were still building the South. I was one of the lucky ones. I survived. Most of the men died before their sentences were up. The chain gang system got so bad that they even sentenced black children as young as six years old to work on the convict lease gang. One little boy's feet rotted off, because he had to work all winter without any shoes.

A lot of African American men were victims just like me. I want all of you to remember this from Chain Gang Charlie: prison ain't fun, whether it was back in the day, as you like to say, or today. Stay out of trouble. Don't give people a reason to send you to jail. At least you have a choice; we didn't.

Today's African American

(Fictional character ZAVIER *shares why he is proud to be African American.)*

ZAVIER
(On the phone.)
I have to go now. Good-bye.
(Hangs up.)
I hope each of you is having a blessed day. I represent the contemporary African American. I am the CEO of a Fortune 500 company. I am young, gifted, and black. When you look at me, you look at black history: a history of people who descended from kings and queens. You see a person whose ancestors came from the continent

where the earliest known man originated. You are looking at a person whose forefathers were survivors; survivors of over two hundred years of enslavement; survivors who had their churches bombed but still found a way to pray; survivors who had crosses burned at their front doors and were forced to use the back door in public places because of Jim Crow laws. We are a race of people who survived after being beaten, arrested, and killed in the fight for civil rights.

I boast of my heritage, because my people rose from forced illiteracy to become doctors, lawyers, teachers, ministers, skilled laborers, accountants, astronauts, PhDs, CEOs, and loving parents who can read bedtime stories to their children. I am today's African American, and I say it loud, "I'm black, and I'm proud!"

BIBLIOGRAPHY

Academy of Motion Picture Arts and Sciences. "Oscar Legacy: Academy Award Ceremonies from 1929 through 2011." Last accessed June 13, 2011. http://www.oscars.org/awards/academyawards/ legacy/ index.html.

Abdul-Jabbar, Kareem and Alan Steinberg. *Black Profiles in Courage.* New York: HarperCollins, 2000.

Adams, Russell L. *Great Negroes Past and Present.* Chicago: Afro-Am Publishing Co., 1969.

Adolf, Arnold. *The Poetry of Black America.* New York: HarperCollins, 1973.

African American Holiday Association. Last accessed January 31, 2008. http://www.africanamericanholidays.org/holidays/index.htm.

African American Registry: A Non-Profit Education Organization. Last accessed June 13, 2011. http://aaregistry.org/.

Altman, Susan. *Encyclopedia of African American Heritage.* 2nd ed. New York: Checkmark Books, 2000.

Altman, Susan. *Extraordinary Black Americans . . . From Colonial to Contemporary Times.* Chicago: Children's Press, 1989.

Apostolic Assemblies of Christ Inc. "About Us." Last accessed June 13, 2011. http://www.apostolicassembliesofchrist.com/aboutus.html.

Bethune, Mary McLeod. "My Last Will and Testament." In *Mary McLeod Bethune: Building a Better World, Essays and Selected Documents*, edited by Audrey Thomas McCluskey and Elaine M. Smith, 58-61. Bloomington: Indiana University Press, 2002.

Bond, Adam L. "United Church of Christ." In *African American Religious Cultures*, edited by Anthony B. Pinn. Vol. 2, 401-403. Santa Barbara: ABC-CLIO, 2009.

Brewster, Charles W. *Rambles about Portsmouth.* 1859. Reprint, Somersworth, NH: New Hampshire Publishing Company, 1971.

Bringhurst, Newell G., and Darron T. Smith, eds. *Black and Mormon.* Champaign, IL: University of Illinois Press, 2006.

Bunche, William. "Strange Harmonies." *American Legacy* 9 (Winter 2004).

Chartier, Courtney. "The Voter Education Project." Last accessed July 13, 2011. http://web.library.emory.edu/blog/voter-education-project.

Cheyney University of Pennsylvania. "History of Cheyney University." Last accessed June 13, 2011. http://www.cheyney.edu/about-cheyney-university/cheyney-history.cfm.

Clark, John Henrik. *American Negro Short Stories.* New York: Hill and Wang, 1966.

Culver, Virginia. "Pilot Marlon D. Green Fought Racial Discrimination." *Denverpost.com*, July 10, 2009, updated February 8, 2010. http://www.denverpost.com/obituaries/ci_12805244.

Cunningham, Valerie. "Whipple, Prince, 1750–1796." In Blackpast. org. Last accessed June 13, 2011. http://www.blackpast.org/?q=aah/whipple-prince-1750-1796.

Diouf, Sylviane A. *Dreams of Africa in Alabama: The Slave Ship Clotilda and the Story of the Last Africans Brought to America.* New York: Oxford University Press, 2009.

Douglass, Frederick. "The Meaning of July Fourth for the Negro." In *The American Constitutional Experience: Selected Readings and Supreme Court Opinions*, edited with introductions by James A. Curry, Richard B. Riley, Richard M. Battistoni, and John C. Blakeman, 66-73. Dubuque, IA: Kendall Hunt Publishing Co., 2000.

Father Divine's International Peace Mission Movement. "Dates from 1876 Pertaining to the Work and Mission of Father Divine." Last accessed June 13, 2011. http://peacemission.info/father-divine/.

Fire Baptized Holiness Church. "Our Logo." Last accessed June 13, 2011. http://www.fbhchurch.org/logo_description.html.

France, Lisa Respers. "Def Jam Changed Music Business, Still a Power at 25." *CNN.com*, November 4, 2009. http://www.cnn.com/2009/SHOWBIZ/Music/11/02/def.jam.anniversary/index.html.

Fred Gray Official Website. Last accessed June 13, 2011. http://www.fredgray.net/background.html.

Gates, Henry Louis Jr., and Cornell West. *The African American Century*. New York: The Free Press, 2000.

Hills Tabernacle Primitive Baptist Church. "Church History." Last accessed July 13, 2011. http://hillstabernaclepbchurch.org/.

Hine, Darlene, William Hine, and Stanley Harrold. *African-American History*. Upper Saddle River, NJ: Pearson Prentice Hall, 2006.

Holt, Rinehart, and Winston, Inc. *African American Literature*. Austin, TX: Harcourt Brace Jovanovich, Inc., 1992.

Hornsby, Alton Jr. *Chronology of African American History*. 2nd ed. Detroit: Gale Research,1997.

Huey, Steve. "The Jackson 5: Biography." *Billboard.com*. Last accessed June 13, 2011. http://www.billboard.com/#/artist/the-jackson-5/bio/4895.

John Conyers Jr. United States Congressman. "Biography." Last accessed June 13, 2011. http://conyers.house.gov/index.cfm?FuseAction=About. Biography.

Kimball, Gregg D. *American City, Southern Place: A Cultural History of Antebellum Richmond*. Athens, GA: University of Georgia Press, 2003.

King, Martin Luther. "The Drum Major Instinct." Last accessed June 13, 2011. http://mlk-kpp01.stanford.edu/index.php/encyclopedia/multimediaentry/doc_the_drum_major_instinct/.

Kisch, John, and Edward Mapp. *A Separate Cinema*. New York: Noonday Press, 1998.

LeFebvre, Catherine. "Remembering Naomi Sims." *Ladies' Home Journal*. Last accessed June 13, 2011. http://www.lhj.com/style/covers/naomi-sims/.

Michael Jackson: The King of Pop, Official Website. Last accessed June 13, 2011. http://www.michaeljackson.com/us/home.

Morrison, Allan. "Black Patriots were Heroes at First Major Battle of Revolution." *Ebony*, February, 1964.

NASA. "NASA's African-American Astronauts Fact Sheet." Last modified September 22, 2009. Last accessed June 13, 2011. http://

www.nasa.gov/audience/foreducators/topnav/materials/listbytype/ African_American_Astronauts.html.

NASA. "Astronaut Biographies: Biographical Data." Last accessed June 13, 2011. http://www.jsc.nasa.gov/Bios/astrobio.html.

National Museum of American History, Smithsonian Institute. "Archives Center Finding Aids: Duke Ellington Collection." Last accessed July 19, 2011. http://americanhistory.si.edu/archives/d5301.htm.

National Park Service U.S. Department of the Interior. "Cuff Whitmore." In "Biographies of Patriots of Color at the Battle of Bunker Hill." http:// www.nps.gov/search/index.htm?query=Cuff+Whitmore&sub1. x=0&sub1.y=0.

Negro League Baseball Players Association. Last accessed June 13, 2011. http://negroleaguebaseball.com/.

Nobel Prize. Last accessed June 13, 2011. http://nobelprize.org/.

Parks, Rosa. "Standing Up for Freedom: Interview with Rosa Parks." Academy of Achievement, June 2, 1995. Last accessed June 14, 2011. http://www.achievement.org/autodoc/page/par0int-1.

PBS. "Race Records." Last accessed June 14, 2011. http://www.pbs.org/ jazz/exchange/exchange_race_records.htm.

PBS. "Rebecca Cox Jackson, 1795–1871." Last accessed June 14, 2011. http://www.pbs.org/wgbh/aia/part3/3p247.html.

PBS. "Maj. Robert H. Lawrence Jr." In "Secret Astronauts." Last accessed June 14, 2011. http://www.pbs.org/wgbh/nova/astrospies/prof-08.html.

Potter, Joan, and Constance Claytor. African American Firsts. Elizabethtown, NY: Pinto Press, 1994.

Rein, Lisa. "Mystery of Va.'s First Slaves is Unlocked 400 Years Later." The Washington Post, September 3, 2006. Last accessed May 9, 2011. http://www.washingtonpost.com/wp-dyn/content/article/2006/09/02/ AR2006090201097.html.

Reynolds, Patrick. "Flashbacks: Bill Bojangles Robinson." Washington Post, May 20, 2007.

Rhode Island College. "Edward Mitchell Bannister." Last accessed June 14, 2011. http://www.ric.edu/bannister/about_emb.php.

Ross, Lawrence C. Jr. *The Divine Nine*. New York: Kensington Publishing Corp., 2000.

Saint Bartley Primitive Baptist Church. "Church History." Last accessed June 14, 2011. saintbartleypbchurch.org/history.html.

Salzman, Jack. *The African American Experience*. New York: Macmillan Publishing, 1993.

Sammons, Mark J., and Valerie Cunningham. *Black Portsmouth: Three Centuries of African-American Heritage*. Lebanon, NH: University of New Hampshire Press, 2004.

Simmons, Russell, and Nelson George. *Life and Def: Sex, Drugs, Money, and God*. New York: Crown Publishers, 2001. Kindle edition.

Smith, Jessie Carney. *Black Firsts*. Detroit: Visible Ink Press, 1994.

Stewart, Jeffrey. *1001 Things Everyone Should Know About African American History*. New York: Broadway Books, 1996.

Swarthmore College. "An Inventory of the Richard Humphreys Foundation Records, 1837–1982." Last accessed June 14, 2011. http://www.swarthmore.edu/library/friends/ead/4059rihu.xml.

Tobin, Jacqueline L., and Raymond Dobard. *Hidden in Plain View*. New York: Doubleday, 1999.

U.S. House of Representatives, Office of the Clerk. "Black Americans in Congress." Last accessed June 14, 2011. http://baic.house.gov/.

Walter Mosley Official Website. Last accessed June 14, 2011. http://www.waltermosley.com/.

Wilson, Eric. "Naomi Sims, 61, Pioneering Cover Girl, Is Dead." *The New York Times*, August 3, 2009. Last accessed June 14, 2011. http://www.nytimes.com/2009/08/04/fashion/04sims.html.

Woodson, Carter G. *The History of the Negro Church*. 1921. Electronic version by the University of North Carolina at Chapel Hill, 2000. Last accessed June 14, 2011. http://docsouth.unc.edu/church/woodson/woodson.html.

Zuczek, Richard. *Encyclopedia of the Reconstruction Era: Greenwood Milestones in African American History*. Volume 2, *M-Z and Primary Documents*. Westport, CT: Greenwood Press, 2006.

INDEX

Colored Intercollegiate Athletic Association. *See* Central Intercollegiate Athletic Association

Colored Methodist Protestant Church, 320

Colored Orphan Asylum, 95

Columbia, 366

Columbia Air Center, 361

Columbia Law School, 244

Columbia University, 102, 419

Columbus laboratory, 367

Colvin, Claudette, 141-42

Commandment Keepers, 323

Compensated Emancipation Act, 484

conductor, 19

Confederate Army, 83

Confederate States of America, 75, 483

Congregationalists, 320

Congressional Black Caucus, 105, 127, 288

Connecticut Historical Society, 75

Connor, Bull, 158

Continental Airlines, 362-63

Conyers, John, Jr., 106-7

Cook, George, 59

Cooke, Sam, 275

Coolidge, Calvin, 123

COOLJC (Church of Our Lord Jesus Christ of the Apostolic Faith), 325, 330

Cooper, Charles "Chuck," 194-96

Cooper, George, 262

Cooper, Oscar, 471

Cooper, Wilhelmina, 495

Copeland, John Anthony, Jr., 42

Corbin, Lloyd, Jr. *See* Djangatolum

CORE (Congress of Racial Equality), 153, 169

Cornell University, 467

Cornish, Samuel, 404

Cornwallis, Charles, 31

Cosby, Bill, 257-58

Cosby Show, The, 258

Council of Women of the Darker Races, 65

coupler, 52

Crandall, Prudence, 173

Creole, 41-42

Crews, Donald, 451

Crisis, 121, 419

Cromwell, Oliver, 29

Crowdy, William, 323

Crum, George, 49

Cuban Giants, 203

Cuffe, Paul, 7

Cullen, Countee (b. Countee Porter), 425

Culpepper, Daunte, 220

Cunningham, Randall, 220

Curbeam, Robert, 366

G

H

I

J

O

Y

Z